Cook & Deal

Great Recipes for Easy Entertaining
Plus
Challenging Bridge Hands

by *DJ Cook*

My sincere appreciation to the many friends
who have made this book possible.

Additional copies of COOK & DEAL
may be obtained by writing:

COOK & DEAL
12 Busbee Road
Biltmore Forest
Asheville, North Carolina 28803

First Edition, First Printing: 1982
Second Printing: 1983
Second Edition, 1988
Third Edition, 1993

Printed in the USA by

WIMMER
The Wimmer Companies, Inc.
Memphis • Dallas

A note to you from the author of COOK & DEAL:

There are 20 million bridge players in North America. All of them eat...and most of them cook! While waiting for the Brie en Croûte to bake or the Brown Bag Apple Pie to finish cooking, I hope that you will enjoy studying some of my favorite bridge-teaching hands.

The recipes include favorites of many of my students. The collection has been carefully chosen and tested for accuracy and excellence. I hope that you will have fun and pleasure putting each recipe to use.

The 60 bridge hands are challenging and instructive. They are favorites not only of mine but also many of my students. From the thousands of bridge hands that I have used in teaching for many years, these hands illustrate the basic principles of Standard American Bridge. The Goren principles of bidding and play presented here should make it possible for anyone to play acceptable bridge in any company. Serious study of these hands could well improve your game and make you a welcome partner in any foursome.

From soufflé to end play, I wish you good luck.

DJ Cook

DJ Cook
Goren Master Teacher
Life Master #236

Dedicated to my sons

With admiration and affection

TABLE OF CONTENTS

PART I

RECIPES

TABLE OF CONTENTS

PART II

BRIDGE HANDS

Jump raise after a pass

Raising partner or rebidding your own suit

1 notrump opening

Jump shift by responder

Bidding with two five card suits

Trump lead

1 notrump opening with a five card major suit

Short club

Response at the two level in hearts

End play

Bidding with two four card suits

1 notrump overcall

Discarding the queen on the king

Forcing the dummy

Percentage

Opening two bid

Uppercut

Pre-emptive opening

Banker's finesse

Take-out double

Barricade response

Lead signal

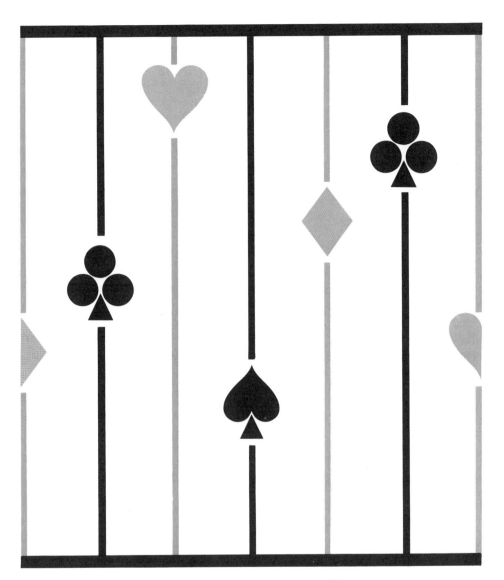

Appetizers

ABC SQUARES

You'll love these . . . everyone does

½ cup blanched almonds,
  finely chopped
6 slices bacon, cooked and
  crumbled
8 ounces very sharp
  Cheddar cheese, grated
  (2 cups)

½ cup onion, grated
2 teaspoons Worcestershire
  sauce
1 cup mayonnaise
1 loaf top quality sandwich
  bread

In blender or food processor separately chop almonds and bacon; grate cheese and onions. Fold in Worcestershire sauce and mayonnaise. Spread mixture on each slice of bread, remove crust and cut into fourths. Freeze. When ready to serve, bake frozen at 400° for 10 minutes. Yield: 5 dozen squares.

Blanche Evans
Vero Beach, Florida

CHEESE SURPRISES

These are popular . . . and for a very good reason

4 ounces sharp Cheddar
  cheese, grated (1 cup)
2 tablespoons butter
½ cup flour, sifted

2 dashes cayenne pepper
1 tablespoon dry sherry
Small pimiento stuffed
  Spanish olives, drained

Allow cheese and butter to soften to room temperature. Cream together cheese and butter. Stir in flour, cayenne and sherry; mix well. Wrap one teaspoon of mixture around each olive, covering completely. Arrange on flat pan, and freeze firm. When frozen, place in plastic bags and seal; return to freezer. To serve, place frozen olives on foil-lined cookie sheet. Bake at 400° about 15 minutes, or until lightly browned. Serve hot. Yield: 30 appetizers.

Evelyn Searles
Harbor Springs, Michigan

HOT CHEESE PUFFS

Bake these puffs straight from the freezer and serve piping hot

1 loaf unsliced French
  bread
¼ pound very sharp
  Cheddar cheese (1 cup)
1 (3 ounce) package cream
  cheese

½ cup butter
¼ teaspoon dry mustard
2 egg whites, stiffly beaten

Remove crust and slice bread into 1 inch cubes. Melt cheese, butter and mustard in top of double boiler; stir well. Remove from heat. Fold egg whites into cheese mixture. Dip bread cubes into cheese mixture scraping off excess with spatula. Place cubes on baking sheet lined with wax paper. Freeze until firm. Transfer to plastic bags; return to freezer. When ready to serve, place frozen cubes on buttered baking sheet. Bake at 400° about 10 minutes, or until puffed and golden brown. Serve hot. Yield: about 40 cheese puffs.

BRIE EN CROÛTE

1 package frozen puff
  pastry shells
3 (4½ ounce) rounds Brie
  cheese
1 egg yolk, beaten

Seedless green grapes,
  apple slices
French bread or assorted
  crackers

Roll out thawed pastry shells for each Brie. Place one shell on bottom of Brie and one shell on top, folding sides to completely cover cheese. Crimp edges together. Rounds may be frozen. To serve, thaw and brush with egg yolk. Bake at 450° for 10 minutes; reduce heat to 350° and bake about 20 minutes more, or until crust is lightly browned. Serve with fruit and French bread or crackers. Each round will serve 4.

BAKED BRIE

1 (16 ounce) wheel of Brie
3 tablespoons apricot
  preserves
1 tablespoon brown sugar
1 tablespoon brandy

¼ cup sliced, blanched
  almonds
1 red apple, sliced
Melba Toast

Place Brie on foil-lined baking dish. Cover with apricot preserves, brown sugar and brandy. Place almonds over top. Bake at 350° for 15 minutes, or until top is golden brown. Serve with apple slices and melba toast. Serves 8 to 10

WATERCRESS AND CHEESE ROLLS

One of Polly's Party Sandwiches

1 (3 ounce) package cream
  cheese, softened
1 teaspoon lemon juice
⅛ cup dairy sour cream
½ teaspoon salt
1 teaspoon chives

1 cup watercress, chopped
18 slices white bread,
  thinly sliced
3 tablespoons butter,
  softened
Watercress for garnish

Blend together cream cheese, lemon juice, sour cream, salt, chives and watercress. Trim crust from bread and roll each slice with rolling pin. Spread bread with butter, then cheese mixture. Roll bread tightly into small logs. Tuck a sprig of watercress in the end of each sandwich. Chill. To serve, slice each roll in half. Garnish. Yield: 36 rolls.

Polly Jernigan, author of *Good! Good!! Good!!!*
Opelika, Alabama

CHUTNEY CHEESE SPREAD

A wonderful blend of flavors

2 (8 ounce) packages cream
  cheese, softened
½ cup Major Grey's
  chutney, chopped fine

1½ teaspoons curry powder
½ teaspoon dry mustard
½ cup toasted chopped
  almonds

Combine all ingredients; blend well. Store in covered jar in refrigerator. The spread improves with age and keeps for weeks. Serve with Pita bread or crackers. Yield: 2½ cups.

Pita Bread:

Split and tear bread into good size bite-pieces. Brush with melted butter and sprinkle with oregano. Bake at 250° for 30 to 40 minutes, or until golden brown.

Gidge Barry
New Canaan, Connecticut

APRICOT AND CREAM CHEESE SPREAD

These are very popular

1 (6 ounce) package dried
  apricots
1¼ cups water
4 tablespoons sugar
1 (8 ounce) package cream
  cheese, softened

Pinch of salt
5 tablespoons butter,
  softened
20 very thin slices of
  sandwich bread, crust
  removed

Place apricots in heavy saucepan with water. Simmer fruit about 20 minutes, stirring frequently. Add sugar and cook 5 minutes longer; mash. Cool. Combine cream cheese, salt and mashed apricots in an electric mixer; blend well. Spread butter on each bread slice; spread apricot mixture on 10 slices and top with remaining 10 slices. Cut into rectangles. May freeze. Yield: 40 small sandwiches.

CUCUMBER CANAPÉS

I keep my freezer filled with these!

1 (8 ounce) package cream
  cheese, softened
1 large cucumber, peeled,
  seeded, grated and
  drained well
1 tablespoon onion, grated
2 tablespoons mayonnaise

¼ teaspoon lemon juice
Dash salt and pepper
10 to 12 thin slices whole
  wheat bread, buttered
5 to 6 thin slices white
  bread, buttered

Combine all ingredients. Blend well. Spread on bread, using three slices for each sandwich. Wrap tightly in foil. Seal in plastic bags and freeze until needed. While slightly frozen, remove crust of bread from sandwiches. Slice into 4 finger size sandwiches; cut these in half, making 40 to 48 bite-size canapés. Thaw completely before serving.

SPINACH DIP

Dunker's Delight

1 (10 ounce) package
  frozen chopped spinach,
  thawed
1 cup mayonnaise*
1 cup dairy sour cream
3 green onions, minced

1 (1.4 ounce) package
  Knorr vegetable soup
  mix
1 (8 ounce) can water
  chestnuts, chopped

Drain spinach thoroughly; blot dry. Mix all ingredients with spinach. Refrigerate several hours. Serve with dip-size Fritos. Also good with celery sticks, carrots, radishes, cauliflower or cucumbers. Stir before serving. Yield: 3 cups.

* 1 cup small curd cottage cheese may be substituted for mayonnaise.

Peggy Williams
Opelika, Alabama

VEGETABLE SANDWICHES
Oh my, these are good!

2 tomatoes, peeled and
  seeded
1 cucumber, peeled and
  seeded
1 green pepper, finely
  chopped
1 onion, finely chopped
1 cup celery, finely
  chopped

2 teaspoons salt
1 envelope unflavored
  gelatin
2 cups mayonnaise
3 medium size loaves very
  thinly sliced bread (very
  fresh), crust removed
  and cut in half

Make the day before serving. Combine all vegetables and chop fine. Place in colander over bowl in which gelatin has been sprinkled. Sprinkle vegetables with salt and let stand for 1 hour or more. This allows juice to drip into gelatin. Heat juice and gelatin; remove from heat and add mayonnaise. Add vegetables and blend. Refrigerate in tightly covered jar. Filling will keep for a week. When ready to prepare, spread vegetable filling on one slice of bread; cover with another slice. Serves 20.

Leila Stringer
Anderson, South Carolina

CURRY DIP FOR FRESH VEGETABLES
Excellent Flavor

1 cup mayonnaise
1 teaspoon curry powder
1 teaspoon tarragon
  vinegar

1 clove garlic, pressed
1 teaspoon horseradish
1 teaspoon grated onion

Mix ingredients together and surround with crisp raw vegetables. This dip looks especially pretty in a hollowed-out red cabbage.

Blanche Evans
Vero Beach, Florida

CHEESE AND BACON WRAP

1 loaf fresh sandwich
  bread, crust removed

1 (11 ounce) can Cheddar
  cheese soup
1 pound bacon, uncooked

Flatten bread with rolling pin. Spread bread with cheese soup and roll up. Cut bacon in half lengthwise; spiral wrap each roll with bacon. Place on rack in pan. Bake at 350° 15 minutes; turn over and bake an additional 15 minutes, or until crisp and brown. Yield: 20 appetizers.

BACON AND WATER CHESTNUTS

8 strips bacon
Dijon mustard
Brown sugar

1 (8 ounce) can water
  chestnuts

Cut bacon strips in half and place on foil-lined pan. Spread each strip with mustard, then sprinkle generously with brown sugar. Place a water chestnut on each piece, roll-up, and secure with wooden pick. Bake at 350° for 25 to 30 minutes, or until bacon is crisp. Drain on absorbent paper.

CHEESE WAFERS

8 ounces extra sharp
  Cheddar cheese, grated
1 cup butter, softened
2 cups flour

1 teaspoon cayenne pepper
½ teaspoon salt
2 cups Rice Crispies

Blend cheese and butter. Add remaining ingredients; mix well. Drop in small rounds on ungreased baking sheet; flatten with fork. Bake at 350° about 15 minutes. Do not let them get too brown. Yield: 7 dozen.

ARTICHOKE HEART SPREAD

A conversation piece

1 (14 ounce) can artichoke
  hearts, drained and
  chopped fine
6 ounces Parmesan cheese,
  freshly grated

1 cup mayonnaise
3 dashes Tabasco
Pinch cayenne pepper
Salt to taste

Combine all ingredients; blend thoroughly. Pour into greased 8 inch square baking pan or quiche dish. Bake at 350° for 30 minutes. Serve hot with assorted crackers. Serves 12.

Gerald Stelter, M.D.
Hendersonville, North Carolina

EGGS EVERGLADES

An elegant appetizer for very special guests

2 envelopes unflavored
  gelatin
1½ cups chicken broth
1 teaspoon curry powder
4 hard-cooked eggs,
  chopped

1½ cups Hellmann's
  mayonnaise
Paprika
Caviar (optional)

Dissolve gelatin in ½ cup broth. Heat 1 cup broth and dissolve curry powder in it. When broth is slightly cooled, add gelatin mixture. Add eggs. Blend in blender, add mayonnaise and reblend. Pour into 3 cup mold, rinsed with cold water, and refrigerate. Unmold when set, sprinkle with paprika, and serve with Triscuits.

Optional: Use a ring mold. Place small bowl in center of ring and fill with black caviar. Serves 14 to 16.

Lazelle Rafferty
Little Compton, Rhode Island

19

GUACAMOLE PIE
Absolutely wonderful

Make the layers on a large serving platter.

1st layer:
**2 (15 ounce) cans refried beans mixed with 1 (1¼ ounce)
package taco seasoning**

2nd layer:
2 cups avocado dip

3rd layer:
1 (4½ ounce) can chopped ripe olives
1 cup green onions with tops, minced
1 small can green chilies, seeded and chopped
1 small jar chopped green olives with pimientos

Mix together.

4th layer:
2 large tomatoes, peeled, chopped, drained well

5th layer:
½ pound grated sharp Cheddar cheese; sprinkle over top.

Drain everything well. Cover and refrigerate several hours or
overnight. Serve with toasted tortilla chips. Serves 20.

Phyllis Holliday
Zionsville, Indiana

AVOCADO DIP

**4 medium size avocados
(chop two; mash two)**
**6 tablespoons picante
sauce hot (in Mexican
food section)**

4 teaspoons lemon juice
2 teaspoons onion, grated
¼ teaspoon seasoned salt
Tortilla chips

Blend all ingredients. Cover and refrigerate several hours.
Serve with tortilla chips. Yield: 2 cups

TEX-MEX CHEESE ROLLS
This one hit the top of the scale

1 (8 ounce) package cream
  cheese, softened
1 (10 ounce) package sharp
  Cheddar cheese, grated
½ cup pecans, chopped

1 large garlic clove,
  pressed
1 (1.25 ounce) package
  Taco seasoning mix

Combine all ingredients but Taco seasoning mix. Mix thoroughly. (A food processor does it well). Wrap mixture in wax paper; refrigerate 1 hour. Divide cheese into 3 rolls. Roll each in Taco seasoning mix until well covered. Cover and refrigerate or freeze. Serve at room temperature with crackers. Each roll serves 6.

Lillian Paxson
Vero Beach, Florida

BEGGARS BOURSIN AU POIVRE
As good as the real thing and maybe better!

1 (8 ounce) package cream
  cheese, softened
2 tablespoons butter
½ teaspoon lemon juice
2 cloves garlic, pressed
1 tablespoon dried parsley

½ teaspoon oregano
⅛ teaspoon cayenne
  pepper
Pinch of salt
1 tablespoon lemon pepper
  marinade

Mix all ingredients but lemon pepper marinade. Blend until smooth. Refrigerate 30 minutes or more, until mixture is firm. Sprinkle lemon pepper on a sheet of wax paper. Using hands, mold cheese into a round ball. Roll cheese in lemon pepper. Cover and refrigerate. Serve with assorted crackers. Serves 6 to 8.

SPINACH AND SALMON ROULADE

Roulade can be made several hours ahead. Reheat, covered with foil, in moderate oven. Roulade yields about 12 slices.

1 package frozen spinach
2 tablespoons water
5 tablespoons butter
⅓ cup flour

1¼ cups milk
4 eggs, separated
2 dashes cream of tartar

Filling:

2 (1 pound) cans red
   salmon, drained
4 shallots, chopped

½ cup mayonnaise
1 tablespoon chopped
   chives

Place frozen spinach in pan with water and cook over medium heat until all liquid has evaporated. Melt butter in separate pan, add flour and stir 1 minute. Add milk gradually, stir until mixture boils and thickens. Quickly stir in beaten egg yolks and spinach; transfer to large bowl. Beat egg whites and cream of tartar until soft peaks form; fold lightly into spinach mixture.

Lightly oil bottom and sides of a 15x10-inch jellyroll pan with vegetable oil; line with wax paper. Lightly oil wax paper.

Pour mixture into prepared pan. Bake at 475° for 15 minutes or until puffed and golden brown. Remove from oven, turn onto wire rack covered with tea towel. Carefully remove wax paper; cool. Spread with filling to 1 inch from edge. Holding tea towel with both hands, gently roll roulade. May be served cold, room temperature or reheated.

Filling:

Remove bones and skin from salmon. Add shallots, mayonnaise and chives; mix well.

Gerald Stelter, M.D.
Hendersonville, North Carolina

TAMALE DIP

A happy hostess . . . guests too!

2 (15 ounce) cans tamales,
    shucked and mashed
1 (15 ounce) can chili
    without beans
½ pound sharp Cheddar
    cheese, shredded
2¼ teaspoon
    Worcestershire sauce

Juice of 1 lemon
¾ teaspoon salt
¼ teaspoon cayenne
    pepper
¼ teaspoon white pepper

Put all ingredients in top of double boiler until dissolved and hot. Place in chafing dish and serve with large corn chips. Serves 15 to 20.

Beverley Wood
Vero Beach, Florida

CHILIES RELLEÑOS

Oh my, are these good!

7 slices white bread,
    buttered, cubed
8 ounces sharp Cheddar
    cheese, grated
8 ounces Monterey Jack
    cheese, grated
1 (4 ounce) can green
    chilies, minced

6 eggs, beaten
2 cups milk
1 teaspoon salt
1 teaspoon oregano
½ teaspoon pepper
½ teaspoon garlic powder
½ teaspoon dry mustard
Paprika for garnish

In bottom of buttered 9×13 inch baking pan place bread. Sprinkle Cheddar cheese, Monterey Jack cheese and chilies over bread. Combine remaining ingredients; mix well. Pour over cheese mixture. Cover and chill 4 hours or overnight. Bake at 350° for 50 to 55 minutes. Let stand 10 minutes. Cut into 1 inch squares. Serves 10 to 12.

PARTY PIZZAS

Serves a crowd and is always a favorite

2 loaves party rye bread,
  sliced
Salad oil
1 (10¾ ounce) can tomato
  soup
1 (6 ounce) can tomato
  paste
1½ teaspoons oregano

1 teaspoon curry powder
12 ounces mozzarella
  cheese, grated
3 (4 ounce) packages
  pepperoni, thinly sliced
Freshly grated Parmesan
  cheese

Brush each slice of bread with salad oil. Make sauce of soup, tomato paste, oregano and curry powder. Spread sauce on bread. Put mozzarella cheese over sauce. Add pepperoni; sprinkle with Parmesan cheese. Bake at 350° for 15 minutes. To serve, cut in half after baking. May freeze before baking. Yield: 60 whole slices.

Lazelle Rafferty
Little Compton, Rhode Island

ENGLISH MUFFIN CANAPÉ

Easy to prepare and absolutely delicious

6 English muffins, split
2 (4½ ounce) cans chopped
  ripe olives
6 ounces extra sharp
  Cheddar cheese, grated
  (1½ cups)

½ cup onion, grated
½ cup mayonnaise
½ tablespoon curry powder
½ teaspoon salt

Mix all ingredients and pile on 12 muffin halves. Place on cookie sheet and freeze. When frozen, place in freezer bags and return to freezer. To serve, cut each half muffin into 8 pieces. They are easier to cut when still a little frozen. Place on broiler pan and broil until bubbly. Yield: 8 dozen.

PEANUT BUTTER STICKS
Good with coffee, tea, lemonade or cocktails

1 large loaf of sandwich
bread, frozen
1 (16 ounce) jar smooth
peanut butter

⅔ cup vegetable oil
2½ tablespoons sugar
1 (8 ounce) can unseasoned
bread crumbs

Remove crust from bread and cut each slice into 8 pieces. Bake sticks at 250° until light brown, about 35 minutes. (Bread sticks may be made ahead and stored in plastic bags). Heat peanut butter, oil and sugar in top of double boiler. Mix well. Place bread crumbs on cookie sheet with sides. Dip bread sticks, a few at a time, into peanut butter mixture. Remove sticks from mixture with slotted spoon. Roll sticks in crumbs. Stack, log fashion, on wax paper to dry. May freeze. Yield: 10 dozen.

ROJAK PETIS
*An unusual combination of textures and flavors makes up
this Malaysian dip.*

⅔ cup crunchy peanut
butter
6 tablespoons dark brown
sugar

½ cup lemon juice
4 tablespoons chili sauce
1 teaspoon soy sauce

Combine all ingredients. Store at room temperature for 24 hours. Refrigerate. Serve with raw vegetables or pineapple chunks. Yield: 1½ cups.

Bali Hyatt
Courtesy of Ruth Fuller
Mountain Lake Club, Lake Wales, Florida

MUSHROOM ROLLS

These always go over BIG

1 loaf thin sliced bread,
  crust removed
½ pound fresh mushrooms,
  finely chopped
¼ cup butter, melted
3 tablespoons flour

1 cup cream
½ teaspoon salt
½ teaspoon onion salt
1 teaspoon lemon juice
3 or 4 tablespoons butter,
  softened

Roll bread slices very thin with rolling pin. Sauté mushrooms in butter for 5 minutes. Stir in flour until well blended. Add cream and cook until thickened, stirring constantly. Add salt, onion salt and lemon juice. Blend well, then cool. Place 1 to 2 teaspoons of mixture on each slice of bread and roll up, seam side down. Butter top of each roll. Freeze an hour; wrap in foil and return to freezer. To serve, cut in thirds and thaw. Bake at 400° for 10 minutes. Serve hot. Yield: 2½ to 3 dozen rolls.

CHICKEN NUGGETS

A wonderful appetizer that should win a prize

4 whole large chicken
  breasts, skinned, boned
Beau Monde seasoning
½ cup butter, melted
1 cup seasoned bread
  crumbs

½ teaspoon onion powder
¼ teaspoon salt
Dash pepper
¼ cup freshly grated
  Parmesan cheese

Cut chicken into pieces the size of a walnut. Shake Beau Monde seasoning over pieces. Dip chicken in butter. Mix crumbs with onion powder, salt, pepper and Parmesan cheese. Dip each chicken piece into crumb mixture. Arrange on cookie sheet and bake at 375° for 15 to 20 minutes, or until nicely browned. Yield: 40 pieces

Marion Logan
St. Louis, Missouri

HOT MUSHROOM SPREAD

All of the testers Loved It!

4 slices bacon
½ pound fresh mushrooms, chopped
1 medium onion, grated
1 clove garlic, pressed
2 tablespoons flour
¼ teaspoon salt

⅛ teaspoon pepper
1 (8 ounce) package cream cheese, cubed
2 teaspoons Worcestershire sauce
1 teaspoon soy sauce
½ cup dairy sour cream

Fry bacon until crisp; drain on paper towels. Crumble bacon, and set aside. Drain and strain bacon drippings, reserving 2 tablespoons for skillet. Add mushrooms, onion, and garlic to skillet; cook, stirring often, until liquid is evaporated. Stir in flour, salt and pepper. Add cream cheese, Worcestershire sauce and soy sauce. Cook, stirring constantly, until cheese melts. Stir sour cream and bacon into mushroom mixture; cook until thoroughly heated, stirring constantly. (Do not boil.) Serve warm with assorted crackers or toast rounds. Yield: 2½ cups.

Grace Bravos
Timonium, Maryland

CAVIAR POTATOES

10 small new potatoes
8 ounces dairy sour cream

2 tablespoons black lumpfish caviar
Chives for garnish

Cook potatoes in their jackets in boiling water to cover until just tender, about 15 minutes. Chill. Slice crosswise into ⅓ to ½ inch slices; make small indentation in middle of each slice. Top each with sour cream and caviar; sprinkle with chives. Yield: 30 appetizers.

HOT CHIPPED BEEF DIP

Very easy and very good

1 (8 ounce) package cream
  cheese, softened
1 cup dairy sour cream
1 (2½ ounce) package dried
  beef, finely chopped
1 tablespoon onion, grated

¼ teaspoon black pepper
¼ teaspoon garlic salt
½ cup chopped pecans
  which have been sautéed
  in 2 tablespoons butter

Combine all ingredients except pecans. Mix well. Turn into buttered shallow serving dish. Top with pecans. Bake at 350° for 20 minutes. Serve hot with Triscuits. Serves 10.

Frances Taylor
Kenilworth, Illinois

LAYERED CRAB OR SHRIMP COCKTAIL SPREAD

Guests gather around this . . . it's a winner

12 ounces cream cheese,
  softened
1 tablespoon
  Worcestershire sauce
1 tablespoon fresh lemon
  juice

1 tablespoon grated onion
Pinch garlic salt
6 ounces chili sauce
8 ounces fresh crabmeat or
  shrimp, cut up
Dried parsley flakes

Blend together cheese, Worcestershire sauce, lemon juice, onion and garlic salt. Spread mixture evenly in an 8 inch quiche dish or shallow serving dish. Spread chili sauce evenly over first layer. Spread crabmeat or cut up shrimp over chili sauce. Sprinkle generously with dried parsley flakes. Cover with plastic wrap and refrigerate a minimum of 12 hours. Serve with crackers. Serves 10 to 12

Marie Gookin
Pittsburgh, Pennsylvania

ASPARAGUS ROLLS

1 loaf fresh sandwich
 bread (26 slices, crusts
 trimmed)
3 to 4 ounces each cream
 cheese, bleu cheese,
 margarine, blended into
 smooth spread

2 (14½ ounce) cans cut
 asparagus spears,
 drained well, mashed
 into pulp
Melted margarine

After trimming crust from bread, roll firmly with rolling pin. Spread each slice with cheese mixture. Place approximately 1 heaping tablespoon mashed asparagus on edge of slice. Roll into a "stick." Brush tops with melted margarine. May be frozen now for later use.

To serve, thaw, if frozen. Cut in desired sizes. Bake at 325° for 12 to 15 minutes or until slightly crisp. Toast under broiler until light brown.

Antoinette Burdett
Asheville, North Carolina

BREWMASTERS SPREAD

12 ounces sharp Cheddar
 cheese, grated
6 ounces warm beer
1 tablespoon
 Worcestershire sauce

1 garlic clove, pressed
¾ teaspoon Tabasco
⅛ teaspoon salt
⅛ teaspoon freshly ground
 pepper

Combine all ingredients in food processor or blender. Mix well. Refrigerate overnight before serving. Serve with crackers. Yield: 2 cups.

PARTY CHEESE BALLS

1 (8 ounce) package cream
   cheese, softened
1 pound sharp Cheddar
   cheese, shredded
4 ounces Roquefort or bleu
   cheese, crumbled
2 teaspoons finely grated
   onion

2 teaspoons Worcestershire
   sauce
2 tablespoons chopped
   stuffed olives
Dash cayenne pepper
1 cup chopped pecans
½ cup parsley, minced

Combine all ingredients but pecans and parsley. Blend thoroughly. Chill several hours or overnight. Form into balls. Mix pecans and parsley on wax paper. Roll cheese balls in this mixture until completely covered. Serve with assorted crackers. Serves 16 to 20.

IMPERIAL CRAB DIP

A party favorite

1 pound fresh crabmeat
2 (8 ounce) packages cream
   cheese
1 cup dairy sour cream
½ cup mayonnaise
2 teaspoons Dijon mustard
3 tablespoons fresh lemon
   juice

4 tablespoons onion, finely
   grated
4 drops Tabasco
4 drops Worcestershire
   sauce
¼ teaspoon salt
8 ounces sharp Cheddar
   cheese, grated (2 cups)

Flake crabmeat; set aside. Combine all remaining ingredients but Cheddar cheese. Carefully fold in crabmeat. Grease two 9 inch quiche dishes or a shallow 2½ quart serving dish; add crabmeat mixture and top with grated cheese. Set oven at 350°. Bake 9 inch quiche dish 20 to 25 minutes; bake 2½ quart dish about 45 minutes. Serve hot with Melba toast or toast rounds. Serves 20.

Lou Steffens
Salisbury, Maryland

HOT CRAB AMANDINE

Good! Good!

1 (8 ounce) package cream
  cheese
1 tablespoon milk
1 tablespoon dry sherry
1 tablespoon horseradish

Dash freshly ground
  pepper
½ pound fresh crabmeat
Almonds, sliced

Soften cream cheese with milk, sherry, horseradish and pepper. Add crabmeat and mix well. Place in 8 inch quiche dish and sprinkle top with almonds. Bake at 350° for 15 minutes, or until bubbly. Serve with Triscuits. Serves 10 to 12.

Sissy Brophy
Grosse Pointe Shores, Michigan

SALMON MOUSSE

Delicious, and simplicity itself

1 (15½ ounce) can Alaska
  red salmon
1 tablespoon unflavored
  gelatin
1 (10½ ounce) can
  consommé
1 tablespoon
  Worcestershire sauce
½ cup mayonnaise
1 small onion, grated

Juice of 1 lemon
1 tablespoon tarragon
  vinegar
Dash soy sauce
Dash Tabasco
Dash garlic salt
Freshly ground pepper to
  taste
Parsley for garnish

Drain and flake salmon. In saucepan, sprinkle gelatin over consommé; let stand 1 minute. Stir over low heat until gelatin is dissolved. Place all ingredients but parsley in blender. Whip until blended. Pour into lightly greased 3 cup mold; chill until firm or overnight. Garnish. Serve with buttery crackers. Serves 12 to 14.

Ellen Bickmore
Vero Beach, Florida

CRABMEAT DIP

Very Popular

½ pound fresh crabmeat
1 cup small curd cottage
   cheese
¼ cup mayonnaise

1 tablespoon onion, grated
1 tablespoon capers
Salt and pepper to taste

Combine all ingredients. Chill several hours before serving. Serve with Triscuits. Serves 8.

Mary Tatham
Tequesta, Florida

TUNA FISH HORS D'OEUVRE MOLD

Lovely for a bridge luncheon too

1 envelope unflavored
   gelatin
¼ cup cold water
2 (6½ ounce) cans white
   meat of tuna, drained
2 cups mayonnaise

2 hard-cooked eggs,
   chopped
½ cup stuffed green olives,
   chopped
2 tablespoons capers
Watercress for garnish

Dissolve gelatin in cold water. Place over very low heat, stirring constantly, until dissolved. Combine tuna fish, mayonnaise, eggs, olives and capers. Add dissolved gelatin and mix. Pour into an oiled 6 cup fish mold. Refrigerate overnight or until firm. Unmold onto a serving platter and garnish with watercress. As a salad luncheon, garnish with avocado slices, peeled tomato wedges and Bibb lettuce. Serves 15 to 20 as an hors d'oeuvre and 6 to 8 as a salad.

BLACK MAGIC
A do-ahead hors d'oeuvre that will be the hit of the party

1 (8 ounce) package cream cheese, softened
⅔ cup dairy sour cream
1 large onion, grated
4 or 5 hard-cooked eggs, grated

1 (3½ ounce) jar Romanoff black lumpfish, Icelandic caviar
Finely chopped parsley

Combine cream cheese and sour cream; beat until smooth. Spread in an 8 inch quiche dish or shallow serving dish to make an even layer. Add a layer of grated onion; then a layer of grated eggs. Cover. Chill 3 hours or more, or overnight. At party time, top with caviar, distributing it to edge of dish; sprinkle with parsley. Serve with toast points. Serves 10.

Dorothy Kohler
Atlanta, Georgia

SMOKED SALMON BALL

1 (15½ ounce) can Alaska red salmon
1 (8 ounce) package cream cheese, softened
1 tablespoon fresh lemon juice
2 teaspoons onion, grated

1 teaspoon horseradish
¼ teaspoon salt
¼ teaspoon liquid smoke
½ cup pecans, chopped
3 tablespoons parsley, minced

Drain and flake salmon; combine with cream cheese, lemon juice, onion, horseradish, salt and liquid smoke. Chill several hours. Combine pecans and parsley. Shape salmon mixture into one large ball or two small ones. Roll in nut mixture. Chill again. Serve with crackers. Serves 10 to 12.

BLEU CHEESE MOLD

A treat for special guests

½ cup water
1 package unflavored
  gelatin
½ cup half and half cream
2 (8 ounce) packages
  cream cheese
2 tablespoons
  Worcestershire sauce

½ cup sour cream or plain
  yogurt
2 ounces bleu cheese,
  crumbled
Sliced pimiento stuffed
  green olives for garnish

Combine water, gelatin and cream in small pan. Whisk on low heat until gelatin is dissolved. In mixer blend remaining ingredients. Add warm gelatin mixture to cheese and combine thoroughly.

Place mixture in 4 cup mold; refrigerate overnight. Unmold and garnish with olives. Serve with carrots, celery, radish roses and assorted crackers. Serves 12.

Gerald Stelter, M.D.
Hendersonville, North Carolina

PRINCETON PÂTÉ

1 pound chicken livers
1 can chicken broth
¾ cup butter, softened
2 tablespoons onion,
  grated

½ teaspoon dry mustard
¼ teaspoon salt
⅛ teaspoon pepper
⅛ teaspoon ground cloves
3 tablespoons bourbon

Bring chicken livers to a boil in chicken broth and simmer for 20 minutes in covered saucepan. Drain; put livers through meat grinder or chop fine in food processor. Mix livers with remaining ingredients and blend well. Pack in a crock and refrigerate until firm. To serve, bring to room temperature for 30 minutes. Serve as a spread with melba toast. Serves 8 to 10.

CRAB PÂTÉ

An excellent combination of flavors

1 can cream of mushroom
  soup
1 envelope unflavored
  gelatin
3 tablespoons cold water
1 (8 ounce) package cream
  cheese, softened

¾ cup mayonnaise
1 small onion, grated
1 cup celery, chopped
½ pound fresh crabmeat
Dash Worcestershire sauce
Dash seasoned salt
Parsley for garnish

Heat soup. Soften gelatin in cold water and dissolve in hot soup. Remove from heat and combine with cream cheese; beat with a mixer until smooth. Add remaining ingredients. Pour mixture into an oiled 4 cup mold and chill several hours or overnight. Unmold and garnish with parsley. Serve with crackers. Serves 12.

CRANBERRY LIVER PÂTÉ

A bit different...delicious

1 pound Braunschweiger
  sausage
1 (8 ounce) package cream
  cheese
½ cup butter

¼ cup cranberry juice
2 teaspoons curry powder
½ teaspoon thyme
½ teaspoon marjoram
¼ teaspoon salt

Have all ingredients at room temperature. Mash sausage in food processor or by hand; beat in cream cheese and butter. Blend in cranberry juice and seasonings. Pack into crock, cover tightly and refrigerate for 2 days. Serve with thin slices toasted French bread, slices of Swiss cheese or stone ground wheat crackers. Cornichons are a fine accompaniment. May freeze. Yield: 3½ cups.

Sally Brooker
Mountain Lake Club
Lake Wales, Florida

PÂTÉ EN GELÉE

A gem of a recipe

1 package unflavored
  gelatin
¼ cup water
1 (10½ ounce) can beef
  consommé
2 tablespoons dry sherry
1 (3 ounce) package cream
  cheese, softened

½ pound liverwurst
1 tablespoon parsley
1 tablespoon onion tops
1 tablespoon capers
3 tablespoons
  Worcestershire sauce
Dash nutmeg

Soak gelatin in cold water. Heat consommé, remove from heat and add gelatin. Cool. Add sherry. Put ½ inch of consommé mixture in lightly greased 2 cup mold. Refrigerate until congealed. Put remaining consommé in blender; add remaining ingredients. Blend until smooth. Pour over congealed consommé and refrigerate until firm. Serve with melba toast or toast triangles. Serves 12.

Patty Bennett
Wilmette, Illinois

PEANUT BUTTER AND CHUTNEY ROUNDS

36 white bread rounds,
  (1½ inch cutter)
½ cup smooth peanut
  butter

½ cup chutney, finely
  chopped
Very small pieces of
  cooked, crisp bacon

Toast bread on both sides. Combine peanut butter and chutney; spread mixture on bread rounds. Bake at 400° for 5 minutes. Top with bacon. Serve hot. Yield: 3 dozen appetizers.

Soups and Salads

BROCCOLI BISQUE

Another winner

1 large head broccoli (use
   flowerets only)
2 cups chicken broth
¼ cup onion, grated
2 tablespoons butter

1 tablespoon flour
1½ teaspoons salt
¼ teaspoon pepper
2 cups half and half cream
Minced parsley for garnish

Steam broccoli until crisp-tender, about 8 minutes. Combine broccoli, broth and onion. Bring to a boil, lower heat and simmer 10 minutes. Process in blender until coarsely chopped. In saucepan, melt butter, blend in flour, salt and pepper. Stir for 2 minutes. Stir in cream. Combine cream sauce and broccoli mixture. Cook over low heat for 10 minutes, stirring constantly, until bisque comes to a boil. Garnish. Bisque can be served hot or cold. Serves 6.

GAZPACHO

A summer delight

4 large tomatoes, peeled
½ large cucumber, peeled,
   seeded
¼ cup green pepper,
   seeded
¼ cup onion
1 large garlic clove,
   pressed
2 (11 ounce) cans V8 juice
3 tablespoons red wine
   vinegar

3 tablespoons olive oil
2 tablespoons medium
   picante sauce
2 teaspoons salt
¼ teaspoon cumin
Dash onion powder
Dash celery salt
Dash celery seed
Chopped parsley for
   garnish

Chop vegetables. Place in blender; add remaining ingredients. Mix well. Cover and refrigerate several hours or overnight. Garnish. Serves 8.

TOMATO BISQUE

Serve piping hot in mugs and pass an appetizer tray

3 cups canned tomatoes
1 tablespoon grated onion
¼ teaspoon celery seed
2 whole cloves
1 bay leaf
¼ cup butter

¼ cup flour
1 quart milk
½ cup Roquefort or bleu
   cheese, crumbled
Salt and pepper to taste
Parsley for garnish

In saucepan combine tomatoes, onion, celery seed, cloves and bay leaf. Cover and simmer gently for 15 minutes. Strain through a fine sieve. Melt butter in saucepan, add flour; blend and stir for 2 minutes. Add milk, stirring constantly until sauce is smooth and thickened. Add cheese and stir until melted. Continue stirring, gradually adding warm tomato mixture. Season with salt and pepper. Serve hot. Garnish. Serves 6.

CRAB BISQUE

Superb for your bridge foursome

1 (11¼ ounce) can green
   pea soup
1 (10¾ ounce) can tomato
   soup
1½ cups half and half
   cream, heated

8 ounces fresh crabmeat
Salt and pepper to taste
1 tablespoon dry sherry in
   each soup bowl
Chopped parsley for
   garnish

Combine soups and heat to boiling point. Over low heat, stir in cream. Flake crabmeat, add salt and pepper and combine with soup. When hot, pour over sherry in soup bowls. Garnish. Serves 4.

BLENDER VEGETABLE SOUP CHILLED

1 (11¼ ounce) can green
  pea soup
2 cups half and half cream
1 teaspoon horseradish
½ teaspoon Accent
½ teaspoon salt

¼ teaspoon curry powder
¼ teaspoon Worcestershire
  sauce
1 small onion, grated
1 carrot, grated
Minced parsley for garnish

Combine all ingredients but parsley. Whirl in blender. Serve well chilled. Garnish with parsley. Serves 4.

TOMATO COB

This chilled soup is excellent when good ripe tomatoes are available

8 large tomatoes
8 tablespoons onion,
  grated
½ teaspoon sugar
1½ teaspoons salt

½ teaspoon Fines Herbes
¼ teaspoon freshly ground
  pepper
Juice of 1 lemon
½ cup chopped parsley

Peel and core tomatoes. Chop tomatoes and onions in blender. Add all remaining ingredients but parsley. Mix well. Chill for several hours in coldest part of refrigerator or place in freezer for ½ an hour. Drain liquid.* Soup should be pulpy.

Dressing:

6 tablespoons mayonnaise
½ teaspoon curry powder
5 drops Worcestershire
  sauce

Minced parsley for garnish

Combine ingredients. Chill. Before serving, fold in chopped parsley. Top with dressing; garnish. Serve ice cold in bouillon cups. Serves 4 to 6.

* 2 cups of delicious tomato juice

Aleka Armour
Lake Forest, Illinois

CREAM OF MUSHROOM SOUP

A lovely compliment to any meal

1 pound mushrooms, finely
  chopped
4 tablespoons butter
2 tablespoons flour

2 cups chicken broth
1½ teaspoons seasoned salt
¼ teaspoon white pepper
½ pint heavy cream

In a 2 quart saucepan sauté mushrooms in butter for 5 minutes. Blend in flour stirring constantly. Slowly add broth, salt and pepper. Simmer for 5 to 10 minutes. Add heavy cream just before serving; heat thoroughly. Serves 5 to 6.

GARDEN SOUP CHILLED

A special dinner calls for an extra special beginning... This chilled soup is an elegant first course

2 tablespoons butter
1 cup chopped green
  onions with tops
1 cup thinly sliced potato
3 cups chicken broth
1 teaspoon dill weed
1 large cucumber, peeled,
  chopped

2 cups shredded lettuce
Salt and freshly ground
  pepper, to taste
1 cup yogurt
Chives for garnish,
  optional

Melt butter in a large saucepan. Add onions and potato and sauté over low heat for 10 minutes. Stir in broth, dill weed, cucumber, lettuce, salt and pepper. Heat to boiling, reduce heat and simmer 15 to 20 minutes. Cool. Add yogurt and stir. Put half of mixture at a time in blender and whip at high speed until smooth, about 30 seconds. Refrigerate for several hours; serve well chilled. Garnish. Serves 6.

Barbara Eitel
Vero Beach, Florida

NINE BEAN SOUP MIX
A great soup ... A great present

To start, mix together in a large container, 1 pound each of nine beans

Lentils
Black Beans
Pinto Beans
Split Peas
Kidney Beans

Black-eyed Peas
Barley Medium
Navy Beans
Great Northern Beans

Mix thoroughly (dry, of course); put into pint jars with fabric tops as gifts. Put recipe inside the jar. Makes 9 pints.

NINE BEAN SOUP

2 cups nine bean soup mix
4 cups water
4 cups chicken broth
1 pound ham hock or 1 pound ham, diced
1 large onion, chopped fine
1 clove garlic, pressed
½ teaspoon salt

1 (16 ounce) can tomatoes chopped in blender with juice
1 (10 ounce) can Mexican tomatoes with green chilies, chopped in blender
Thin lemon slices

Wash 2 cups bean mix and place in a large soup pot. Cover with water 2 inches over beans and soak overnight. Drain; add 4 cups water, chicken broth, ham hock, onion, garlic and salt. Cover and bring to a boil, reduce to simmer and cook 2 to 2½ hours, or until tender. Add chopped tomatoes and simmer 30 minutes, stirring occasionally.

Some like the soup "as is" with the beans whole; others like the soup placed in a blender and chopped for a few seconds. Top with lemon slices. Serves 8.

Joy Satcher
Cocoa, Florida

CHIPPEWA SOUP

This deliciuos soup can be prepared the day before serving

1 (11¼ ounce) can green
  pea soup
1 (10¾ ounce) can tomato
  soup
1 (10½ ounce) can beef
  consommé
½ cup water

1 cup half and half cream,
  heated
1 teaspoon curry powder
2 tablespoons dry sherry
Chopped parsley for
  garnish

With a whisk, combine green pea soup and tomato soup; add consommé and water. Heat to boiling point. Stir in remaining ingredients. Serve very hot. Garnish. Yield: 5 cups.

Miriam Dirks
Asheville, North Carolina

AVOCADO SOUP

2 cups peeled avocados,
  sliced
2 cups chicken broth
½ teaspoon grated onion
1 cup dairy sour cream
1 cup light cream

½ teaspoon lemon juice
¼ teaspoon salt
Freshly ground pepper
Paprika
Chopped parsley
Chopped scallion tops

In electric blender combine avocados, broth and grated onion. Process just until puréed. Pour into large bowl, beat in sour cream, light cream, lemon juice, salt and pepper to taste. Mix until smooth. Refrigerate. Garnish with paprika, parsley and scallion tops. Yield: 5 cups.

Sis Kantrow
Baton Rouge, Louisiana

BANANA FREEZE

A frozen fruit salad that everybody likes!

1 (8 ounce) can crushed
  pineapple
1 teaspoon unflavored
  gelatin
3 tablespoons pineapple
  syrup
1⅓ cups miniature
  marshmallows
2 tablespoons lemon juice

1 tablespoon maraschino
  cherry juice
½ cup maraschino cherries,
  quartered
1 cup mashed bananas
⅓ cup mayonnaise
1 cup heavy cream,
  whipped

Drain pineapple. Soften gelatin in pineapple syrup. Melt marshmallows in lemon juice and cherry juice over hot water. Dissolve gelatin in hot marshmallow mixture, blending thoroughly. Cool until partly thickened, then fold in well drained cherries, bananas and mayonnaise. Fold in pineapple. Blend in whipped cream. Pour into 9×5 inch pan; freeze until firm. Serves 8.

Trudy Jackson
Opelika, Alabama

AMBROSIA SALAD

This is a favorite at our house.

1 (11 ounce) can mandarin
  oranges, sliced
1 cup pineapple chunks,
  sliced
1 cup maraschino cherries,
  sliced

1 cup coconut
2 cups miniature
  marshmallows
1 cup dairy sour cream

Drain fruit. Combine all ingredients and chill several hours. Serves 8

Vernice Rufus
Tuberville, South Carolina

RIBBON SALAD

Dazzle your holiday company with this one

2 (3 ounce) packages lime flavor gelatin
5 cups boiling water
4 cups cold water
1 (3 ounce) package lemon flavor gelatin
½ cup miniature marshmallows
1 cup pineapple juice

1 (8 ounce) package cream cheese
1 (20 ounce) can crushed pineapple
1 cup heavy cream, whipped
1 cup mayonnaise
2 (3 ounce) packages raspberry flavor gelatin

Dissolve lime gelatin in 2 cups boiling water; add 2 cups cold water. Pour into 14 × 10 × 2 inch pan. Chill until partially set.

Dissolve lemon gelatin in 1 cup boiling water in top of double boiler; add marshmallows and stir to melt.

Remove from heat; add drained pineapple juice and cream cheese.

Beat until well blended and stir in pineapple. Cool. Fold in whipped cream and mayonnaise. Chill until thickened.

Pour in layer over lime gelatin. Chill until almost set.

Dissolve raspberry gelatin in 2 cups boiling water; add 2 cups cold water. Chill until syrupy. Pour over pineapple layer. Chill until firm. Serves 20.

My Sister, Cherry Sue Jackson
Opelika, Alabama

HONEY-MUSTARD DRESSING FOR AVOCADO & SPINACH SALAD

6 tablespoons oil
2 tablespoons cider
vinegar
2 tablespoons honey
2 tablespoons Dijon
mustard

2 tablespoons toasted
sesame seeds
1 garlic clove, minced
½ teaspoon black pepper

Combine all ingredients; shake well. Keep in refrigerator. Pour on salad just before serving. Serves 6.

Salad:

2 avocados, cut up
2 bunches spinach, torn

6 slices bacon, cooked
crisp & crumbled
3 green onions, diced

Curtis Martin
Wichita Falls, Texas

FRESH PEAR SALAD

Fresh Pears
Lemon juice
Cream cheese
Mayonnaise

Seedless green grapes,
halved
½ cup French dressing
¼ cup chutney, minced

Peel, core and halve ripe pears. Brush cut side of pear with lemon juice. Soften cream cheese with mayonnaise to make soft enough to spread. Place pears, cut side down, on bread board, and cover outside surface with softened cheese. Stud pears with grapes all over cheese, pressing cut side of grapes well into cheese. Chill. Mix French dressing and chutney together and serve with salad.

TURKEY APRICOT SALAD

Call for a reservation...they have the best food in town

½ cup dried moist pack
  apricots
2 tablespoons poppy seed
2 tablespoons honey
2 tablespoons Dijon
  mustard
⅓ cup of salad oil
⅓ cup fresh lemon juice
½ teaspoon fresh lemon
  peel, grated

4 cups cubed cooked
  turkey breast (see index)
1 large tart apple, peeled
  and chopped
¼ cup green onions,
  minced
Seedless grapes, apple
  slices, orange slices,
  avocado for garnish

Cut apricots into quarters. Marinate in next six ingredients for 30 minutes to soften. Add turkey, apple and onions, toss lightly. Chill thoroughly. Serve on lettuce leaf and garnish with fruit. Serves 4 to 6.

Allied Arts Guild Restaurant
The Palo Alto Auxiliary for the benefit of
Children's Hospital at Stanford, California

COLE SLAW SOUFFLÉ

1 (3 ounce) package lemon
  gelatin
1 cup boiling water
½ cup mayonnaise
2 tablespoons vinegar
½ teaspoon salt
½ cup cold water

2 cups cabbage, finely
  chopped
¾ cup carrots, shredded
¾ cup celery, diced
3 tablespoons green
  pepper, diced
1 tablespoon onion, grated

Dissolve gelatin in boiling water. Add mayonnaise, vinegar, salt and cold water. Blend with rotary beater. Refrigerate until partially congealed. Whip again with rotary beater until fluffy. Add vegetables, mix thoroughly, and pour into 1½ quart lightly oiled mold or 8 individual molds. Chill until firm.

Patricia Jordan
Asheville, North Carolina

MELON AND GINGER ALE SALAD

2 (3 ounce) packages lemon
　Jell-O
1 cup boiling water
¾ cup lemonade
　concentrate, frozen
2 cups ginger ale
1 cup honeydew melon
　balls
1 cup cantaloupe melon
　balls

1 cup seedless green
　grapes, sliced
4 ounces cream cheese
½ cup pecans or walnuts,
　chopped
1 cup mayonnaise
1 cup heavy cream,
　whipped

Dissolve Jell-O in boiling water. Stir until well mixed. Add lemonade and ginger ale. Place in refrigerator to thicken while preparing fruit. Form cream cheese into small balls and roll in nuts. Oil a 3 quart ring mold or 12 individual molds. When Jell-O begins to thicken, fold in fruit. Pour into mold. Place cream cheese balls into gelatin mixture at regular intervals. Refrigerate 3 hours or more, until firm. Serve with mayonnaise folded into the whipped cream. Serves 12.

STRAWBERRIES AND CREAM

1 (6 ounce) package wild
　strawberry gelatin
1 cup boiling water
2 (10 ounce) packages
　frozen strawberries and
　juice

1 (16 ounce) can crushed
　pineapple, with juice
3 bananas, mashed
1 cup of nuts, chopped
1 pint dairy sour cream

Dissolve gelatin in boiling water. Add strawberries, pineapple and bananas. Pour half of mixture into a 9×9 inch pan. Chill until firm. Combine nuts and sour cream; spread over congealed gelatin. Cover with remaining gelatin mixture that is at room temperature. Chill. Cut in squares to serve. Serves 12.

PEACH HALVES WITH CREAM CHEESE

10 large peach halves
8 ounces cream cheese,
  softened
1½ tablespoons brandy

½ teaspoon garlic powder
2 to 3 tablespoons peach
  juice
½ cup toasted almonds

Drain peaches, reserving juice. Combine cream cheese, brandy and garlic powder. Add enough juice to make a creamy filling. Fill peach halves and sprinkle with almonds.

CRANBERRY SALAD AND RAW CRANBERRY RELISH
Deserves a blue ribbon

1 package unflavored
  gelatin
¼ cup cold water
1¼ cups boiling water

1 teaspoon sugar
1½ cups raw cranberry
  relish
½ cup pecans, chopped

Dissolve gelatin in cold water. Add boiling water to gelatin mixture. Stir until blended. Cool. Add remaining ingredients. Pour into individual molds. Refrigerate until firm. Serves 6.

RAW CRANBERRY RELISH
A wonderful accompanient for meat

4 cups cranberries
2 Delicious apples
Orange peel of ½ an
  orange

2 large oranges
1½ cups sugar

Put cranberries, apples and orange peel through coarse blade of food processor. Cut orange sections into small pieces; add to cranberry mixture. Add sugar; mix well. Refrigerate. Relish will freeze for months. Yield: 5 cups.

Elizabeth Salter
Auburn, Alabama

EMERALD PARTY SALAD

Beautiful and delicious

2 (3 ounce) packages lime
   flavor Jell-O
3½ cups boiling water

½ cup diced pineapple
½ cup slivered almonds
1 cup dairy sour cream

Dissolve gelatin in boiling water. Jell slightly. Add pineapple, almonds and sour cream. Pour into 9 to 10 individual molds. Refrigerate until firm. Serve with dressing.

Dressing:

1 tablespoon butter
1 tablespoon flour
¼ cup sugar, skimpy
1 egg yolk
5 ounces warm pineapple
   juice

Pinch of salt
1 egg white
1 tablespoon sugar
½ cup heavy cream,
   whipped

In top of double boiler, melt butter, add flour; mix until smooth and stir 2 to 3 minutes. Add sugar, egg yolk mixed with a little pineapple juice and salt. Stir and add remaining pineapple juice. Stir constantly until mixture is thick; simmer a few more minutes. Remove from heat. Cool. Beat until just blended, egg white with sugar; add to pineapple mixture. Fold in whipped cream. Refrigerate.

SAUCY APPLE SALAD

¼ cup small red cinnamon candies, ("red hots")
1 (3 ounce) package cherry flavor gelatin
1 cup boiling water
1½ cups sweetened applesauce
1 (8 ounce) package cream cheese, softened
½ cup nuts, chopped
½ cup celery, finely cut
½ cup mayonnaise type salad dressing
Frosted grapes (see index)

Mix cinnamon candies and gelatin. Add boiling water; stir to dissolve. Stir in applesauce. Pour half of mixture into an 8 inch square pan. Chill until firm. Blend together cream cheese, nuts and celery; add salad dressing. Spread in a layer over firm apple mixture. Pour on remaining apple mixture. Chill until firm. Garnish with frosted grapes. Serves 6.

THREE-DAY-AHEAD COLE SLAW

Perfect for the barbecue crowd

1 medium size head of cabbage, shredded
1 medium size onion, minced
1 green pepper, chopped fine
1 (4 ounce) jar pimiento, chopped fine

Dressing:

½ cup honey
½ cup vinegar
½ cup oil
2 teaspoons sugar
2 teaspoons salt
½ teaspoon mustard seed
Dash pepper

Place cabbage, onion, pepper and pimiento in large bowl; mix. Put all ingredients for dressing in saucepan. Bring to a boil. Immediately pour over cabbage mixture and refrigerate, covered. Stir occasionally and serve three days later. Keeps well for at least a week. Serves 8.

Barbara Eitel
Vero Beach, Florida

TOMATOES LUTECE

The restacking is different and attractive. The marinade is delicious

8 firm ripe tomatoes
1 clove garlic, crushed
1 teaspoon salt
1 teaspoon sugar
¼ teaspoon black pepper
¼ cup olive oil

2 tablespoons tarragon or
  cider vinegar
2 tablespoons mustard
  (Dijon type)
¼ cup chopped parsley

Peel and slice tomatoes crosswise into ¼ inch thick slices. Restack and place in a shallow serving dish. Combine all ingredients but parsley in small jar. Cover and shake well. Pour over tomatoes. Cover lightly and refrigerate. Let stand at room temperature for 20 minutes before serving. Sprinkle parsley over top of tomatoes. Serves 8.

Carol Porter
Lake Zurich, Illinois

HOT CHICKEN SALAD

Good for a bridge luncheon or any time

2 cups diced cooked
  chicken
1 cup mayonnaise
2 tablespoons lemon juice
2 cups chopped celery
2 teaspoons grated onion
½ teaspoon salt
Few dashes cayenne
  pepper

½ cup chopped toasted
  almonds
4 ounces grated sharp
  Cheddar cheese (1 cup)
1 cup finely crushed potato
  chips

Combine all ingredients but cheese and potato chips. Mix well. Place in 2 quart buttered baking dish. Sprinkle with cheese and top with potato chips. Bake at 350° for 30 to 35 minutes. Serves 4 to 6.

Dottie Neville
Jupiter, Florida

CURRIED CHICKEN SALAD

An immediate family favorite

4 cups cubed cooked breast
  of chicken
1 (8 ounce) can sliced
  water chestnuts
2 cups seedless green
  grapes
1 cup celery, chopped
1 cup sliced almonds,
  toasted (save ¼ cup for
  garnish)

1 cup mayonnaise
½ cup dairy sour cream
2 teaspoons curry powder
1 teaspoon soy sauce
4 tablespoons lemon juice
Bibb lettuce
1 (13 ounce) can chunk
  pineapple, drained

Combine first 5 ingredients. Mix mayonnaise, sour cream, curry powder, soy sauce and lemon juice; blend well. Toss mayonnaise mixture with chicken and chill several hours. To serve, spoon onto Bibb lettuce and sprinkle with pineapple chunks and remaining almonds. Serves 8.

Helen Warren
Vero Beach, Florida

TOMATO ASPIC

2 envelopes unflavored
  gelatin
3½ cups V-8 juice
4 tablespoons lemon juice
4 tablespoons
  Worcestershire sauce

2 tablespoons horseradish
½ cup sliced pimento
  stuffed olives
1 teaspoon salt
Few dashes Tabasco

Dissolve gelatin in ½ cup V-8 juice. Heat 3 cups V-8 juice to boiling; remove from heat, add gelatin; stir until dissolved. Add remaining ingredients. Pour into 4 cup oiled mold. Refrigerate until firm. Serves 6 to 8.

SPINACH SALAD
Superb!

Salad:

1 pound fresh spinach,
washed and stemmed
½ cup sliced fresh
mushrooms
12 water chestnuts, sliced
6 slices cooked bacon,
crumbled

½ cup Gruyere or Swiss
cheese
Red onion slices for
garnish

Dressing:

¼ cup wine vinegar
2 tablespoons chutney
2 tablespoons Dijon
mustard
2 teaspoons sugar

1 clove garlic, pressed
¼ teaspoon salt
⅛ teaspoon pepper
⅓ to ½ cup vegetable oil

Mix all salad ingredients in a large bowl. In blender or food
processor, mix all dressing ingredients except oil. Add oil
slowly, beating continuously. When ready to serve, stir dressing well and toss with spinach mixture. Garnish. Serves 8.

Margaret Z. Larsen
Nantucket, Massachusetts

MARINATED BROCCOLI

2 heads of broccoli (use
flowerets only)
1½ cups cider vinegar
½ cup vegetable oil
¼ cup cold water

2 tablespoons sugar
1 clove garlic, pressed
1 tablespoon dill seed
1 teaspoon salt
½ teaspoon pepper

Combine all ingredients. Cover and refrigerate several hours
or overnight. Stir occasionally. Serves 8.

MARINATED MUSHROOM SALAD

If you like mushrooms you'll love this salad!

1 pound fresh mushrooms,
  sliced
2 tablespoons finely
  chopped onion
2 tablespoons lemon juice
2 teaspoons sugar
¼ teaspoon freshly ground
  pepper

⅓ cup heavy cream
¼ cup dairy sour cream
¼ teaspoon salt
¼ teaspoon dry mustard
Romaine lettuce
Tomato wedges
Coarsely ground pepper

In a medium mixing bowl toss together the mushrooms, onion, lemon juice, sugar and pepper. Chill at least 30 minutes but not more than 4 hours. Whip the heavy cream. Stir together sour cream, salt and dry mustard; fold in whipped cream. Stir into mushroom mixture. Spoon mixture onto 6 romaine-lined salad plates. Garnish with tomato wedges; top with coarsely ground pepper. Serves 6.

Jan Lee
Neenah, Wisconsin

VEGETABLE MÉLANGE

Fix this one day to serve the next . . . delicious

1 head of broccoli
1 head of cauliflower
4 carrots, diagonally sliced
2 small zucchini squash,
  thinly sliced
1½ cups Wesson oil
1 cup cider vinegar

1 tablespoon dill seed
1 tablespoon Accent
1 tablespoon sugar
1 teaspoon salt
1 teaspoon garlic salt
1 teaspoon pepper

Divide broccoli and cauliflower into bite-size flowerets. Combine all vegetables. Blend remaining ingredients; pour over vegetables. Cover and chill 24 hours. Lift vegetables occasionally to distribute dressing. Yield: 2 quarts.

Lucy Wagner
Cincinnati, Ohio

MARINATED BLACK-EYED PEAS

Don't wait for the New Year!

3 (16 ounce) cans black-
  eyed peas, drained
1 cup vegetable oil
½ cup wine vinegar
4 tablespoons onion,
  grated

1 clove garlic, pressed
1 teaspoon salt
⅛ teaspoon pepper
5 dashes Tabasco
Onion rings
Green pepper rings

Combine all ingredients but onion rings and green pepper rings. Cover and marinate in refrigerator for 3 days. Drain slightly before serving. Reserve marinade; place in serving bowl to be used as additional dressing. Garnish with onion rings and pepper rings. Yield: 6 cups.

Rebecca Alexander
Vero Beach, Florida

BROCCOLI SALAD MOLD

This is a tasty combination

1 head broccoli, separated
  into flowerets, chopped
1 envelope unflavored
  gelatin
½ cup water
1 cup chicken broth
⅔ cup mayonnaise

⅓ cup dairy sour cream
1 tablespoon lemon juice
1 tablespoon onion, grated
¼ teaspoon seasoned salt
3 hard-boiled eggs, chopped
Lettuce
Cherry tomatoes

Steam broccoli over boiling water until tender. Soften gelatin in water over low heat; add chicken broth and stir until dissolved. Add mayonnaise, sour cream, lemon juice, onion and seasoned salt; blend. Refrigerate until mixture begins to thicken. Add broccoli and eggs; fold into gelatin mixture. Pour into 4½ cup mold. Chill until firm. Unmold and serve on lettuce; garnish with cherry tomatoes. Serves 8.

POTATO SALAD

Potato salad is best made from new potatoes cooked in their jackets

3 pounds potatoes
1 cup mayonnaise
½ cup onions, grated
2 tablespoons red wine
  vinegar
2 tablespoons Dijon-style
  mustard

1 tablespoon parsley,
  minced
1 tablespoon lemon-pepper
  seasoning
2 teaspoons dried dillweed
4 hard-cooked eggs, diced
Sliced radishes, optional

Cook potatoes just until tender, about 20 minutes, in boiling salted water. Drain; peel potatoes and cut into bite-size pieces. Place in large bowl. Combine mayonnaise, onions, vinegar, mustard, parsley, lemon-pepper and dillweed. With a wooden spoon, gently blend mayonnaise mixture with potatoes and hard-cooked eggs. Cover and refrigerate several hours. Stir lightly before serving. Serves 8 to 10.

CALICO BEAN SALAD

Wonderful for a buffet supper

1 (16 ounce) can red
  kidney beans
1 (16 ounce) can French-cut
  green beans
1 (16 ounce) can yellow
  wax beans
½ cup onion, minced

½ cup green pepper,
  minced
½ cup salad oil
½ cup cider vinegar
¾ cup sugar
1 teaspoon salt
½ teaspoon pepper

Drain beans and place in a glass bowl. Add onions and green pepper. Mix oil and vinegar with sugar, salt and pepper. Pour over bean mixture. Blend thoroughly. Cover and refrigerate several hours. Serves 10.

AVOCADO WITH HOT DRESSING

2 peeled avocados, halved
  and pitted
2 teaspoons lemon juice
4 slices bacon, crisply
  cooked and crumbled
2 tablespoons chili sauce
2 tablespoons
  Worcestershire sauce

2 tablespoons vinegar
4 teaspoons sugar
2 tablespoons butter,
  melted
Crisp greens

Brush cut surfaces of avocado with lemon juice. Place bacon in each avocado well. Combine all remaining ingredients, heat and pour over avocado halves. Serve on crisp greens. Serves 4.

CAVIAR DRESSING

1 (3 ounce) package cream
  cheese, softened
½ cup Hellman's
  mayonnaise

1 cup dairy sour cream
2 teaspoons onion, grated
1 (3½ ounce) jar black
  lumpfish caviar

Combine cream cheese, mayonnaise, sour cream and onion. Mix well. Gently stir in caviar. Store dressing in a covered container. If dressing seems too thick, add a small amount of half and half cream. Serves 6.

Salad for Caviar Dressing:

1 head of leaf lettuce torn
  into small pieces or an
  equal amount of Bibb
  lettuce

1 peeled and chopped
  tomato
1½ cups orange sections
1 sliced avocado

Patt La Montagne
Rockledge, Florida

58

SALMON SALAD WITH CUCUMBER DRESSING

1 (10¾ ounce) can tomato soup
1 (8 ounce) package cream cheese, softened
2 tablespoons unflavored gelatin
½ cup cold water

1 (15½ ounce) can red salmon, drain and flake
1 green pepper, chopped fine
1 small onion, grated
1 cup celery, cut fine
1 cup mayonnaise

Heat soup in top of double boiler. Add cream cheese; stir until melted. Dissolve gelatin in cold water and add to soup mixture. Remove from heat; add remaining ingredients. Mix well. Pour into oiled fish mold and chill several hours.

Cucumber Dressing:

½ cup heavy cream, whipped
1 cup mayonnaise
2 tablespoons lemon juice
¼ teaspoon salt

⅛ teaspoon white pepper
1 small cucumber, peeled, seeded, chopped fine, well drained

Fold whipped cream into mayonnaise; stir in lemon juice, salt, pepper and cucumber. Chill. Serve separately with salmon. Serves 8.

ZESTY SALAD DRESSING

½ cup wine vinegar
4 tablespoons vegetable oil
1 tablespoon chili sauce
1 teaspoon Fines Herbes

1 teaspoon cracked pepper
½ teaspoon paprika
¼ teaspoon sugar
1 clove garlic, crushed

Combine all ingredients. Place in a covered jar and shake well. Refrigerate. Yield: about 1 cup.

WATERCRESS SALAD DRESSING

1 bunch watercress, tops
  only (about 2 cups)
1 bunch parsley, tops only
  (about 2 cups)
3 green onions, minced
⅛ cup vinegar
1 cup safflower oil
3 egg yolks

½ teaspoon Aćcent
½ teaspoon horseradish
1 teaspoon Vege-Sal
  seasoned salt (available
  at health food store)
¼ teaspoon Worcestershire
  sauce
Pinch of dry mustard

Blend all ingredients in blender. If dressing is too thick, thin with ice water, adding a very small amount at a time. Yield: 2½ cups.

Peggy Fulenwider
Denver, Colorado

CELERY SEED DRESSING

Wonderful on avocado and grapefruit, Bibb lettuce or any fruit

½ cup sugar
1 teaspoon dry mustard
1 teaspoon salt
⅛ cup vinegar

1 cup vegetable oil
1 tablespoon celery seed
¼ cup onion, finely grated

Mix sugar, mustard, salt and vinegar. Add oil gradually, and beat with electric mixer until well blended. Add celery seed and onion; mix well. Refrigerate. Dressing will keep for weeks under refrigeration. Yield: 1½ cups.

Elizabeth Salter
Auburn, Alabama

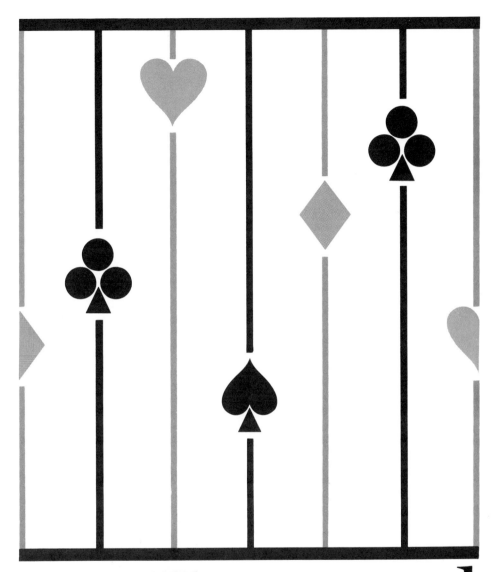

Eggs and Cheese

POPOVER PANCAKE

It's fun to watch it pop and it's mighty good too!

½ cup flour
½ cup milk
2 eggs, slightly beaten
¼ cup butter

2 tablespoons
    confectioners' sugar,
    sifted
Juice of 1 lemon

Combine flour, milk and eggs; beat lightly. The batter will be slightly lumpy. Put butter into 12 inch round frying pan with heatproof handle. Place pan in 425° oven until very hot. Pour batter into hot pan, return to oven, and bake 20 minutes, or until pancake is puffed all around sides of pan and golden brown. Remove from oven and sprinkle with confectioners' sugar and lemon juice. Serve immediately. Serves 2 to 3.

WELSH RAREBIT

2 teaspoons butter
½ cup light beer
2 cups (8 ounces) sharp
    Cheddar cheese, grated
1 egg, beaten
⅛ teaspoon dry mustard
½ teaspoon salt

½ teaspoon Worcestershire
    sauce
Few dashes cayenne
    pepper
Few dashes paprika
4 tomato slices
4 English muffins, halved
    and toasted

Melt butter in top of double boiler. Stir in beer. Add cheese; stir constantly, over low heat, until cheese is melted. Stir in egg. Combine mustard, salt, Worcestershire sauce, cayenne pepper and paprika; stir into cheese. When smooth and hot, serve over tomato slices and muffins. Serves 4.

ZIPPY CHEESE OMELET

Outstanding!

½ cup picante sauce
4 ounces sharp Cheddar
   cheese, grated (1 cup)
4 ounces Monterey Jack
   cheese, grated (1 cup)
6 eggs

1 cup dairy sour cream
2 ripe tomatoes, peeled
   and chopped
Parsley, minced
Picante sauce (in Mexican
   food section)

Pour ½ cup picante sauce into a lightly greased 9 inch quiche dish or pie pan; sprinkle cheeses over sauce. Place eggs in container of an electric blender; process until blended. Add sour cream, and process until well blended. Pour egg mixture over cheeses. Bake, uncovered, at 350° for 30 to 35 minutes. Sprinkle tomatoes and parsley over top. Serve omelet with additional picante sauce. Serves 6.

Suzanne Meyer
Seminole, Florida

SOUFFLÉED FRENCH TOAST

For a special-occasion breakfast

1 long loaf French bread
   (about ½ pound)
8 large eggs, well beaten
3 cups half and half cream
4 tablespoons sugar
Dash of nutmeg

¾ teaspoon salt
1 tablespoon vanilla
2 tablespoons butter
Confectioners' sugar
Maple syrup

Generously grease a 9 x 13 inch baking dish. Cut bread into 1½ inch cubes and arrange in single layer. Combine eggs, cream, sugar, nutmeg, salt and vanilla. Mix well. Pour over bread and dot top with butter. Cover and refrigerate overnight. Bake uncovered at 350° for 45 to 50 minutes, until bread is puffed and lightly browned. Sift with confectioners' sugar and serve with maple syrup. Serves 6.

Julie Crump
Blowing Rock, North Carolina

TOMATO PIE

This is a good one!

1 deep dish (9 inch)
  unbaked pie shell
3 ripe tomatoes, peeled
4 tablespoons sweet
  onions, grated
Seasoned salt and pepper,
  to taste

4 ounces Swiss cheese,
  grated (1 cup)
1 cup mayonnaise
2 ounces freshly grated
  Parmesan cheese (½ cup)
½ cup dairy sour cream

Bake pie shell at 425° about 10 minutes, or until lightly browned. Remove from oven. Slice tomatoes onto crust adding onions, salt and pepper as you go. Sprinkle with Swiss cheese. Mix mayonnaise, Parmesan cheese and sour cream; spread this mixture evenly over tomato slices, making sure to seal edges of the pie crust. Bake at 350° about 25 minutes. Serves 6.

Wendy Higgins
New York City

CHEESE SOUFFLÉ

Served every Monday to the bridge players at the
Woman's Athletic Club of Chicago

¼ cup butter
¼ cup flour
1 cup milk
½ teaspoon salt
6 ounces sharp Cheddar
  cheese, grated

4 egg yolks, beaten
4 egg whites, beaten stiff
2 tablespoons Parmesan
  cheese
4 (10 ounce) individual
  buttered casseroles

Melt butter; blend in flour and cook 2 to 3 minutes. Heat milk and add slowly to butter-flour mixture. Add salt. Cook until thick; add cheese and stir until cheese is melted. Remove from heat and stir in egg yolks. Cool. Fold in beaten egg whites. Spoon into 4 casserole dishes and sprinkle with Parmesan cheese. Place casseroles in pan of water. Bake at 375° for 25 to 30 minutes. Serves 4.

This recipe is included by special permission of the club.

GREEN CHILIE CHEESE PIE

Do make this soon! It is special!!

1 deep dish (9 inch) pie shell
6 ounces Monterey Jack cheese, grated (1½ cups)
4 ounces sharp Cheddar cheese, grated (1 cup)
1 (4 ounce) can green chilie peppers, drained, seeded, chopped
⅛ cup grated onions, well drained
⅛ cup chopped tomatoes, well drained
⅛ cup chopped mushrooms
1 cup half and half cream
3 eggs
¼ teaspoon salt
⅛ teaspoon cumin
Dash of Worcestershire sauce

Pierce bottom and sides of pie shell with fork; bake at 400° for 10 minutes. Remove from oven. Lower oven temperature to 350°.

Sprinkle all of Monterey Jack cheese and ½ cup of Cheddar cheese over bottom of cooked pie crust. Sprinkle chilie peppers over cheese. Add onions, tomatoes and mushrooms.

Pour half and half in blender; add remaining ingredients. Blend 20 seconds. Pour into pie crust; sprinkle remaining ½ cup Cheddar cheese over filling.

Bake 40 to 45 minutes, or until tested done with fork. Let stand 15 minutes before cutting. Serves 6.

Frances Biddinger
Sebastian, Florida

CHEESY GREEN ONION QUICHE

A gem of a recipe

1 deep dish (9 inch)
  unbaked pie shell
8 slices bacon, cooked and
  crumbled
3 ounces Cheddar cheese,
  shredded (¾ cup)
3 ounces Swiss cheese,
  shredded (¾ cup)

4 eggs, beaten
1 cup dairy sour cream
½ cup half and half cream
¼ cup green onions, sliced
1 tablespoon flour
¾ teaspoon salt
⅛ teaspoon pepper
Dash red pepper

Pierce bottom and sides of pie shell with a fork. Bake at 400°
for 3 minutes; remove from oven, and gently pierce shell
again. Return to oven for 5 minutes longer. Sprinkle bacon
and cheese into pie shell. Combine remaining ingredients and
mix well. Pour over cheese mixture. Bake at 375° for 40 to 45
minutes, or until set. Yield: one 9 inch quiche.

Grace Bravos
Timonium, Maryland

CHEESE PUDDING

Guests always want the recipe

5 slices bread, buttered
¾ pound sharp Cheddar
  cheese, shredded
4 eggs, beaten slightly

2 cups milk
½ teaspoon dry mustard
½ teaspoon salt
Pinch cayenne pepper

Tear bread into small pieces; add cheese. Place in bottom of 2
quart casserole. Mix eggs, milk and seasonings together. Pour
over bread and cheese mixture; push down to cover. Place in
refrigerator overnight before cooking. When ready to cook,
put casserole dish in pan of water and bake at 350° for 60
minutes. The pudding keeps very well and will not fall if not
served immediately. Serves 4 to 6.

Barbara Carlson
Glens Falls, New York

QUICK QUICHE
First place winner in the Dairy Food Contest

1 (8 ounce) can crescent rolls
½ teaspoon mustard
8 ounces Lorraine Swiss cheese, grated (2 cups)
6 slices bacon, cooked and crumbled

4 eggs
1 cup half and half cream
⅛ teaspoon salt
Dash white pepper

Fit crescent rolls into greased 9 inch pie plate, pressing together perforated edges. Brush on mustard and pierce dough with fork repeatedly. Bake at 400° for 3 minutes. Remove from oven and press dough down with fork. (Dough will be puffy at this point.) Return to oven for 4 minutes more. Remove and press down again. Crust will never be soggy if these steps are followed. Sprinkle cheese and bacon on crust. Mix remaining ingredients and pour over cheese mixture. Bake at 350° about 55 minutes, or until set. Cool slightly before cutting. Serves 6.

Patt LaMontagne
Rockledge, Florida

SPINACH QUICHE
A savory blend of ingredients

1 package frozen spinach soufflé, thawed
2 eggs, beaten
3 tablespoons milk
2 teaspoons onion, grated
Dash of salt

¼ pound fresh mushrooms, sliced
4 ounces Swiss cheese, grated
1 deep dish (9 inch) unbaked pie shell

Mix all ingredients and pour into pie shell. Place shell on cookie sheet. Bake at 400° about 45 minutes. Serves 5 to 6.

Susan Mallinson
Vero Beach, Florida

CHEESE CRISP

Nice! This will please eight of you.

2 cups avocado dip (see index)
8 ripe tomatoes
Salt
1 pound sharp Cheddar cheese, grated
1 pound Monterey Jack cheese, grated

2 avocados, thinly sliced
Lime juice
Oil for frying
8 flour tortillas
2 (10 ounce) cans tomatoes with green chilies

Make avocado dip and refrigerate. Peel, seed and finely chop tomatoes; lightly salt and place in colander to drain. Grate cheese and blend together; cover and refrigerate. Slice avocados into thin slices, sprinkle with lime juice, cover and refrigerate.

Heat 1 inch of oil in skillet. Fry tortillas over medium heat, turning 2 or 3 times with tongs. This will make them brown evenly and become crisp. Drain on paper towels.

When all tortillas are cooked, place on foil-lined cookie sheets and mound each one with cheese all over top; use cheese generously. Bake at 350° until cheese melts, about 8 minutes.

To assemble: Place each tortilla on serving plate, put a mound of avocado dip in center and sprinkle tomatoes evenly over cheese. Arrange slices of avocado over tomatoes. Serve with tomatoes and green chilies sauce. Serves 8.

Cookie Smith
Vero Beach, Florida

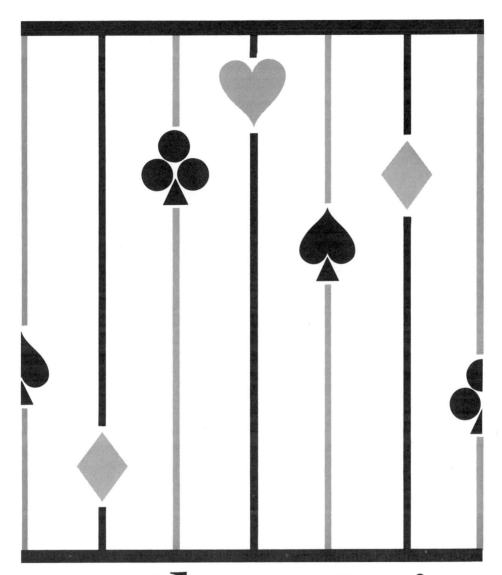

The Main Course

CHICKEN 'N' SWISS

4 whole chicken breasts,
   split, skinned and boned
6 ounces Swiss cheese,
   grated
1 (10¾ ounce) can cream of
   chicken soup
⅓ cup dry white wine

1 cup packaged herb
   stuffing mix, crushed
6 tablespoons butter or
   margarine, melted
Chopped parsley for
   garnish

Place chicken in lightly greased 13 × 9 inch baking dish. Sprinkle with cheese. Combine soup and wine; pour over Swiss cheese. Evenly spoon dressing over all. Drizzle butter over crumbs. Bake, covered, at 350° for 35 minutes; uncover and bake an additional 10 to 15 minutes, or until chicken is tender. Garnish. Freezes well. Serves 6.

CHICKEN PICCATA

A wonderful dinner for family or company with little effort

3 whole chicken breasts,
   halved, boned, skinned
⅓ cup flour
1½ teaspoons salt
¼ teaspoon pepper

4 tablespoons butter
4 tablespoons lemon juice
1 lemon, thinly sliced
3 tablespoons chopped
   fresh parsley

Place each piece of chicken between sheets of wax paper and with a rolling pin flatten to ¼ inch thickness. In a shallow dish combine flour, salt and pepper; add chicken, one piece at a time, dredging to coat. In a large skillet, melt butter over medium heat. Sauté chicken until golden brown, about 8 minutes on each side. Remove chicken, drain on paper towels; keep warm. Add lemon juice and lemon slices to pan drippings in skillet; cook until thoroughly heated. Spoon sauce over chicken and sprinkle with parsley. Serves 4.

CHICKEN IN PASTRY
Elegant dish for special occasions

6 chicken breast halves,
  skinned and boned
2 green onions with tops,
  minced
1 clove garlic, pressed
¾ pound fresh mushrooms,
  chopped
4 tablespoons butter,
  melted

¼ teaspoon salt
1 (10 ounce) package
  Pepperidge Farm frozen
  pastry shells, thawed
1 egg, beaten
½ cup currant jelly
¼ cup dry sherry

Place each chicken breast half between 2 sheets of waxed paper. Flatten chicken to ¼ inch thickness using a rolling pin; set aside. Sauté onion, garlic and mushrooms in butter until tender; drain. Stir in salt.

Roll out each pastry shell to a 6½ inch circle; spread 1 heaping tablespoon onion mixture on each, leaving a ½ inch border. Place 1 chicken breast half over vegetable mixture. Moisten edges of pastry with water; roll up jellyroll fashion. Place seam side down on a lightly greased 15 × 10 inch pan, pressing edges to seal. Brush with egg; bake at 425° for 30 minutes, or until golden brown.

Combine jelly and sherry in a small saucepan; cook over low heat, stirring constantly, until jelly melts. Serve with chicken. Serves 6.

Phyllis Garrett
Monett, Missouri

CHICKEN DELIGHT

*There's nothing like a chicken casserole for
honest-to-goodness good eating*

3 cups medium noodles
¼ cup green pepper,
  chopped
¼ cup minced onion
2 tablespoons butter
1 (10¾ ounce) can cream of
  chicken soup
1 cup dairy sour cream
¼ cup milk

⅛ cup sliced ripe olives
½ teaspoon salt
⅛ teaspoon white pepper
1½ cups diced cooked
  chicken
¼ cup blanched almonds,
  slivered
1 tablespoon minced
  parsley

Cook noodles in boiling salted water; drain. Sauté green pepper and onion in butter until tender. Add soup and next 6 ingredients. Gently stir in noodles. Turn into greased 1½ quart casserole; sprinkle with almonds and parsley. Bake at 350° for 35 to 40 minutes, or until hot and almonds are lightly browned. Serves 6.

CHICKEN DIVAN

*In many home recipe files this is an old favorite, but to younger cooks it
can be a delightful new addition*

4 whole chicken breasts
1 head broccoli
2 (10½ ounce) cans cream
  of chicken soup
¾ cup mayonnaise
1 teaspoon lemon juice

4 ounces sharp Cheddar
  cheese, grated (1 cup)
1 cup toasted bread crumbs
2 tablespoons melted
  butter

Boil chicken breasts in well seasoned water until tender. Bone chicken into large pieces, then slice. Cook broccoli just until tender-crisp, about 8 minutes. Drain and place in a 13 × 9 inch baking dish. Place chicken on broccoli. Combine soup, mayonnaise and lemon juice. Pour soup mixture over chicken and sprinkle with cheese. Mix crumbs with butter and spoon over top. Bake at 350° about 35 minutes. Serves 8.

RIJSTTAFEL

For a glamrous dinner...an East Indian chicken curry

4 slices bacon, diced
¼ cup grated onion
¼ cup celery, minced
½ clove garlic, minced
2 tablespoons vegetable oil
¼ cup flour, sifted
½ cup applesauce
3 teaspoons curry powder
3 tablespoons tomato paste
1 tablespon sugar

1 tablespoon lemon juice
2 chicken bouillon cubes
   dissolved in 1¼ cups hot
   water
Salt to taste
1 cup light cream
3 cups cubed cooked
   chicken
Hot fluffy rice

In saucepan, sauté bacon until crisp. Remove bacon and bacon grease. Put onion, celery and garlic in vegetable oil; sauté for 10 minutes. Blend in flour and cook mixture over low heat, stirring frequently, for 5 minutes. Add bacon and mix. Add applesauce, curry powder, tomato paste, sugar, lemon juice, bouillon cubes and water. Salt to taste. Cook the mixture, covered, over low heat for 25 to 30 minutes.

To serve curry sauce, add cream; stir. Add chicken and heat mixture through. Serve over rice with the usual accompaniments. The sauce doubles easily and freezes well. Add cream and chicken just before serving. Serves 6.

The ceremony of serving this dish is part of its charm. The accompaniments, which are served in separate dishes, are referred to as a "5 boy curry", or a "7 boy curry", or a "12 boy curry" etc., each boy representing one dish.

Suggested curry accompaniments:

Chutney
Crisp bacon bits
Chopped peanuts
Candied ginger
Grated coconut
Chopped cucumber

Banana chips
Currant jelly
Sliced avocado
Snipped parsley
Raisins
Sieved hard-cooked eggs

BAKED CHICKEN SOUFFLÉ

9 slices white bread, crust removed
4 cups diced cooked chicken
½ pound fresh mushrooms, sliced
¼ cup butter
1 (8 ounce) can water chestnuts, drained, sliced
½ cup mayonnaise
9 slices sharp Cheddar cheese
4 eggs, well beaten
2 cups milk
1 teaspoon salt
1 can mushroom soup
1 can celery soup
1 (2 ounce) jar pimiento, cut fine
2 cups diced bread, buttered

Line a 10 × 13 inch buttered baking pan with the bread slices. Top with chicken. Cook mushrooms in butter for 5 minutes. Spoon over chicken. Add water chestnuts and dot with mayonnaise. Top with cheese. Combine eggs, milk and salt; pour over chicken. Mix soups and pimiento; spoon over mixture. Cover with foil; refrigerate several hours or overnight. Bake, covered, at 350° for 1½ hours. Uncover and top with diced bread and brown 15 minutes more. Serves 9.

CRISPY CHICKEN

A family favorite

5 whole chicken breasts, halved, skinned, boned
1 teaspoon salt
¼ pound margarine, melted
5 cups corn flakes, crushed
3 additional tablespoons margarine, melted

Sprinkle chicken with salt. Dip chicken in margarine and then into corn flake crumbs. Line 10 × 14 inch baking pan with foil. Place chicken, one layer deep, in pan. Sprinkle remaining crumbs on top of chicken and drizzle additional margarine over crumbs. Bake, uncovered, at 350° for 45 minutes. Serves 6 to 8.

Janice Beuttell Cook
Menlo Park, California

CHICKEN TETRAZZINI

Popular everywhere with everybody

½ pound fresh mushrooms,
  sliced
6 tablespoons butter
½ pound thin spaghetti
2½ tablespoons flour
2 cups hot chicken broth
¾ teaspoon salt
¼ teaspoon freshly ground
  pepper

⅛ teaspoon nutmeg
1 cup heavy cream, heated
3 tablespoons dry sherry
2 cups cooked chicken, cut
  into large pieces
½ cup freshly grated
  Parmesan cheese

Sauté mushrooms in 3 tablespoons butter over moderately high heat; shake the pan so the mushrooms are coated without scorching. continue to cook, uncovered, shaking pan occasionally, for 3 to 4 minutes until soft but not browned. Cook spaghetti in boiling salted water just until tender, about 6 minutes; stir occasionally. Rinse under cold running water and drain.

Melt remaining butter in another saucepan. Stir in flour until smooth. Gradually add hot chicken broth stirring constantly until thickened; add salt, pepper and nutmeg. Remove from heat. Stir in heated heavy cream and sherry.

Combine the sauce with mushrooms and spaghetti in large saucepan. Toss over low heat for a minute or two. Add chicken pieces and mix well. Place mixture in large buttered baking dish; cover with cheese. Bake at 350° for 20 to 30 minutes, or until hot and lightly browned. Serves 6.

CHICKEN AND CHIPS

4 whole chicken breasts
1 (7 ounce) bag potato
　chips
8 ounces sharp Cheddar
　cheese, grated
1 (4 ounce) jar diced
　pimiento, drained

¾ cup sliced toasted
　almonds
2 (10½ ounce) cans
　mushroom soup
1 cup chicken broth

Boil chicken breasts in well seasoned water until tender. Bone chicken into large pieces, then slice. Crush potato chips. Put a layer of potato chips in a greased 3-quart casserole; add a layer of chicken, cheese, pimiento and almonds. Pour on half of soup and broth mixture. Repeat, saving some chips and almonds for topping. Bake at 325°, uncovered, for 30 minutes. Serves 8.

Polly Jernigan
Opelika, Alabama

CHICKEN BREASTS WITH ORANGE SAUCE
A gourmet's delight

3 whole chicken breasts,
　boned, split, skinned
1 teaspoon salt
¼ cup butter
2 tablespoons flour
2 tablespoons sugar

¼ teaspoon dry mustard
¼ teaspoon cinnamon
⅛ teaspoon ginger
1½ cups orange juice
3 cups cooked rice,
　optional

Sprinkle chicken with ½ teaspoon salt. Melt butter in large skillet; add chicken and brown both sides. Remove from skillet. Add flour, sugar, mustard, cinnamon, ginger and remaining ½ teaspoon salt to drippings in pan; stir to a smooth paste. Slowly add orange juice and cook, stirring constantly, until mixture thickens and comes to a boil. Add chicken breasts. Cover; simmer over low heat until chicken is tender, about 25 to 30 minutes. Serve with rice. Serves 4 to 6.

THE BEST COMPANY CHICKEN CASSEROLE

4 cups cooked chicken
breasts, cut into large
pieces
3 cups cooked rice
1 can water chestnuts,
sliced
1 can cream of celery soup
½ can chicken broth
1 medium size onion,
grated

1 cup mayonnaise
1 (4 ounce) jar pimiento,
diced
1 teaspoon curry powder
1 teaspoon salt
1 (10 ounce) package
frozen French style
green beans

Combine all ingredients; mix well. Turn into a greased 3-quart casserole. Bake at 325° for 40 to 50 minutes. May be prepared the day before serving or frozen for several weeks. Serves 12.

Ruth Keller
Asheville, North Carolina

SAUTÉED CHICKEN LIVERS WITH BRANDY
Classic in its simplicity

1 pound chicken livers
½ cup flour
½ teaspoon salt
½ teaspoon freshly ground
pepper

½ teaspoon paprika
Pinch thyme
¼ cup butter, melted
6 ounces chicken broth
¼ cup brandy

Dredge chicken livers in flour that has been seasoned with salt, pepper, paprika and thyme. Sauté in butter over medium heat for 10 minutes; turn livers once to evenly brown. Add chicken broth and simmer about 5 minutes longer. Warm brandy; light and pour over chicken livers. After flaming, stir and serve. Serves 4.

Goodwin C. Tyler
St. Paul, Minnesota

ELEGANT CHICKEN

It is!

3 large chicken breasts,
   boned and skinned
½ cup all-purpose flour
2 teaspoons salt

2 teaspoons paprika
½ cup milk
4 cups hot, cooked rice
Lemon cream sauce

Cut chicken breasts into ½ inch strips. Combine flour, salt and paprika. Dip chicken strips into milk, then roll in seasoned flour. Heat fat ½ inch deep in skillet. Add chicken strips and fry until golden brown. To serve, mound rice on serving dish, top with lemon cream sauce and fried chicken strips.

Lemon Cream Sauce:

¼ cup butter
¼ cup all-purpose flour
1 teaspoon salt
¼ teaspoon paprika
2 chicken bouillon cubes

1½ cups water
1 cup heavy cream
3 to 4 teaspoons lemon
   juice

Melt butter in saucepan. Blend in flour, salt, paprika and cut-up bouillon cubes. Gradually add water and cook, stirring constantly, until mixture thickens and comes to a boil. Add cream and heat to serving temperature. Stir in lemon juice. Serves 6.

HONEY-BAKE CHICKEN

1 broiler-fryer, cut up, or 3
   breasts, split and
   skinned
¼ cup butter

½ cup honey
¼ cup prepared mustard
1 teaspoon salt
1 teaspoon curry

Wash and dry chicken. Melt butter in shallow baking pan. Stir into butter the remaining ingredients. Roll chicken into butter mixture, coating both sides. Arrange meaty side up in single layer in baking pan. Bake at 375° for 1 hour, or until chicken is tender and richly glazed. Serves 4.

CHICKEN FIESTA

4 cups cooked breast of
  chicken, cubed
1 (4 ounce) can peeled
  green chilies, diced
1 pound Cheddar cheese,
  shredded (reserve 1½
  cups for topping)
½ cup ripe olives, sliced

1 can cream of mushroom
  soup
1 can cream of chicken
  soup
1 cup milk
1 tablespoon onion, grated
1 (10 ounce) package corn
  tortilla chips
Picante sauce, optional

Combine all ingredients but tortillas. Layer bottom of a buttered 9 x 13-inch baking pan with half of tortillas. Layer half of chicken mixture, remaining tortillas, then remaining chicken. Cover with reserved cheese. Bake, uncovered, at 350° for 40 minutes. Serve with picante sauce. Serves 8.

CHICKEN ROLLS WITH FRUIT AND WALNUTS

This delicious blend of flavors is easy to prepare

3 slices bread, toasted,
  cubed
¼ cup dark raisins
1 (8 ounce) can crushed
  pineapple, drained
  (reserve juice)
½ cup walnuts, chopped,
  toasted
¼ teaspoon cinnamon

4 chicken breasts
  (5 to 6-ounce each),
  boned, skinned
1 tablespoon vegetable oil
¾ cup reserved pineapple
  juice
½ cup tomato catsup
¼ teaspoon ginger
¼ teaspoon pepper

For stuffing, combine toast, raisins, pineapple, walnuts and cinnamon. Flatten chicken to uniform thickness. Place about ½ cup of stuffing across center of each chicken breast; fold ends to center and secure with wooden pick. Lightly brown chicken in oil on all sides. Combine remaining ingredients; pour over chicken. Simmer, uncovered, 20 to 30 minutes, basting occasionally. Remove picks before serving. Serve with sauce. Serves 4.

Alice Cook
Asheville, North Carolina

*CRANBERRY GLAZED CHICKEN

6 whole chicken breasts,
boned, split, skinned
Salt and pepper to taste
1 (12 ounce) can whole
cranberries

1 (8 ounce) bottle Russian
salad dressing
1 envelope dry onion soup
mix

Line a 13 × 9 inch baking pan with heavy foil. Arrange chicken
in pan. Add salt and pepper. Combine cranberries, salad
dressing and onion soup mix; mix well. Pour sauce over
chicken. Bake at 350° for 1 hour, or until chicken is tender.
Serves 6 to 8.

* For apricot-glazed chicken, substitute 1 (10 ounce) jar of apricot
preserves for the cranberries.

TURKEY BREAST
Cooked in chicken broth and seasoned in a tangy marinade

1 (6 pound) frozen turkey
breast
2 (10¾) ounce cans chicken
broth
2 cups water
2 onions, each stuck with 4
cloves

1 celery stalk with leaves,
cut up
4 carrots, peeled, cut up
2 teaspoons salt
10 whole peppercorns
1 bay leaf

Thaw and rinse turkey breast. In an 8 quart kettle, combine
remaining ingredients; add turkey breast. Bring to boiling,
reduce heat, and simmer, covered, for 2 hours. Remove from
heat.

Let stand, frequently basting with broth, for 1½ hours, or
until cool enough to handle; or refrigerate overnight, covered.
Remove skin. Slice, cube, etc.

SHRIMP AND DEVILED EGGS

About the best thing you've ever tasted

8 eggs, deviled
1½ pounds medium-size
  shrimp, peeled and
  deveined
4 tablespoons butter
4 tablespoons flour
¼ teaspoon salt

2 cups half and half cream
4 ounces sharp Cheddar
  cheese, shredded (1 cup)
Several dashes cayenne
  pepper
Crushed fresh potato chips

In 8 individual casserole dishes, place deviled eggs. Add shrimp to boiling water for 1 minute. Drain; place in ice water for 1 minute. Arrange shrimp around deviled eggs.

Melt butter in heavy saucepan, blend in flour and salt. Over low heat, stir constantly, for 3 minutes. Add cream, continue stirring until mixture thickens. Add cheese and cayenne pepper and cook until cheese melts. Pour over eggs and shrimp. Sprinkle top with potato chips. Bake at 350° for 30 minutes. Serves 8.

Deviled Eggs:

8 hard-cooked eggs
2 tablespoons mayonnaise
2 tablespoons mustard
  (Dijon type)
¼ teaspoon salt

2 teaspoons vinegar
Several dashes cayenne
  pepper
¼ teaspoon dry mustard
⅛ teaspoon onion powder

Cut eggs in half, lengthwise. Remove yolks and mash until fine and crumbly. Add remaining ingredients and blend until smooth. Fill hollow of egg whites. Chill.

Gil True
Vero Beach, Florida

HERBED SHRIMP

Splurge and enjoy

2 pounds raw medium
   shrimp, peeled and
   deveined
1 cup butter
1 teaspoon basil, crushed
1 teaspoon tarragon,
   crushed

1 clove garlic, pressed
1 cup fine, dry bread
   crumbs
½ teaspoon salt
¼ teaspoon pepper
Parsley for garnish

Add shrimp to boiling water for 1½ minutes. Drain. Place shrimp in ice water for a minute. Divide shrimp into six individual bakers. cream butter with all remaining ingredients. Mix well and spread over shrimp. Bake at 350° for 18 to 20 minutes. Garnish. Serves 6.

TUNA FLORENTINE STRATA

Tuna was never tastier

2 (6½ ounce) cans solid
   white tuna, drained
⅓ cup chopped scallions
1 (10 ounce) package
   frozen chopped spinach,
   thawed and drained well
4 ounces Swiss cheese,
   shredded (1 cup)
1 tablespoon lemon juice

1 teaspon salt
¼ teaspoon thyme
6 slices bread, crust
   removed and cubed
6 eggs
2 cups milk
½ teaspoon dry mustard
⅛ teaspoon cayenne
   pepper

In a large bowl mix tuna, scallions, spinach, cheese, lemon juice, ¼ teaspoon salt and thyme. Layer half of bread cubes in buttered 2 quart soufflé dish, top with half of tuna mixture, repeat with remaining bread cubes and tuna. Combine eggs, milk, dry mustard, cayenne pepper and remaining ¾ teaspoon salt; pour over tuna. Let stand 2 hours or longer. Place baking dish in larger pan and add 1 inch of water. Bake at 350° uncovered for 50 to 60 minutes, or until a knife inserted in center comes out clean. Let stand for 5 minutes. Serves 8.

Jane Stelter
Hendersonville, North Carolina

SHRIMP ELEGANTÉ

This will delight your foursome

1 (14 ounce) can whole artichoke hearts	1 tablespoon Worcestershire sauce
¾ pound shrimp	¼ cup dry sherry
¼ pound fresh mushrooms, sliced	¼ cup freshly grated Parmesan cheese
2 tablespoons butter	Paprika
1½ cups cream sauce	Hot fluffy rice (see index)

Drain artichokes and cut in half. Arrange on bottom of buttered shallow baking dish. Rinse shrimp, boil for 1 minute, rinse again, shell and devein. Add shrimp in a layer over artichoke hearts. Add mushrooms which have been sautéed in butter for about 6 minutes.

To cream sauce, add Worcestershire sauce and sherry. After blending well, pour mixture over shrimp. Sprinkle top with Parmesan cheese and paprika.

Bake at 375° for 20 minutes, or until mixture is hot. Serve over hot rice. Serves 4.

Cream Sauce:

3 tablespoons butter	Dash white pepper
3 tablespoons flour	1½ cups half and half cream, scalded
½ teaspoon salt	

Melt butter in saucepan over low heat. Stir in flour blending until smooth; cook 2 to 3 minutes. Add salt and pepper. Slowly add cream, continue stirring, and cook until mixture thickens. Yield: 1½ cups.

SALMON LOAF

Don't pass by this one!

1 (1 pound) can Alaska red salmon
1 (11 ounce) can celery soup
1 cup cracker crumbs
2 eggs, beaten
5 tablespoons onion, grated
2 tablespoons parsley, minced
1 stalk celery, minced
4 tablespoons mayonnaise
5 to 6 dashes Tabasco
¼ teaspoon pepper
Olive sauce
Minced parsley
Paprika

Drain, skin, bone and flake salmon, reserving oil. Stir in ½ can soup, salmon oil and cracker crumbs. Combine remaining ingredients, but olive sauce, parsley and paprika and add to salmon mixture. Place in 8½ × 4½ inch greased loaf pan. Bake at 350° for 45 minutes. Serve with olive sauce. Garnish with parsley and paprika. Serves 4 to 5.

Olive Sauce:

½ can celery soup
½ cup milk
1 tablespoon cornstarch
2 tablespoons mayonnaise
10 pimiento stuffed olives, slices
1 tablespoon olive juice

Blend soup, milk and cornstarch. Cook until smooth and thick. Remove from heat and stir in mayonnaise, olives and juice.

Phyl Miller
Johnson City, Tennessee

SOLE VÉRONIQUE

6 fillets of sole	2 tablespoons flour
Salt and freshly ground	1 cup milk
pepper to taste	1 cup seedless green
½ cup dry white wine	grapes
2 tablespoons butter	Minced parsley for garnish

Place fillets in buttered 9 × 13 inch baking dish. Add salt and pepper. Pour wine over fish. Cover pan with foil and bake at 350° for 15 minutes. Melt butter; add flour and cook for 2 to 3 minutes. Add milk and cook until thick, stirring constantly. Pour off juice from fish and add to cream sauce, mixing well; add half of the grapes to sauce. Pour sauce over fish and place under broiler just long enough to brown surface. Place rest of grapes around fillets before serving. Garnish with parsley. Serves 6.

SALMON CROQUETTES

A wonderful entrée with little effort

1 (1 pound) can Alaska	¼ teaspoon salt
red salmon	¼ teaspoon fresh ground
1 tablespoon mayonnaise	pepper
1 egg, beaten	8 saltine crackers, coarsely
1 teaspoon lemon juice	crushed
⅛ teaspoon baking powder	Minced parsley for garnish
2 tablespoons chopped	
parsley	

Drain salmon. Remove skin and bones; flake. Add remaining ingredients but parsley. Mix well and chill. Make into four patties. In a heavy skillet add ½ inch oil. Heat to 375°. A simple test, when no frying thermometer is available, can be made with a small cube of bread. If the cube browns in sixty seconds, the oil will be around 375°. Add croquettes and fry 2 to 3 minutes. Drain on absorbent paper before serving. Serves 4.

Frances Watkins
Anderson, South Carolina

POT ROAST IN FOIL

3 pound sirloin tip roast
1 pint fresh mushrooms,
  sliced and sautéed in
  butter

1 (10¾ ounce) can golden
  mushroom soup
1 package dry onion soup
  mix
1 cup dry sherry

Line roasting pan with 2 large pieces of heavy foil. Place meat in center of foil. Combine remaining ingredients; pour over roast. Bring edges of foil together and seal completely so that no juice can escape. Bake at 325° for 3 hours. Rice is a fine accompaniment. Serves 6.

GRINGO CASSEROLE

Borders on the terrific!

1 medium onion, grated
1 clove garlic, crushed
1 tablespoon vegetable oil
1½ pounds lean ground
  chuck
1 (8 ounce) can tomato
  sauce

⅓ cup water
1½ tablespoons chili
  powder
1 teaspoon oregano
⅛ teaspoon ground cloves
1 (8 ounce) package corn
  chips

Topping:
2 cups finely shredded
  lettuce
Fresh tomatoes, diced

4 ounces sharp Cheddar
  cheese, grated (1 cup)

Sauté onion and garlic in oil until golden. Add ground chuck and brown. Drain off fat. Add tomato sauce, water, chili powder, oregano and ground cloves. Return to stove over low heat and blend ingredients. Place ½ of corn chips in buttered 2 quart baking dish. Spoon half of meat mixture over chips. Repeat, ending with meat. Bake at 325° for 20 minutes, or until heated thoroughly. Remove from oven and garnish with lettuce, tomatoes and cheese. Serves 6.

ALL AMERICAN MEAT LOAF
This is a winner from coast to coast

1½ pounds ground chuck
1 egg, beaten
½ cup dry bread crumbs
5 tablespoons onion, grated
⅓ cup half and half cream

¼ cup Heinz 57 Sauce
3 tablespoons fresh parsley, minced
¾ teaspoon salt
⅛ teaspoon pepper

Combine all ingredients; mix lightly. Place loaf in greased 8½ × 4½ inch pan. Bake at 350° for 1 hour. Serves 5.

CALIFORNIA BEEF-NOODLE BAKE
A great family dish-guests too!

1 pound ground chuck
½ cup onion, grated
1 tablespoon butter, melted
2 (8 ounce) cans tomato sauce
1 teaspoon sugar
¾ teaspoon salt
¼ teaspoon garlic salt
¼ teaspoon pepper
4 cups uncooked medium noodles

1 cup cream style cottage cheese
1 (8 ounce) package cream cheese, softened
¼ cup dairy sour cream
⅓ cup finely chopped green onions
¼ cup finely chopped green pepper
¼ cup grated Parmesan cheese

Sauté beef and onion in butter until browned. Stir in tomato sauce, sugar, salt, garlic salt and pepper. Remove from heat. Cook noodles according to package directions; drain. Combine cottage cheese, cream cheese, sour cream, onions and pepper. In a 2 quart casserole, spread half of noodles; top with a little of meat sauce; cover with cheese mixture; then cover with rest of noodles and remaining meat sauce. Sprinkle with Parmesan cheese. Bake, uncovered, at 350° for 30 to 35 minutes, or until hot. May freeze. Serves 8.

Janice Beuttell Cook
Menlo Park, California

BEEF EN CROÛTE

The long list of ingredients just means that it's good . . .
it is easy to prepare

1 cup onion, grated	2 tablespoons flour
1 tablespoon oil	½ cup dairy sour cream
1½ pounds ground chuck	1 (17¼ ounce) package
1 teaspoon salt	Pepperidge Farm Puff
1 teaspoon pepper	Pastry
1 teaspoon garlic powder	1 cup melted butter
1 tablespoon	1 cup dry bread crumbs
Worcestershire sauce	¼ cup chopped parsley
¼ cup white wine	

Sauté onions in oil; add meat and cook until lightly browned.
Drain. Add salt, pepper, garlic powder, Worcestershire sauce
and wine. Simmer until most of the liquid is absorbed. Stir in
flour; add sour cream and blend. Cool to room temperature.

Thaw pastry 20 minutes. Flour board and rolling pin. Unfold
pastry and cut each pre-rolled sheet into quarters. Roll each
piece of pastry to 6×6 inch square. Brush each square with
melted butter and sprinkle with 2 tablespoons bread crumbs.

Spoon about 3 heaping tablespoons of meat mixture on each
square and spread to within 1 inch of edge. Fold pastry over
filling; fold in margins. Brush with butter. Place on lightly
buttered baking sheet, seam side down.

Bake at 375° for 25 to 30 minutes. Before serving, pour sauce
over, and top with parsley. Serves 8.

Continued on next page

Sauce for Pastry:

¼ cup white wine
½ cup water
2⅓ tablespoons cornstarch
1 cup beef consommé

½ cup fresh mushrooms, sliced
¼ cup green onions, minced

Add wine and water to cornstarch in top of double boiler gradually, whisking well. Stir in consommé and mushrooms. Cook and stir until thickened and clear. Serve over pastry. Sprinkle with onions.

Allied Arts Guild Restaurant
The Palo Alto Auxiliary for the benefit of
Children's Hospital at Stanford, California

LUCY'S SPAGHETTI MEAT SAUCE

None better . . . makes a lot . . . freeze some

3 large onions, chopped
2 cloves garlic, minced
¼ stick butter
¼ cup oil
3 pounds ground chuck
1 pound fresh mushrooms, sliced
2 (28 ounce) cans Italian tomatoes

1 (12 ounce) can tomato paste
1 tablespoon chili powder
1 tablespoon sugar
¼ teaspoon each of marjoram, oregano, basil, thyme
3 bay leaves
Salt and pepper to taste

Cook onion and garlic in butter and oil until clear. Add meat and brown. Stir in sliced mushrooms. Combine tomatoes, tomato paste and all seasonings; add to meat mixture. Simmer, uncovered, until thick; at least 3 hours. When cool, put in refrigerator. Before reheating to serve, or freezing, skim off fat. Serve over very thin spaghetti. Serves 10 to 12

Lucy Jones
Vero Beach, Florida

CHARLEY'S CHILI

It should win the Championship Chili Cook-off this year

6 tablespoon vegetable oil, divided
3 pounds lean beef, diced or coarsely ground
2 cups coarsely chopped onion, loosely packed
2 tablespoons garlic, finely chopped
4 cups beef broth
1 (6 ounce) can tomato paste

5 tablespoons chili powder
1 to 2 teaspoons red pepper flakes
1 teaspoon oregano
1 teaspoon ground cumin
1 teaspoon salt
Few grindings black pepper
1 (14 ounce) can dark red kidney beans

In a large skillet heat 4 tablespoons oil over medium-high heat. Add beef and brown in 3 batches, transferring to a Dutch oven with slotted spoon. Drain liquid from skillet. Add remaining oil to skillet; cook onions and garlic 5 minutes, stirring frequently. Stir onions and garlic into meat. Add remaining ingredients except beans.

Bring to a boil; reduce heat, half cover pot and simmer 1½ hours, stirring occasionally. Add beans 15 minutes before meat is done. Degrease before serving. Yield: 2 quarts.

Charles Fairchild
Lakewood, Ohio

HERBED SPAGHETTI CASSEROLE

Beef and pork are an excellent combination for this fine sauce

1 pound ground chuck
1 pound hot bulk pork
  sausage
1 cup chopped onion
2 cloves garlic, pressed
2 (15 ounce) cans tomato
  sauce
1 (12 ounce) can tomato
  paste
1 (6 ounce) can
  mushrooms, drained and
  sliced
2 cups water
¼ cup chopped fresh
  parsley
1 tablespoon brown sugar
1½ teaspoons oregano
¼ teaspoon thyme
1 bay leaf
1½ teaspoons chili powder
1½ teaspoons salt
16 ounces thin spaghetti,
  cooked, drained

Combine beef, sausage, onion and garlic in 6 quart heavy saucepan. Cook until meat is brown; drain drippings. Add remaining ingredients. Bring to boil, reduce heat, cover and simmer for 2 hours, stirring occasionally. Remove bay leaf. Combine sauce and cooked spaghetti; toss until well blended. Place in a large greased casserole. Bake at 350° about 20 minutes, or until hot. May freeze. Serves 8.

Charlotte Hagar
Vero Beach, Florida

CHEESE STUFFED SHELLS FLORENTINE

A really good family dinner

1 (12 ounce) package
    Jumbo Shells
1 pound ground chuck
1 tablespoon vegetable oil
1 (32 ounce) jar marinara
    sauce
1 (10 ounce) package
    frozen chopped spinach,
    drain well
1 pound Ricotta cheese

8 ounces Mozzarella
    cheese, divided
1 egg, beaten
2 tablespoons Italian
    seasoning
1 (6 ounce) package
    Provalone cheese
1 pound sweet Italian
    sausage

Cook shells according to package directions. Drain and rinse with cold water. Brown beef in oil; pour off drippings. Add marinara sauce to meat.

Combine spinach and Ricotta cheese; mix thoroughly. Add 4 ounces of Mozzarella cheese, egg and Italian seasoning to spinach mixture; blend well.

Spoon a small amount of meat sauce into greased 9×13 inch baking dish. Using a teaspoon, place spinach-cheese mixture in each shell. Place shells on top of meat sauce. Spoon remaining sauce over mixture.

Slice Provalone cheese and cover sauce; sprinkle remaining Mozzarella cheese over all. Slice sausage and arrange around sides of casserole. Bake at 350° for 30 minutes. May freeze. Serves 10.

Marge Dunkelberger
Sebastian, Florida

CONTINENTAL GOULASH
A wonderful dish for entertaining

2½ pounds sirloin tip beef, cut into 1 inch cubes
2 tablespoons vegetable oil
2 beef bouillon cubes dissolved in 1½ cups boiling water
½ garlic clove, crushed
1 tablespoon Hungarian paprika
5 tablespoons butter
5 tablespoons flour
¼ cup tomato purée
16 ounces noodles, boiled
Parsley for garnish

Sear beef in vegetable oil. Add bouillon mixture and garlic. Cover and cook over medium heat for 1½ to 2 hours, or until meat is tender. Stir in paprika. Make a roux of butter and flour; stir in a little broth from beef and add to beef mixture to thicken goulash. Add tomato purée and stir until smooth and heated through. Serve over hot noodles. Garnish. Serves 6.

Edith McCarthy
Vero Beach, Florida

VEAL PAPRIKA
Company caliber

2 pounds boned veal stew meat, in 1½ inch cubes
½ cup flour
2 tablespoons butter
2 tablespoons vegetable oil
2 garlic cloves, pressed
1 tablespoon paprika
1 teaspoon salt
¼ teaspoon pepper
½ cup water
1 cup dairy sour cream
8 ounces broad noodles, cooked
⅓ cup toasted slivered almonds
1 tablespoon poppy seeds

Lightly dredge veal in flour. To hot butter and oil, in Dutch oven, add veal and sauté until it begins to brown; add garlic and brown well. Sprinkle veal with paprika, salt and pepper. Add water. Simmer, covered, 1 hour, or until tender. Stir in sour cream; simmer 5 minutes. Arrange cooked noodles in a ring on a warm serving platter. Spoon veal into center; top with almonds and poppy seeds. Serves 6.

Susan Johnson
Bemedji, Minnesota

VEAL CORDON BLEU

8 thin veal scallopine
4 thin slices baked ham
4 thin slices Swiss cheese
3 eggs, beaten
¼ cup dry white wine
½ teaspoon thyme

Salt and pepper to taste
30 saltine crackers,
  crushed
4 tablespoons butter,
  melted
¼ cup dry white wine

Place veal between sheets of wax paper and pound until very thin. Put ham on 4 slices of veal, cover with cheese, and top with remaining veal slice.

Combine eggs, ¼ cup wine, thyme, salt and pepper. Dip each veal "sandwich" in egg mixture, then in cracker crumbs. Sauté in heated butter about 8 minutes, turning once, until meat is browned and cheese is melted. Remove from skillet to a heated platter.

Add ¼ cup wine to skillet. Simmer sauce for 30 seconds; pour over veal. Serve at once. Serves 4.

Ruth Breese
Vero Beach, Florida

LAMB CARDINAL

Epicurean

¼ cup currant jelly
¼ cup tarragon vinegar
½ cup catsup
1 tablespoon butter
1 teaspoon Worcestershire
  sauce

¼ teaspoon Accent
Salt and pepper to taste
8 to 12 thin slices cold
  cooked lamb
1 tablespoon Marsala wine

In an iron skillet put jelly, vinegar, catsup, butter and Worcestershire sauce. Cook until jelly is melted and all is well blended. Add Accent, salt and pepper to taste. Add lamb slices and cook, uncovered, over low heat for 20 minutes. Just before serving, add wine to the sauce. Stir. Serves 4 to 6.

LAMB AND WILD RICE CASSEROLE
Pamper your guests with this regal dish

½ cup flour
1 teaspoon salt
½ teaspoon pepper
1 teaspoon paprika
2 pounds lamb cut in
  pieces
½ stick butter

2 onions, grated
1 (16 ounce) can tomatoes
1 pound fresh mushrooms,
  sliced
Lots of chopped parsley
1 cup dairy sour cream
Cooked wild rice

Mix together flour, salt, pepper and paprika. Put in paper bag; add lamb pieces and toss until lightly coated. In skillet, melt butter, add lamb and onions; brown. Transfer to a 2 quart casserole, add tomatoes and bake at 350° for 30 minutes. Add mushrooms and bake 30 minutes longer. Remove from oven. Put lots of parsley on top, a large dollop of sour cream and serve over rice. Can be prepared ahead of time and reheated. Serves 6.

Carolyn McCluney
St. Louis, Missouri

TEXAS CHOW

1½ pounds ground chuck
2 (10 ounce) cans
  tomatoes and green
  chilies
1 teaspoon chili powder
1 teaspoon basil
1 teaspoon sugar

1 (8 ounce) package wide
  noodles, cooked
1 cup dairy sour cream
4 ounces cream cheese,
  softened
2 teaspoons freeze-dried
  chives

In a Dutch oven brown beef. Remove from heat; drain liquid. Stir in tomatoes and green chilies, chili powder, basil and sugar. Layer noodles and beef mixture in a greased 9 × 13 inch baking pan. Mix sour cream, cream cheese and chives together and spread over top of mixture. Bake at 325° for 20 minutes. Serves 8.

COMPANY HAM LOAF

1½ pounds smoked ham,
  ground
1½ pounds lean pork,
  ground
4 eggs, beaten
1½ cups cornflakes,
  crushed

1½ cups milk
⅛ teaspoon pepper
4 teaspoons Dijon mustard
½ cup brown sugar
⅔ cup pineapple juice

Combine ham, pork, eggs, cornflakes, milk and pepper. Mix well. Shape into 2 loaves and place in greased loaf pans. Spread mixture of mustard and sugar on top of loaves and pour pineapple juice over each one. Bake at 350° for 1½ hours. Baste loaves several times during baking. Serves 10.

GLAZED HAM BALLS

1½ pounds smoked ham,
  ground
1 pound lean ground pork
2 cups Waverly cracker
  crumbs

2 eggs, beaten
1 cup milk
Juice of 1 lemon and lemon
  peel, grated

Glaze:

1 cup brown sugar
½ cup water

½ cup vinegar
1 teaspoon dry mustard

Mix ham, pork, crumbs, eggs, milk, lemon and peel. Shape into 16 balls. Place in greased shallow baking dish. In saucepan heat glaze ingredients until sugar is dissolved. Pour over ham balls. Bake, uncovered, at 325° for 1½ hours, spooning glaze over ham balls two or three times. Serves 8.

Peggy Young
Centerville, Iowa

96

PORK À L'ORANGE

Vegetable oil
4 center-cut pork chops
1 (6 ounce) can frozen
orange juice concentrate,
thawed

6 ounces dry white wine
1 teaspoon dried oregano
1 teaspoon dried sweet
basil
Slivered almonds

In a heavy skillet heat a small amount of vegetable oil. Add pork chops and fry until nicely browned on both sides. Place in a flat, uncovered baking dish. Set aside. Combine orange juice, wine, oregano and basil. Pour over pork chops. Place in 350° oven and cook for 30 minutes. Sprinkle the top of chops liberally with almonds, spoon sauce over almonds, and cook 30 minutes longer, or until sauce thickens slightly. Serve with sauce spooned over the chops. Serves 4.

PORK CHOPS, CRANBERRIES AND APPLESAUCE

Bon Appetit!

6 pork chops, cut 1½
inches thick
1½ teaspoons salt
½ teaspoon freshly
ground pepper
⅛ teaspoon thyme
2 eggs, beaten
1 cup dry bread crumbs
3 tablespoons butter

2 teaspoons chopped onion
1 cup applesauce
1 cup canned whole
cranberries
½ cup hot water
1 tablespoon
Worcestershire sauce
2 tablespoons sugar

Trim fat from chops; rub with mixture of salt, pepper and thyme. Dip chops in eggs, then in crumbs, coating well. Melt butter in heavy skillet; sauté onions 2 minutes. Add chops and brown on both sides. Mix together applesauce, cranberries, hot water, Worcestershire sauce and sugar. Pour over chops. Cover and bake at 350° for 50 minutes, or until chops are tender; remove cover for last 15 minutes. Serves 6.

Gordon Leland
Meriden, New Hampshire

PORK BARBECUE

This is an absolute treasure of a recipe

7 pound pork loin
Salt and pepper
1 (10 ounce) bottle Heinz
 57 sauce

1 (14 ounce) bottle catsup
1 (16 ounce) bottle red hot
 barbecue sauce

Have butcher split bone and cut off excess fat. Line roasting pan with foil. Place meat on rack in pan; add salt and pepper. Bake, covered, overnight, at 225° for 9 to 10 hours.

Remove from oven and cool. Pull meat apart; chop slightly. Combine sauces in large saucepan. Simmer for a few minutes; remove from heat. Add meat and mix well; marinate several hours.

Before serving, place barbecue in large casserole to heat. For supper serve barbecue in buns. For a cocktail party serve with small party rolls, split, buttered and heated. May freeze. Serves 20 for supper and 40 for cocktails.

Carolyn Davis
Asheville, North Carolina

Ida Yancey
Atlanta, Georgia

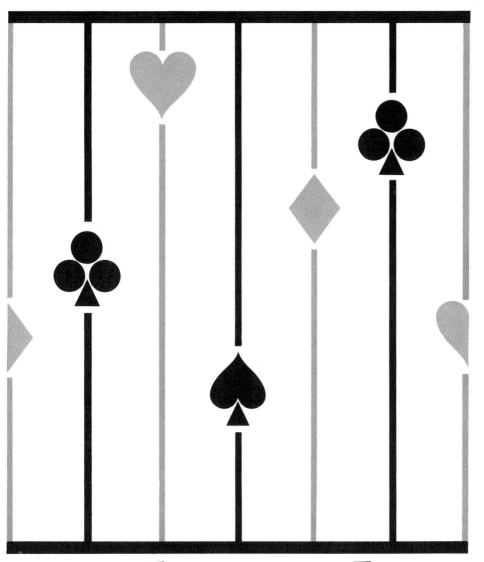

Side Dishes

APPLE FRITTERS

The secret of a good fritter is the batter

6 tablespoons flour
4½ tablespoons water
1 egg, separated
1 tablespoon vegetable oil
Pinch of salt

3 tart apples, sugared
(peel, core, cut into
eighths)
Confectioners' sugar for
topping

Mix flour gradually with water; add egg yolk and oil beaten together with salt. Rest dough at least 2 hours, covered and refrigerated. Just before using batter, beat well until smooth. Beat white of egg until stiff but not dry; fold into dough. Dip apple slices into batter and fry in deep fat heated to 375°. Fritters will take 4 to 5 minutes to brown. Drain on absorbent paper. Dust with confectioners' sugar. Serves 4.

BANANA SCALLOPS

Good served with a meat course

Vegetable oil
1 teaspoon salt
1 egg, slightly beaten

6 firm bananas
¾ cup crushed corn flakes

For deep fat frying have deep kettle ½ to ⅔ full of vegetable oil. For shallow frying have 1 inch of vegetable oil in frying pan. Heat oil to 375°, or until a 1 inch cube of bread will brown in about 40 seconds. It is important to have oil at correct temperature before frying. Add salt to egg. Peel bananas and slice crosswise into pieces 1 inch thick. Dip into egg. Drain. Roll in corn flake crumbs. Fry in hot oil 1½ to 2 minutes, or until brown and tender. Drain well. Serve very hot. Serves 6.

CURRANT GLAZED PEACHES
Serve hot with meats or poultry

1 (1 pound, 13 ounce) can
  peach halves
Brown sugar

Fresh lemon juice
2 tablespoons currant jelly

Drain peaches thoroughly; arrange, cut side up, in shallow buttered baking dish. Place a teaspoon of brown sugar in center of each peach, and drizzle about ½ teaspoon lemon juice in each. Broil 4 inches from heat until lightly browned. Melt currant jelly; spoon over browned peaches and broil a minute or two longer, until glazed. Serves 5 to 6.

PASTA WITH FRESH BROCCOLI
Different, distinctive and delicious

1 head broccoli
½ teaspoon salt
1 (8 ounce) box twists or
  sea-shell pasta
½ cup olive oil
6 tablespoons butter
4 garlic cloves, pressed

½ teaspoon cayenne
  pepper
3 ripe tomatoes, peeled
  and quartered
½ cup freshly grated
  Parmesan cheese

Divide broccoli into bite-size flowerets. Steam with salt until crisp-tender, about 8 minutes. Cook pasta according to package directions. Drain. Heat olive oil, butter, garlic and pepper; pour over pasta, lightly toss, then add broccoli. Recipe can be prepared to this point and kept warm. When ready to serve, toss pasta mixture with tomatoes and sprinkle with Parmesan cheese. Serve on warm plates. Serves 6.

NOODLE CASSEROLE

1 (8 ounce) package thin
  egg noodles
Salt
1 cup cottage cheese
1 cup dairy sour cream
½ cup half and half cream
1½ teaspoons
  Worcestershire sauce

4 tablespoons onion,
  grated
1 clove garlic, pressed
½ teaspoon salt
⅛ teaspoon pepper
4 to 5 dashes Tabasco
1 cup corn flakes, crushed
2 tablespoons butter

Cook noodles in boiling salted water. Drain. Toss noodles with cheese, sour cream, cream and Worcestershire sauce. Blend in onion, garlic and seasonings. Pour into buttered 2 quart casserole. Top with cornflakes and dot with butter. Bake at 350° for 20 minutes, covered. Uncover and bake 5 to 10 minutes longer. Serves 8.

FETTUCCINE
Invite Alfredo . . . He'll love it

1 (8 ounce) package
  fettuccine green noodles
2 shallots, crushed with
  garlic press
1 tablespoon butter
1 cup chicken broth
½ cup heavy cream
1 cup dairy sour cream

¼ cup freshly grated
  Parmesan cheese
1 tablespoon chives,
  chopped
Freshly ground pepper to
  taste
Fresh chopped parsley for
  garnish

Cook fettuccine according to package directions. Drain and rinse with cold water. Set aside. In large saucepan, sauté shallots in butter; stir in chicken broth and boil for 3 to 4 minutes. Remove from heat. Add heavy cream slowly. Add fettuccine, sour cream, Parmesan cheese, chives and pepper. Toss thoroughly. Return to low heat; stir until hot. Garnish. Serve immediately on warm plates. Serves 4.

MACARONI MOUSSE WITH FRESH MUSHROOM SAUCE

A tasty combination

8 ounces macaroni, cooked
2 cups milk, scalded
4 slices bread, cubed
¼ pound butter
1 small jar pimiento
4 eggs, beaten
2 tablespoons parsley, minced

½ teaspoon salt
¼ pound sharp Cheddar cheese, grated
1½ teaspoons minced onion
Mushroom sauce

Place cooked macaroni in greased 2 quart casserole. Pour milk over bread and butter. Add pimiento, eggs, parsley, salt, cheese and onion; blend. Pour over macaroni and mix well. Bake at 350° for 30 to 40 minutes. Serve with mushroom sauce. Serves 8.

Mushroom Sauce:

¼ pound butter
¾ pound fresh mushrooms, sliced
1½ tablespoons flour

½ teaspoon salt
¼ teaspoon paprika
Pinch marjoram
1 cup half and half cream

In a large frying pan, melt butter; add mushrooms and sprinkle with flour. Toss and cook over medium heat, stirring occasionally, for 8 to 10 minutes. Season with salt, paprika and marjoram; slowly stir in cream. Cook and stir until mixture thickens. Yield: 2¼ cups.

Charlotte Hagar
Vero Beach, Florida

MUSHROOM CASSEROLE

Keep this in mind for guest dinners

1 pound fresh mushrooms,
  coarsely sliced
¼ cup butter
8 slices white bread,
  buttered
½ cup onion, grated
½ cup celery, minced
½ cup green pepper,
  minced

½ cup mayonnaise
¾ teaspoon salt
¾ teaspoon pepper
2 eggs, slightly beaten
1½ cups milk
1 (10¾ ounce) can
  mushroom soup
¼ pound sharp Cheddar
  cheese, grated (1 cup)

Sauté mushrooms in butter. Cut 3 slices of bread into 1 inch squares; place in 9 × 13 inch baking casserole. Combine mushrooms with onions, celery, green pepper, mayonnaise, salt and pepper and place on top of bread squares. Cut 3 more slices of bread into 1 inch squares and place on top of mushroom mixture. Combine eggs and milk and pour over all. Refrigerate several hours or overnight. An hour before cooking, spoon mushroom soup over mixture. Cut 2 slices bread into ½ inch squares; place on top of soup. Sprinkle cheese over all. Bake at 300° for 60 to 70 minutes. Serves 8.

Helen Warren
Vero Beach, Florida

FLUFFY RICE

Each grain stands out dry and separate

1 cup washed rice
1 teaspoon salt

Deep kettle with 6 cups
  boiling water

Add rice slowly to salted boiling water so as not to disturb the boiling; boil 10 minutes. Drain in colander; rinse with fresh boiling water. Set colander over saucepan of hot water and steam rice, covered with a dish towel and lid, for 15 minutes. Yield: 3½ cups.

WILD RICE WITH MUSHROOMS AND ALMONDS

Excellent with game or poultry

1 cup wild rice	½ pound fresh mushrooms,
¼ cup butter	thinly sliced
2 tablespoons parsley,	¾ teaspoon salt
finely chopped	¼ teaspoon pepper
1 tablespoon chives or	Dash nutmeg
green onions, chopped	½ cup toasted slivered
1 tablespoon onion, grated	almonds

Cook wild rice. This may be done ahead for rice freezes well. In a large skillet, melt butter and sauté parsley and onions for 3 minutes. Add mushrooms and cook for 5 minutes over low heat, stirring frequently. Add salt, pepper and nutmeg. Stir in cooked wild rice and almonds. Serves 6.

WILD RICE

Double the recipe . . . wild rice freezes beautifully

1 cup wild rice   **1 teaspoon salt**

Place rice in large saucepan; cover with boiling water. Let stand for 1 hour. Drain. Repeat the procedure two more times. Place rice and salt in large saucepan. Cover with boiling water and cook about 20 minutes, uncovered. Drain and rinse with fresh boiling water. Set colander and rice over saucepan of hot water and steam rice, covered with a dish towel and lid, for 15 minutes or longer. Serves 4 to 5.

GARLIC CHEESE GRITS

A true Southern dish . . . a marvelous alternative to potatoes

1 cup grits
4 cups boiling water
1 teaspoon salt
½ cup butter
1 (6 ounce) roll garlic
cheese

2 eggs, beaten
½ cup milk
Dash cayenne pepper
Corn flake crumbs
Butter to dot on crumbs

Cook grits in boiling salted water until thick. Remove from heat. Stir in butter and cheese until melted. Mix eggs, milk and pepper; add to grits and stir well. Pour into buttered casserole and cover with crumbs. Dot with butter. Bake, uncovered, at 350° for 45 to 55 minutes. Serves 6.

TWICE BAKED POTATOES

Do keep your freezer filled with these . . . they are really good!

8 large baking potatoes
Vegetable oil
¼ cup butter
1 cup dairy sour cream

1 egg, beaten
1½ teaspoons salt
⅛ teaspoon white pepper
Paprika

Rub potatoes with vegetable oil. Place on rack and bake at 400° for 1 hour. Cut a long oval slice from potatoes; scoop out pulp. Combine butter, sour cream, egg, salt and pepper; blend well. Add to potato pulp and mix thoroughly. Pile filling back into 6 shells, piling high. Sprinkle with paprika. Wrap in foil and place in plastic bags; freeze. To serve, it is unnecessary to thaw. Remove foil, place potato on rack; bake at 400° about 40 minutes. Serves 6.

SWEET POTATOES AND MARSHMALLOW BAKE

An old friend...as popular as ever

6 large sweet potatoes
  (about 3 pounds)
3 tablespoons brown sugar
3 egg yolks, beaten
2 tablespoons butter,
  melted
1 tablespoon baking
  powder

1 teaspoon salt
½ teaspoon allspice
Dash ground cloves
1 cup orange juice
½ cup chopped pecans
Marshmallows

Put unpeeled potatoes in boiling water to cover and cook, covered, 35 to 40 minutes. Cool; peel and put them through a ricer or mash them with a potato masher. Blend all ingredients but marshmallows. Place in deep buttered casserole. Bake at 350° for 30 to 40 minutes. Remove from oven; cover top with marshmallows. Continue baking until marshmallows are puffed and brown. Serve immediately. Serves 6 to 8.

BOURBON SWEET POTATOES

Inviting company fare

4 large sweet potatoes
4 tablespoons brown sugar
4 tablespoons butter,
  melted
2 ounces orange juice
1½ ounces bourbon

¼ teaspoon salt
¼ teaspoon pumpkin pie
  spice
Dash ground cloves
¼ cup pecans, finely
  chopped

Put unpeeled potatoes in boiling water to cover and cook, covered, 35 to 40 minutes. Cool; peel and put them through a ricer or mash them with a potato masher. Combine sweet potatoes with remaining ingredients except pecans. Mix well. Spoon into buttered 1 quart casserole. Sprinkle pecans over top. Bake at 375° for 25 to 30 minutes. Serves 4 to 6.

AUNT LENOIRS' BAKED BEANS

These were my favorites when I was in grade school...many years later they still are!

4 cups Great Northern beans	**1 tablespoon salt**
1 cup sugar	**1 pound salt pork, cut-up in 2 inch pieces**

Soak beans overnight. Drain. Place beans in large roaster; mix in sugar, salt and salt pork. Barely cover with water. Cover and bake at 250°, about 6 hours. If needed, add boiling water, a cup at a time. Uncover the last hour. Serves 8 to 10.

Mary June Burd
Chevy Chase, Maryland

KAHLÚA BEANS

Great flavor

2 (1 pound) cans oven baked beans	**2 tablespoons chili sauce**
½ cup Kahlúa	**1½ teaspoons mustard**
	1 teaspoon dark molasses

Combine ingredients. Refrigerate several hours or overnight. Spoon into 1 quart casserole and bake at 350° for 50 minutes. Serves 4.

HOMINY AND GREEN CHILIES

An extraordinary side dish

2 (15½ ounce) cans hominy, drained	**6 ounces dairy sour cream**
2 (4 ounce) cans green chilies	**4 tablespoons onion, grated**
6 ounces Cheddar cheese, grated	**½ teaspoon chili powder**

Combine all ingredients. Put in a greased 1 quart casserole. Bake at 400° for 20 minutes. Serves 6 to 8.

Hilda Digges
Asheville, North Carolina

PINEAPPLE CURRIED FRUIT

Really good! Serve with meats, fowl and wild game

**1 (20 ounce) can pineapple   1 teaspoon curry powder
chunks, unsweetened**

Drain pineapple and reserve syrup. Place syrup in heavy saucepan; stir in curry powder and mix well. Add pineapple. Cover and cook over medium heat until most of the juice is absorbed and mixture cooks down (about 1 hour). Stir occasionally; watch carefully the last few minutes of cooking and stir so it does not stick and burn bottom of pan. Serve hot or cold. Keeps well under refrigeration. Serves 3 to 4.

Peggy Fulenwider
Denver, Colorado

PEACHES AND MINCEMEAT

Place canned peaches in buttered baking dish. Fill centers with mincemeat. Cover bottom of dish with peach juice. Bake at 300° for 15 to 20 minutes, or until hot.

PINEAPPLE PLEASURE

An excellent accompaniment to chicken, turkey, ham, pork

**½ cup butter   3 eggs, beaten
4 slices white bread   1 (20 ounce) can
½ cup sugar   unsweetened pineapple
3 tablespoons flour   chunks, undrained**

Melt butter in saucepan over low heat. Cut off crust; cube bread. Add bread to melted butter; toss. Mix sugar and flour together, add eggs and blend well. Mix in pineapple with juice. Pour pineapple mixture into 1½ quart buttered casserole. Sprinkle bread cubes over top. Bake uncovered at 350° for 50 to 60 minutes. Serve hot. Serves 4 to 6.

Anne Gregg
Vero Beach, Florida

PINEAPPLE AND CHEESE CASSEROLE

1 (20 ounce) can pineapple
  chunks, reserve juice
3 tablespoons flour
3 tablespoons sugar
3 tablespoons pineapple
  juice

6 ounces sharp Cheddar
  cheese, grated (1½ cups)
30 Ritz crackers, crushed
4 tablespoons butter,
  melted

Slice pineapple chunks in half; arrange on bottom of buttered 9 x 5 inch casserole. Stir together flour and sugar; sprinkle over pineapple. Drizzle pineapple juice over flour mixture; distribute cheese over the top. Combine crackers and butter and spread over cheese. Cover and bake at 350° for 15 minutes; uncover and bake an additional 10 minutes. Serve hot. Serves 6 to 8.

Ann McGlinn
Haverford, Pennsylvania

PICKLED CUCUMBERS

2 large cucumbers
1 cup sugar
1 cup cider vinegar
½ teaspoon celery seed
Salt to taste

Fresh ground pepper to
  taste
Thin slices of 1 small
  onion, optional
2 tablespoons chopped
  parsley

Peel cucumbers and groove them with a silver fork. Slice thin. Combine sugar, vinegar, celery seed, salt and pepper; stir until sugar is dissolved. Pour brine over cucumbers; add onions. Chill for a few hours. Garnish with parsley. Serves 6 to 8.

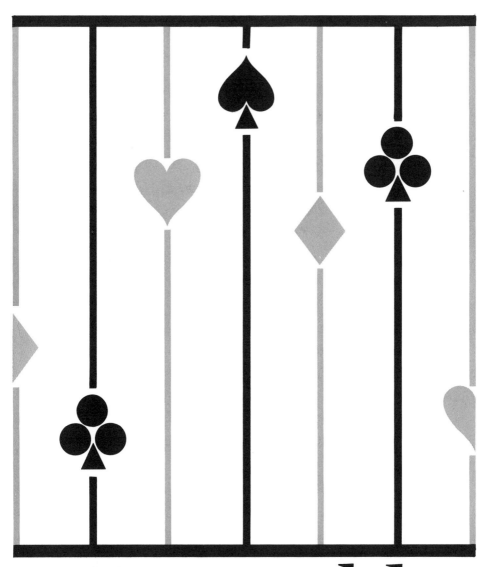

Vegetables
and Sauces

ARTICHOKE SPINACH CASSEROLE

This was a prize winner . . . it deserved the honor

1 (14 ounce) can artichoke
  hearts
2 (10 ounce) packages
  frozen chopped spinach,
  thawed
1 teaspoon salt
¼ teaspoon pepper

1 (8 ounce package) cream
  cheese, softened
2 tablespoons butter,
  melted
¼ cup milk
⅓ cup freshly grated
  Parmesan cheese

Drain artichoke hearts and slice in quarters. Place artichokes in 1½ quart buttered casserole. Press spinach in a sieve to remove moisture. Season with salt and pepper. Arrange spinach over artichokes. Beat cream cheese, butter and milk with an electric mixer until smooth and blended; spoon over spinach. Top with Parmesan cheese. Bake, covered, at 350° for 30 minutes; bake 10 minutes longer uncovered. Serves 6.

CAULIFLOWER WITH SHRIMP AND PECANS

*This annual variety of the cabbage becomes quite elegant
and it is very good*

1 large head cauliflower,
  cut into flowerets
1 (10¾ ounce) can cream of
  shrimp soup
1 cup dairy sour cream

½ teaspoon salt
¼ teaspoon white pepper
⅓ cup broken pecans
2 tablespoons butter,
  melted

Cook cauliflower in small amount of boiling water for 6 to 8 minutes or until crisp-tender. Drain. Place flowerets in buttered 2 quart casserole. Combine soup, sour cream, salt and pepper; mix well. Pour over cauliflower. Over low heat, cook pecans in butter until lightly brown; sprinkle over top of soup mixture. Bake at 350° for 20 to 25 minutes or until bubbly. Yield: 6 servings.

Dottie Neville
Jupiter, Florida

BESSIE PICKENS' STEWED TOMATOES
An old-country favorite

3 (14½ ounce) cans stewed
   tomatoes, top quality
2 heaping tablespoons dark
   brown sugar
2 chopped green onions,
   using tops

2 slices white bread with
   crust
Salt and pepper to taste

Pour tomatoes into 8×8 inch buttered baking dish. Sprinkle brown sugar and onions over top. Tear bread into small pieces and add to tomato mixture. Combine. Bake at 350° for at least 60 minutes, or until bubbling and liquid has been absorbed. Serves 4 to 5.

Peggy Fulenwider
Denver, Colorado

BROCCOLI AND FRIENDS
A dish such as this gives vegetables real importance!

3 (10 ounce) packages
   frozen chopped broccoli
½ cup butter, melted
1 (8 ounce) package cream
   cheese, softened
½ cup scallions, minced
Juice of ½ lemon
Salt and pepper to taste

1 teaspoon Worcestershire
   sauce
2 cups herb seasoned
   stuffing croutons
1 (13 ounce) can artichoke
   bottoms, rinsed (7 to 9
   count)

Cook broccoli as directed on package. Drain thoroughly; add ½ of the butter, cream cheese, scallions, lemon juice, salt and pepper, Worcestershire sauce; mix well. Mix remaining butter with croutons. Spoon half of broccoli mixture into buttered 2 quart casserole; cover with thinly sliced artichoke bottoms; add remaining broccoli, covering artichokes. Top with croutons. Bake at 325° for 30 minutes. If prepared in advance, bake at 325° about 1 hour. Serves 8.

Lillian Paxson
Vero Beach, Florida

COMPANY CAULIFLOWER
Layered with sour cream and cheese, it sauces itself as it bakes

1 head cauliflower
Salt and pepper to taste
1 cup dairy sour cream

4 ounces grated sharp
  Cheddar cheese, (1 cup)
2 teaspoons toasted
  sesame seed*

Rinse head of cauliflower; break into flowerets. Cook, covered, in small amount of boiling salted water until tender, about 10 minutes; drain well. Place half the cauliflower in a 1 quart casserole; season with salt and pepper. Spread with ½ cup sour cream; sprinkle with ½ cup cheese. Top with 1 teaspoon sesame seed. Repeat layers. Bake at 350° until heated through, about 10 minutes. Serves 4.

* To toast sesame seed, place in shallow pan in 350° oven for 3 to 4 minutes or until browned, shaking occasionally. Watch carefully.

BROCCOLI CASSEROLE

1 large head of broccoli
  (use flowerets only)
1 (10¾ ounce) can cream of
  mushroom soup
1 egg, beaten
1 cup mayonnaise

1 small onion, grated
8 ounces sharp Cheddar
  cheese, grated
Pinch of salt
Bread crumbs
Melted butter

Place broccoli in saucepan. Cook, covered, in small amount of water for 5 minutes; drain. Mix broccoli with soup, egg, mayonnaise, onion, cheese and salt. Place in 2 quart buttered casserole. Cover with crumbs and butter. Bake at 350° for 35 to 40 minutes. Serves 8.

Nancy Forester
Asheville, North Carolina

BAKED TOMATOES

4 large ripe tomatoes
1 teaspoon mustard
¼ cup bread crumbs
1 tablespoon onion, grated

¼ teaspoon salt
¼ teaspoon curry powder
2 teaspoons butter, melted

Cut tops off tomatoes; then halve crosswise. Place tomatoes in buttered shallow baking dish; cover with mustard. Combine remaining ingredients and place on top of each tomato. Bake at 400° for 10 to 15 minutes. If tops are not brown, place under broiler for 2 to 3 minutes. Serves 4.

COUNTRY-FRIED GREEN TOMATOES
A Southern treat

4 large firm green
  tomatoes, cut in thick
  slices
½ cup corn meal

Salt and fresh ground
  pepper
4 tablespoons bacon fat or
  vegetable oil

Dredge tomatoes with corn meal; sprinkle with salt and pepper. Heat bacon fat in large heavy skillet and fry tomato slices, turning to brown both sides. Drain on paper towels. Serve hot. Serves 4.

CORN PUDDING
A delicious accompaniment

6 ears of corn
½ cup butter, melted
5 eggs

2 cups half and half cream
1 tablespoon sugar
Salt and pepper to taste

Scrape kernels from fresh corn; add to melted butter. Beat eggs and fold into corn; add cream, sugar, salt and pepper. Pour into 2 quart casserole; set in pan of water. Bake at 300° for 1 hour and 15 minutes. Serves 8.

Margaret Hanes
Atlanta, Georgia

BROCCOLI EGG PUFF

1 large head of broccoli
(use flowerets only)
2 tablespoons flour
½ teaspoon baking powder
Pinch of salt
5 eggs, beaten
1 cup cream-style cottage
cheese

4 slices bacon, crisp
cooked, drained and
crumbled
2 ounces Cheddar or Swiss
cheese, grated (½ cup)

Place broccoli in saucepan. Cook, covered, in small amount of water for 5 minutes; drain. Set aside. In small mixing bowl stir together flour, baking powder and salt; set aside. In medium mixing bowl beat eggs. With wire whisk or rotary beater, beat in flour mixture. Stir in cottage cheese and bacon. Evenly spread broccoli in bottom of buttered 8 × 8 inch pan. Pour egg mixture over broccoli. Bake uncovered, at 350° for 20 minutes. Sprinkle with cheese. Bake 3 minutes more, or until center is almost set and cheese is melted. Let stand 5 minutes before serving. Serves 6.

Gladys Tolsma
Williamsville, New York

"WEINKRAUT"

Welcome this old friend in a new guise

1 small onion, grated
¼ cup butter, melted
2 tablespoons brown sugar
½ teaspoon salt
1 teaspoon vinegar

1½ cups dry white wine
1 cup chicken broth
1 small potato, grated
1 quart sauerkraut,
drained

In large saucepan, add onion to butter and cook until just tender. Add sugar; stir until melted. Add remaining ingredients and cook, uncovered, for 30 minutes. Serves 6.

Elaine Putney
Vero Beach, Florida

BLENDER HOLLANDAISE SAUCE

Little effort . . . big reward

4 egg yolks
2 tablespoons lemon juice
Pinch cayenne pepper

¼ teaspoon salt
½ pound butter

Place egg yolks, lemon juice, pepper and salt in blender. Melt butter in saucepan over low heat until bubbling, and keep hot. Do not allow it to burn. Cover blender and turn motor on low speed. Immediately remove cover and pour in hot butter in steady stream. When all butter is added, turn off motor. Yield: 1¼ cups.

AMANDINE GARNISH

Excellent with fish, green beans, etc.

½ cup butter
½ cup almonds, slivered

1 teaspoon lemon juice

Melt butter; add almonds. Stir and sauté over low heat until lightly browned. Remove from heat and stir in lemon juice.

EL DIABLO MUSTARD

1 loosely packed cup of
   good dry mustard
1 cup cider vinegar

1 cup sugar
3 eggs, beaten

Soak mustard and vinegar for 12 hours. Add sugar and eggs and cook in top of double boiler over simmering water for 20 minutes. Beat frequently with hand beater to prevent lumping. Place in sterile jars, cover and refrigerate. Mustard will keep indefinitely under refrigeration. Yield: 2½ cups.

Delicious with ham, hot dogs, etc. Good as an appetizer with small chunks of sharp Cheddar cheese speared with wooden picks.

Lazelle Rafferty
Little Compton, Rhode Island

COCKTAIL SAUCE

Just right

1 cup chili sauce
4 tablespoons catsup
2 teaspoons horseradish
1½ teaspoons
  Worcestershire sauce

Several dashes Tabasco
Freshly ground pepper to
  taste
Lemon wedges

Mix all ingredients thoroughly. Refrigerate. Serve with lemon wedges. Yield: 1¼ cups.

BARBEQUE SAUCE

A super sauce for chicken, ribs and beef

1 cup chili sauce
¼ cup cider vinegar
¼ cup Worcestershire
  sauce
1 cup water
4 tablespoons dark brown
  sugar

3 tablespoons lemon juice
1 teaspoon chili powder
1 teaspoon celery seed
7 drops Tabasco
1 teaspoon salt
¼ teaspoon pepper

In heavy saucepan combine all ingredients. Heat to boiling, stirring constantly. Simmer, uncovered, 10 to 15 minutes to blend flavors. Yield: 2½ cups.

JEZEBEL SAUCE

*Delicious with any meat, hot or cold and good with
cream cheese and crackers too*

1 (10 ounce) jar apple jelly
1 (10 ounce) jar pineapple
  preserves

1 (5 ounce) jar horseradish
½ teaspoon dry mustard
Few grindings black pepper

Mix all ingredients thoroughly. Refrigerate. The sauce will keep for months under refrigeration. Yield: 3 cups.

Alice McCue
Vero Beach, Florida

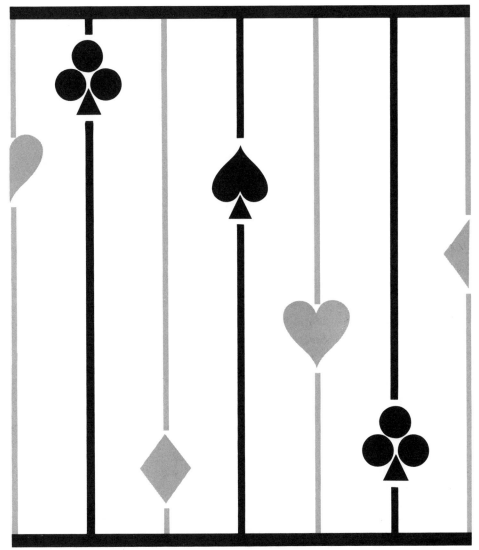

Breads

PEACH MUFFINS
You'll love these!

2 cups flour
½ cup sugar
2 teaspoons baking powder
½ teaspoon baking soda
½ teaspoon salt
½ teaspoon cinnamon
½ teaspoon nutmeg
Dash of ground mace

1 egg, beaten
⅓ cup vegetable oil
⅓ cup milk
1 (8 ounce) carton peach
  yogurt
½ cup dried peaches, finely
  chopped

Combine first 8 ingredients in large bowl; make a well in center of mixture. Combine egg, oil, milk, yogurt and dried peaches; add to dry ingredients, stirring just until moistened. Spoon into greased muffin pans, filling two-thirds full.

Topping:

4 tablespoons flour
4 tablespoons brown sugar
4 tablespoons pecans,
  chopped

1 teaspoon cinnamon
4 tablespoons butter,
  softened

Combine flour, brown sugar, pecans and cinnamon in small bowl. Cut butter into flour mixture until mixture resembles coarse meal; sprinkle 1 heaping teaspoon over each muffin.

Bake at 400° for 20 minutes, or until golden. Serve warm. Yield: 18 muffins.

Grace Bravos
Timonium, Maryland

BANANA ORANGE MUFFINS
Light, tender and delicious

2 cups flour
1½ teaspoons baking
  powder
1½ teaspoons baking soda
¼ pound butter
1 cup sugar
2 eggs

2 large bananas, mashed
⅓ cup buttermilk or dairy
  sour cream
Grated peel of 1 orange
Juice of 1 orange
1 teaspoon vanilla extract

Sift dry ingredients; set aside. Cream butter and sugar; add eggs one at a time. Add bananas and mix well. Stir in flour mixture alternately with remaining ingredients. Fill well-greased muffin pans ⅔ full. Bake at 350° for 25 minutes. Serve hot. Yield: 2 dozen muffins.

Mary Higgins
Duluth, Minnesota

BLUEBERRY MUFFINS

2 cups cake flour
2 teaspoons baking powder
⅓ cup sugar
½ teaspoon salt
2 eggs
¾ cup milk
4 tablespoons butter,
  melted

1 cup fresh blueberries,
  lightly floured
1 teaspoon lemon peel,
  finely grated
Sugar for topping

Have all ingredients at room temperature. Sift dry ingredients into large bowl. In separate bowl, beat eggs until frothy, add milk and melted butter; mix well. Make a well in center of flour mixture. Pour in liquid ingredients. Immediately stir with a fork . . . quickly and lightly, just to blend. Fold in blueberries and lemon peel before dry ingredients are completely moist. Batter should be lumpy. Fill well-greased muffin pans ⅔ full. Sprinkle tops of muffin with sugar. Bake at 400° about 20 minutes. Serve hot. Yield: 14 muffins.

PERPETUAL MUFFINS

Take 6 to 8 to a friend...a lovely treat

3 cups All-Bran cereal	2½ cups flour
1 cup boiling water	2½ teaspoons baking soda
2 cups buttermilk	½ teaspoon salt
1½ cups sugar	Raisins, blueberries,
2 eggs, beaten	optional
½ cup vegetable oil	

Cover cereal with boiling water. Add buttermilk, sugar, eggs and oil. Mix. Sift together flour, soda and salt. Add to cereal mixture. Stir until just mixed; do not overmix. Cover bowl and refrigerate. Muffin batter keeps for 6 weeks. Do not stir again.

To bake, place batter in greased muffin cups in cold oven. Bake at 400° for 20 minutes. A few raisins or blueberries may be added to batter. Serve hot. Yield: 3 dozen muffins.

Fleur Piper
Wichita Falls, Texas

APPLESAUCE BREAD

1st prize at the county fair

2 cups flour, sifted	½ cup butter
1 teaspoon baking powder	¾ cup sugar
1 teaspoon salt	2 eggs
1 teaspoon soda	1 teaspoon vanilla extract
1 teaspoon cinnamon	1 cup applesauce
½ teaspoon nutmeg	½ cup walnuts, chopped

Sift together dry ingredients. Cream butter and sugar; beat in the eggs and vanilla. Blend in dry ingredients gradually. Add applesauce and walnuts and mix only until blended. Pour into well-greased 9 x 5 inch pan. Push batter up into corners of pan, leaving the center slightly hollowed. For well-rounded loaf, allow to stand 20 minutes before baking. Bake at 350° for 55 to 60 minutes. Cool thoroughly before slicing. Serves 12.

BANANA BREAD
This has been one of my favorites for years

1 cup sugar	2 cups flour, sifted
½ cup butter	1 teaspoon baking soda
2 eggs, beaten	½ teaspoon salt
3 tablespoons buttermilk	½ cup pecans, chopped
1 cup mashed bananas (about 3)	

Cream sugar and butter. Add eggs, buttermilk and bananas. Add flour, baking soda and salt, stirring just enough to mix. Fold in pecans. Pour into 2 greased 7½ × 3½ inch loaf pans. Bake at 350° for 45 minutes. Cool 15 minutes. Remove from pans to rack. Freezes well. Yield: 2 loaves.

Cherry Sue Jackson
Opelika, Alabama

APRICOT NUT BREAD
Ideal for tea party sandwiches when sliced thin and spread with butter

1 cup dried apricots	2 tablespoons butter, melted
1½ cups warm water	
2 cups flour	1 egg, beaten
2 teaspoons baking powder	¼ cup water
¼ teaspoon baking soda	½ cup orange juice
¼ teaspoon salt	½ cup chopped walnuts
1 cup sugar	

Cover apricots with warm water and let soak for 30 minutes. Drain; cut into small pieces. Sift flour, baking powder, baking soda and salt into large bowl. In another bowl combine sugar, butter, egg, ¼ cup water and orange juice. When well mixed, add to dry ingredients; add apricots and walnuts. Mix just until flour is dampened. Pour into greased and floured 8½ × 4½ inch loaf pan. Bake at 350° for 50 to 60 minutes. Cool in pan for 10 minutes. Remove from pan to rack to finish cooling. Wrap in foil. Yield: 1 loaf.

SWEDISH KRINGLE

A delicious little coffee cake. It is pretty, very crusty and delicate, with a delightful almond flavor.

Bottom crust:

½ cup unsalted butter
1 cup flour, unsifted

1 tablespoon water

Top layer:

1 cup water
½ cup unsalted butter
1 cup flour, unsifted

3 eggs
½ teaspoon almond extract

Frosting:

1 cup confectioners' sugar,
  sifted
1½ tablespoons unsalted
  butter

½ teaspoon almond extract
1 tablespoon milk
½ cup sliced toasted
  almonds

To make bottom crust:

Using two knives, cut butter into flour; stir in water. Mix thoroughly until mixture holds together; use your hands if necessary. On ungreased baking sheet, pat dough into desired shape — a strip or a horseshoe is nice (about 3 inches wide and 14 inches long).

To make top layer:

Place water in heavy saucepan with butter; heat to boiling. Remove from heat and immediately stir in flour smoothly. Beat in eggs, one at a time, beating hard until well-blended. Add almond extract. Using a small spatula and a spoon, spread top layer dough over the bottom crust, lightly sealing top layer dough to the bottom. Bake at 350° for 55 to 60 minutes, or until golden and puffed up. Cool on rack. Pastry will flatten somewhat on cooling.

Continued on next page

To make frosting:

In a small bowl, blend confectioners' sugar, butter and almond extract. Add enough milk to make a spreading consistency and frost pastry with mixture; press almonds into frosting. Cut crosswise into strips. Heat to serve. Yield: 8 servings.

Nancy Canady
Tyler, Texas

DILLY BREAD

Here is a beautiful bread you'll be proud to serve.

1½ packets dry yeast
½ cup warm water
2 cups cottage cheese, large curd
4 tablespoons sugar or honey
2 tablespoons dry onion flakes
2 tablespoons butter
3 teaspoons dill weed
1½ teaspoons salt
½ teaspoon baking soda
2 eggs, beaten
4½ to 5 cups flour (a mixture of white and wheat is excellent)
Melted Butter

Soften yeast in water. Heat cottage cheese to just lukewarm. Add sugar, onion, butter, dill weed, salt, soda, eggs and softened yeast. Add 2 cups flour and beat well. Add more flour; turn out on board and knead for 10 minutes. (This dough will be slightly sticky). Put in greased bowl and let rise until double. Punch down and let rise again. Punch down; divide into loaves. Put into well greased 9 × 5 inch loaf pans. Let rise until double. Bake at 350° about 50 minutes. Cover with foil after first 20 minutes. Turn out of pans on rack to cool. Brush with melted butter. Yield: 2 loaves

Martha Orr Hassel
Kenilworth, Illinois

PUMPKIN NUT BREAD

Excellent

3 cups sugar
3½ cups flour, unsifted
1 teaspoon baking powder
2 teaspoons baking soda
1½ teaspoons salt
¾ teaspoon cinnamon
¾ teaspoon nutmeg
¾ teaspoon allspice
½ teaspoon cloves
4 eggs, well beaten
1 cup vegetable oil
⅔ cup water
1 (1 pound) can pumpkin
1 cup coarsely chopped
    walnuts or pecans

Mix all dry ingredients in large bowl. Add eggs, oil, water and pumpkin; mix until well blended. Add nuts. Pour batter into 4 buttered and floured 7½ × 3½ inch loaf pans. Bake at 350° for 50 to 60 minutes, or until tester comes out clean. Cool for 10 minutes; remove to rack. Freezes well. Yield: 4 loaves.

Helen Warren
Vero Beach, Florida

FRENCH BREAD WITH HERB BUTTER

Be organized
Double the recipe . . . eat one . . . freeze one

½ cup butter, softened
1 tablespoon dry parsley
1 tablespoon dry chives
2 teaspoons dry sweet
    basil
½ teaspoon lemon juice
3 dashes Tabasco
Medium size loaf of French
    bread

Combine butter, herbs and seasonings and mix well. Cut bread in thin slices but do not cut it all the way through; leave bottom crust undisturbed. Butter each slice generously. Wrap bread in aluminum foil and warm in 350° oven for a few minutes. Just before serving, open foil for a short time to brown crust. Yield: 1 loaf.

GINGERBREAD GEMS
They are!

4 ounces cream cheese,
  softened
2 teaspoons frozen orange
  juice concentrate,
  thawed
1 egg, slightly beaten
4 tablespoons light
  molasses
½ cup water

1½ cups Bran Chex cereal
¼ cup butter, softened
½ cup brown sugar
1¼ cups sifted flour
¾ teaspoon baking soda
½ teaspoon salt
½ teaspoon cinnamon
½ teaspoon ginger

Combine cream cheese and orange juice. Set aside. Mix together egg, molasses and water. Stir in Bran Chex. Let stand 5 minutes. Mix butter and sugar until creamy. Sift together dry ingredients; add to creamed mixture alternately with Chex mixture. Stir until just moistened. Fill greased muffin pans ⅓ full. Divide cream cheese mixture among muffins. Top with remaining batter, sealing cream cheese in center. Bake at 350° for 20 to 25 minutes, or until top springs back when lightly touched. Yield: 12 muffins.

QUICK WHEAT
10 minutes to the oven!

3 cups whole wheat flour
1 cup dark brown sugar
2 teaspoons baking soda
¼ teaspoon salt

¾ cup currants* or raisins
2 cups buttermilk
1 tablespoon butter,
  melted

Combine first five ingredients. Add buttermilk; mix until blended. Pour into two 8½ × 4½ inch greased loaf pans. Bake at 375° for 30 minutes. Turn out and brush with butter. Yield: 2 loaves.

* Buy currants when in season and freeze them.

ZUCCHINI BREAD

3 eggs, beaten
1 cup salad oil
1 cup sugar
1 cup brown sugar
3 teaspoons maple
 flavoring
2 cups coarsely shredded
 zucchini (3 medium size)
2½ cups flour

2 teaspoons baking soda
½ teaspoon baking powder
2 teaspoons salt
3 teaspoons cinnamon
½ cup wheat germ
⅓ cup sesame seeds
1 cup pecans or walnuts,
 coarsely chopped

Combine eggs, oil, sugars and maple flavoring. Beat until foamy and thick. Stir in zucchini. Mix together remaining ingredients; add to batter and stir until just blended. Pour into 2 greased and floured 8½ × 4½ inch loaf pans. Bake at 350° for 60 minutes, or until bread tests done. Cool in pan for 10 minutes. The bread improves with a few days "aging" in refrigerator. Slices well when cold. Yield: 2 loaves.

Barbara Morrison
Vero Beach, Florida

RAISIN BEER BREAD

Wonderful toasted for breakfast

3 cups self-rising flour,
 sifted
3 tablespoons sugar
1 cup dark seedless raisins

1 (12 ounce) can beer,
 room temperature
4 tablespoons butter,
 melted

Mix together flour, sugar, raisins and beer; stir thoroughly. Pour into greased 8½ × 4½ inch loaf pan. Pour 3 tablespoons butter over batter. Bake at 375° for 35 to 40 minutes. Turn out and brush with remaining butter. Yield: 1 loaf.

Evelyn Converse
Vero Beach, Florida

SOUR CREAM CRESCENTS

This is a very popular recipe, and no wonder!

1 cup dairy sour cream	½ cup sugar
1½ packages dry yeast	½ teaspoon salt
⅓ cup warm water	4 cups flour, sifted
1 cup butter or margarine, softened	2 eggs, well beaten

Heat sour cream in top of double boiler over simmering water until it becomes slightly yellow around edges. (Separation of cream will not affect product.) Dissolve yeast in warm water; let stand 5 to 10 minutes.

Combine butter, sugar and salt in large bowl. Pour heated sour cream over butter mixture and stir until butter is melted. Cool to lukewarm; blend in 1 cup flour, beating until smooth. Stir dissolved yeast and add, mixing well. Add 1 cup of remaining flour and beat until smooth. Add eggs and beat until thoroughly blended. Add remaining 2 cups flour; again, beat thoroughly. Cover bowl and refrigerate 6 hours or overnight. (There is not time limit at this point, and any remaining dough can be wrapped in foil and used as needed.)

Divide dough into fourths. On lightly floured surface, roll each portion into a round ¼ inch thick. Cut each round into 12 wedge-shaped pieces. Roll up each wedge beginning at wide end. Place rolls on greased baking sheets with points underneath. Curve into crescents. Let rise in warm place for 1 hour, or until light. Do not cover. Bake 15 minutes at 375°, or until golden brown. Yield: 4 dozen.

Lilli Jackson
Opelika, Alabama

PARSLEY PASTRY SHELLS

Filled with chicken salad, this won the 1985 Dairy Days Grand Prize in Cocoa, Florida — it deserved the honor.

½ cup butter, softened
1 (3 ounce) package cream
  cheese with chives,
  softened

1½ cups flour
½ cup parsley, chopped
¼ teaspoon salt

Cream together butter and cream cheese until smooth. Blend in flour, parsley and salt. Divide dough into 12 pieces and press each piece into muffin cups, to form individual pastry shells. Bake at 350° for 20 minutes, or until golden. Cool before filling. Serves 12.

Nina Bruner
Merritt Island, Florida

POPOVERS

Big puffs with nothing but air inside

1 cup milk
2 eggs
1 cup Wondra flour
  (Gold Medal)

2 teaspoons sugar
¼ teaspoon salt
1 tablespoon butter,
  melted

Have ingredients at room temperature. Combine all ingredients in blender, beat at high speed for 30 seconds; stop and scrape down sides and resume mixing for 20 seconds. Spray custard cups with vegetable spray. Fill cups ½ full with batter. Place on cookie sheet and bake at 425° for 10 minutes; reduce heat to 375° and bake 30 minutes more. Cut a slit into side of each popover; do not remove from oven. Turn heat off and let popovers remain in oven 10 minutes more. May freeze; reheat at 375° for 5 to 7 minutes. Yield: 6 popovers.

June Starkey
Darby, Montana

WHOLE WHEAT REFRIGERATOR ROLLS

These could be the highlight of your next dinner . . . plain or fancy

2 cups milk
¾ cup sugar
1½ teaspoons salt
½ cup butter
2 packages dry yeast

1 egg, beaten
3 cups whole wheat flour
3 to 4 cups flour
½ cup butter, melted

Scald milk. Add sugar, salt, butter and stir until dissolved. Cool to lukewarm; pour into electric mixer bowl. Add yeast and stir until dissolved. Stir in egg; add whole wheat flour and mix until smooth. Mix in 1½ to 2 cups of remaining flour and turn out onto floured surface; gradually add remaining flour, until dough is easy to handle. Kneading is not necessary.

Form into a ball and place in greased bowl, turning to grease entire surface of dough. Cover tightly with double layer of wax paper, then damp cloth. Place in refrigerator until needed, up to one week. Dampen cloth occasionally and punch down dough periodically.

To bake, roll dough on floured surface to ½ inch thickness, cut into 2 inch circles, brush with melted butter and fold over. Cover rolls with damp cloth and let rise in warm place until double in bulk, about 1½ hours. Bake on greased baking sheet at 400° for 12 to 15 minutes, or until golden. Yield: 4 dozen rolls.

Hilda Chapin
Lookout Mountain, Tennessee

CAPE COD CRANBERRY NUT LOAF

My Christmas present one year — one of my favorite gifts

2 cups flour
1½ teaspoons baking
  powder
½ teaspoon baking soda
1 teaspoon salt
2 tablespoons butter,
  melted
⅞ cup orange juice
1 egg, beaten

⅞ cup white sugar
3 tablespoons light brown
  sugar
1 tablespoon grated orange
  peel (optional)
1 cup whole cranberries,
  uncooked
Flour
½ cup chopped walnuts

Sift together flour, baking powder, soda and salt. Set aside. Melt butter and add to orange juice. In large bowl, stir together egg and sugars. Add flour mixture and orange juice mix alternately to egg and sugar, starting and ending with flour. Add orange peel. Fold in cranberries which have been lightly floured; stir in walnuts. Pour batter into greased and floured 9 x 5 inch loaf pan. Bake at 350° for 60 minutes. Invert. Keep in refrigerator or freeze. Yield: 1 loaf.

Grace O'Keeffe
Osterville, Massachusetts

CARAMEL ROLLS

Great "sticky buns" in about 35 minutes!

1 (8 ounce) package
  Pillsbury crescent
  dinner rolls
4 tablespoons butter,
  softened

½ cup brown sugar
2 teaspoons water
½ cup pecans, chopped

Slice rolls into 9 pieces. Lay flat and place in a foil-lined pan. Combine butter, sugar and water. Add pecans and mix well. Cover rolls with brown sugar mixture. Bake at 350° for 30 minutes. Yield: 9 rolls.

Elizabeth Glenn
Asheville, North Carolina

CORN BISCUITS
So easy and very, very good

½ cup butter or margarine   **1 (8 ounce) can cream corn**
1½ cups Bisquick

Melt butter in 13 x 9 inch baking pan. Combine Bisquick and corn. Drop batter by teaspoonfuls into baking pan; turn over to coat all sides. Bake at 400° for 15 to 20 minutes. Watch after 15 minutes; they should be lightly browned. Serve hot. Yield: 2 dozen biscuits.

Blanche Evans
Vero Beach, Florida

CHILIE CORNBREAD

3 large eggs
¼ cup corn oil
1 cup cornmeal
2½ teaspoons baking powder
½ cup sour cream

8 ounces cream style corn
1 (4 ounce) can chopped green chilies
6 ounces sharp Cheddar cheese, grated

With an electric mixer beat eggs until frothy. Add oil, cornmeal, baking powder and sour cream; beat until smooth. Stir in corn, chilies and cheese. Pour into buttered 8 x 8 inch pan. Bake at 350° for 1 hour or until tester comes out clean. Serve warm.

Hilda Digges
Asheville, North Carolina

LEMON TEA BREAD

Wonderful with fruit salad

1 cup sugar
½ cup butter
2 eggs, slightly beaten
1½ cups flour
1 teaspoon baking powder
¼ teaspoon salt

½ cup milk
Juice and grated peel of 1
  lemon
½ cup walnuts, finely
  chopped

Glaze:

¼ cup super-fine sugar   Juice of 1 lemon

Cream together sugar and butter. Stir in beaten eggs. Sift flour, baking powder and salt; stir into creamed mixture alternately with milk. Add lemon juice, peel and nuts. Pour batter into buttered 9×5 inch loaf pan. Bake at 325° for 50 to 60 minutes, or until loaf test done. While bread is baking, mix sugar and lemon juice together for glaze. When bread is done, remove from oven and pierce surface with small skewer to make small holes. Spoon glaze over hot bread before removing from pan. Cool on wire rack; cut into thin slices. Yield: 1 loaf.

TOAST ROUNDS

1 small loaf sandwich
  bread

6 tablespoons butter,
  melted

Cut bread into rounds with 1½ inch cutter. Brush with melted butter. Place on cookie sheet. Bake at 350° for 10 to 12 minutes. May freeze. Yield: 6 dozen.

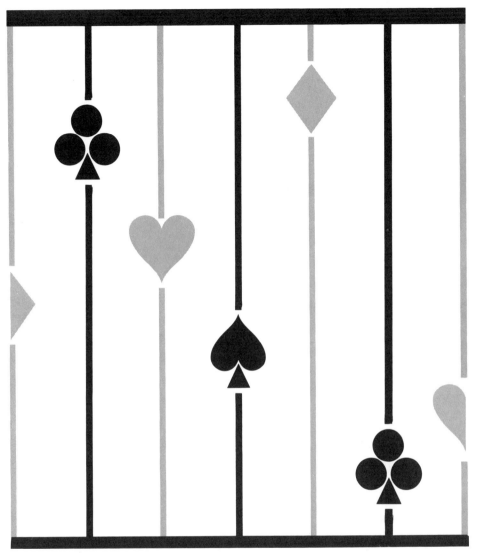

Sandwiches

FRENCH MARKET SANDWICHES
A freezer filled with ham and cheese

9 croissants
½ cup butter, softened
½ cup mustard
2 tablespoons onion, grated
1 tablespoon Worcestershire sauce
3 tablespoons poppy seeds
1 pound shaved baked ham
½ pound Swiss cheese, sliced thin

Slice croissants in half horizontally. Combine butter, mustard, onion, Worcestershire sauce and poppy seeds; mix well. Spread on half of each croissant. Top with ham and slice of cheese, cut to fit. Put halves together. Wrap individually in foil. May freeze. To serve, not frozen, bake in foil at 325° for 15 to 20 minutes. To serve if frozen, bake in foil about 35 minutes. Serves 9.

Mary Tatham
Tequesta, Florida

BROILED MUSHROOM SANDWICHES
Delicious for a bridge luncheon or a company snack.

1 cup finely chopped fresh mushrooms
2 tablespoons butter
12 thin slices bread, lightly buttered
12 slices tomatoes, ½ inch thick
¼ pound sharp cheese, shredded
1 egg, slightly beaten
½ teaspoon salt
6 strips bacon

Sauté mushrooms in butter for 5 minutes. Use a large cookie cutter and cut circles from bread. Top with tomato slice. Mix cheese, egg, salt and mushrooms together and spread over tomato. Cut bacon strip in half and place a piece on each sandwich. Place under broiler until cheese mixture is bubbly and bacon crisp. Serves 6.

TUNA BOATS

This is a great recipe

4 ounces sharp Cheddar
   cheese, cubed (1 cup)
2 hard boiled eggs, diced
1 (6½ ounce) can solid
   white tuna, drained
2 tart apples, chopped
½ cup mayonnaise
3 tablespoons chopped
   stuffed olives
3 tablespoons celery
   chopped

2 tablespoons onion,
   grated
3 tablespoons green
   pepper, minced
2 tablespoons pickle relish
Dash Tabasco
3 to 4 tablespoons
   blanched toasted
   almonds, optional
8 sourdough French rolls
Butter, softened

Combine all ingredients except roll and butter. Cut off tops of
rolls and scoop out centers. Lightly brush inside of each roll
with butter. Pile tuna mixture high into each roll shell. Bake
at 350° for 20 to 25 minutes. Serve hot. If made early in the
day, wrap in foil and refrigerate. Serves 8.

TUNA-APPLE SANDWICH

And it makes a wonderful salad too!

1 (3 ounce) package cream,
   cheese, softened
5 tablespoons mayonnaise
3 tablespoons parsley,
   minced
1 tablespoon lemon juice

½ teaspoon salt
2 (6½ ounce) cans solid
   white tuna, drained
1 large tart apple, peeled
   and finely chopped

Combine cheese, mayonnaise, parsley, lemon juice and salt;
mix until smooth. Stir in tuna and apple until well blended.
Cover and refrigerate mixture to use up within 3 days. Yield:
2½ cups filling.

GRILLED VEGETARIAN SANDWICH
This is a fine way to dress up a sandwich!

½ cup mayonnaise
2 teaspoons Dijon mustard
⅛ teaspoon garlic powder
8 slices bran bread
1 cup alfalfa sprouts
1 avocado, thinly sliced

4 slices Cheddar cheese
4 thin slices tomato
1 cup sliced mushrooms
8 thin slices green pepper
4 thin slices onion
Softened butter

In a small bowl blend mayonnaise, mustard and garlic powder. Spread generously on bread slices. Top each of 4 bread slices with one-fourth of the alfalfa sprouts, avocado, cheese, tomato, mushrooms, green pepper and onion. Top with remaining bread slices. Spread both sides with butter. In frying pans or electric skillet, grill sandwiches on both sides until cheese melts and bread is golden brown. Serves 4.

Fleur Piper
Wichita Falls, Texas

CREAM CHEESE VEGETABLE SANDWICH

1 (8 ounce) package cream
  cheese
½ cup peeled grated
  cucumber, drain well
¼ cup green pepper,
  minced
¼ cup celery, finely
  chopped

1 medium size onion,
  grated
1 cup carrots, grated
1 tablespoon mayonnaise
½ teaspoon salt
Minced parsley for garnish

Combine all ingredients but parsley. Cover and refrigerate several hours. Serve on thin sliced whole wheat bread, crust removed. Excellent as an appetizer served with buttered toast rounds or Triscuits. Yield: 2½ cups.

LOUISVILLE "HOT BROWN" TURKEY SANDWICH

Special "house" lunch of the old Brown Hotel, in Louisville, Kentucky

4 tablespoons butter
5 tablespoons flour
½ teaspoon salt
⅛ teaspoon white pepper
1 cup half and half cream
1 cup turkey or chicken
  broth
½ cup freshly grated
  Parmesan cheese
2 egg yolks, whipped

2 tablespoons cream
8 slices trimmed toast
Sliced breast of turkey for
  4 servings
Parmesan cheese for
  topping
8 slices cooked bacon
Wedges of peeled tomatoes
Parsley

Melt butter, stir in flour, salt and pepper. Gradually add cream and broth, stirring until smooth and thickened. Add cheese and stir with a whisk to help melt the cheese and keep the sauce smooth while it thickens. Blend together the egg yolks and cream. Add a little of the sauce to egg yolks, stirring constantly, then return the mixture to the rest of the sauce and cook until well heated.

For each "Hot Brown" place 2 slices toast on a flameproof dish. Cover toast with a liberal amount of turkey. Pour a generous amount of sauce over turkey and toast. Sprinkle with Parmesan cheese. Place entire dish under broiler until sauce is speckled brown and bubbly; remove from broiler. Top with 2 pieces of bacon. Garnish with tomato wedges and parsley. Serve hot. Serves 4.

Note: To serve in individual dishes, reserve 1 piece of toast. Cut it into toast points and place around the edge of the dish just before serving.

SEA SANDWICH

A hostess's dream ... delicious, easy and make the day before serving

1 pound fresh crabmeat
6 ounces Swiss cheese,
  cubed (1½ cups)
3 tablespoons green
  pepper, chopped fine
2 tablespoons onion,
  grated

½ teaspoon salt
¼ cup mayonnaise
1 teaspoon lemon juice
6 soft hamburger rolls (top
  quality)
Butter, softened

Flake crabmeat. Add cheese, pepper, onion and salt; toss and blend. Mix mayonnaise and lemon juice; add to crabmeat. Slice rolls twice; butter lightly. Place crabmeat mixture on each layer. Wrap individually in aluminum foil. Refrigerate. To serve, bake in foil at 350° for 20 minutes. May freeze; thaw before baking. Serves 6.

Virginia Soderberg
St. Paul, Minnesota

BREADLESS SANDWICH

The Earl would have liked this!

1 head lettuce
1 cup mayonnaise
¼ cup creamy Italian
  dressing
Slices of cooked chicken
  breasts

Slices of tomatoes
4 ounces sharp Cheddar
  cheese, grated (1 cup)
Fresh Parmesan cheese,
  grated

For each of 4 sandwiches, place a ¾ inch slice of lettuce on a baking pan. Mix mayonnaise and Italian dressing and put 2 tablespoons over each lettuce slice. Top with chicken and tomato slices. Mix Cheddar cheese with remaining dressing and cover each sandwich with this mixture; sprinkle each with Parmesan cheese. Place 3 inches under broiler until cheese melts. Serves 4.

Lucy Jones
Vero Beach, Florida

FROSTED SANDWICH LOAF
Absolutely elegant!

1 loaf (16 ounce) day-old
  bread, unsliced
½ cup butter, softened

Sliced stuffed olives and
toasted almonds for
garnish

Trim crusts from unsliced loaf of bread; cut loaf into four lengthwise slices. Butter each slice and spread with filling in order given below; place one on top of the other in form of a whole loaf. Coat top and sides of loaf with cream cheese frosting. Garnish. Chill loaf for 30 minutes, then cover with damp cloth. Chill several hours. Serves 8.

Shrimp Salad Filling:

2 hard-cooked eggs,
  chopped
1⅓ cups chopped shrimp
¼ cup celery, minced

¼ cup mayonnaise
2 tablespoons lemon juice
¼ teaspoon salt
Dash pepper

Cheese-Pecan Filling:

3 ounces cream cheese,
  softened
1 cup pecans, chopped

1 (8 ounce) can crushed
pineapple, well drained

Chicken-Bacon Filling:

8 slices crisp bacon,
  crumbled
1 cup cooked chicken,
  finely chopped
¼ cup mayonnaise

1 tablespoon pimiento,
minced
¼ teaspoon salt
⅛ teaspoon pepper

Cream Cheese Frosting:

2 (8 ounce) packages cream
  cheese

½ cup cream

Beat with an electric mixer until smooth and fluffy.

TEA PARTY SANDWICHES

Too good to be left out

Avocado:

2 avocados, very ripe	2 dashes pepper
2 hard-cooked eggs, grated	½ teaspoon curry powder
2 tablespoons lemon juice	6 tablespoons mayonnaise
1 teaspoon salt	

Mash avocados to a rough purée. Add remaining ingredients and blend thoroughly. Cover with plastic wrap and refrigerate. Yield: 2 cups filling.

Chicken Salad:

2 cups minced, cooked chicken	1 tablespoon Durkee's sauce
1 cup finely chopped celery	½ teaspoon salt
1 cup finely chopped apples	¼ teaspoon white pepper
5 tablespoons mayonnaise	2 teaspoons lemon juice
	¼ teaspoon onion powder

Combine chicken, celery and apples. Add remaining ingredients and blend thoroughly. Cover. May be refrigerated overnight. Yield: 4 cups filling.

Egg Salad:

6 hard-cooked eggs, chopped	1 teaspoon mustard
6 tablespoons mayonnaise	½ teaspoon celery seed
2 ounces pimiento stuffed olives, chopped	¼ teaspoon salt
	¼ teaspoon pepper
	¼ teaspoon onion powder

Combine all ingredients. Blend well. Cover and refrigerate several hours. Yield: 2 cups filling.

Continued on next page

Orange Marmalade Spread:

2 (3 ounce) packages cream
  cheese
4 tablespoons orange
  marmalade
¼ cup chopped pecan
  meats, toasted
½ teaspoon salt
½ teaspoon paprika

Soften cream cheese. Combine remaining ingredients with cheese and blend well. Spread on thin slices of buttered bread, crust removed, and cut into finger size sandwiches. Yield: about 1 cup filling.

Olive and Nut:

2 (3 ounce) packages cream
  cheese
2 teaspoons lemon juice
1 teaspoon onion juice
¼ cup mayonnaise
½ cup pimiento stuffed
  olives, chopped
½ cup pecans, finely
  chopped
Several dashes cayenne
  pepper
¼ teaspoon seasoned salt

Soften cream cheese; add remaining ingredients and blend well. Refrigerate several hours. Yield: 1½ cups filling.

Ham Salad:

1 cup ground cooked ham
3 tablespoons minced
  green pepper
2 tablespoons minced
  sweet pickles
2 teaspoons mustard
4 tablespoons mayonnaise
2 tablespoons Durkee's
  sauce
2 tablespoons minced
  onion
1 hard-cooked egg, chopped
¼ teaspoon salt
¼ teaspoon pepper

Combine all ingredients. Blend well. Refrigerate several hours. Yield: 1½ cups filling.

SWISS TUNA GRILL

1 (6½ ounce) can white
  tuna, drained
2 ounces Swiss cheese,
  shredded (½ cup)
½ cup celery, diced
2 tablespoons onion,
  grated

¼ cup mayonnaise
¼ cup dairy sour cream
Dash of pepper
8 slices rye bread
Butter, softened
Pickles and olives for
  garnish

Combine all ingredients; mix well. Spread filling on 4 sides of rye bread. Top each with another slice of rye. Butter outside of both sides. Grill in frying pan until both sides are toasted and filling is heated through. Serve with garnish. Yield: 4 sandwiches.

Polly Jernigan
Opelika, Alabama

CHUTNEY AND CHICKEN

A delicious combination

1 (8 ounce) container
  whipped cream cheese
3 tablespoons commercial
  chutney, minced
½ teaspoon curry powder
2 cups cooked chicken
  breasts, chopped

Commercial croissants, cut
  in half horizontally and
  lightly buttered
Alfalfa sprouts

Combine cream cheese, chutney and curry powder; blend. Add chicken and mix well. Spread mixture on bottom halves of croissants. Top with alfalfa sprouts and tops of croissants. Serves 6 to 8.

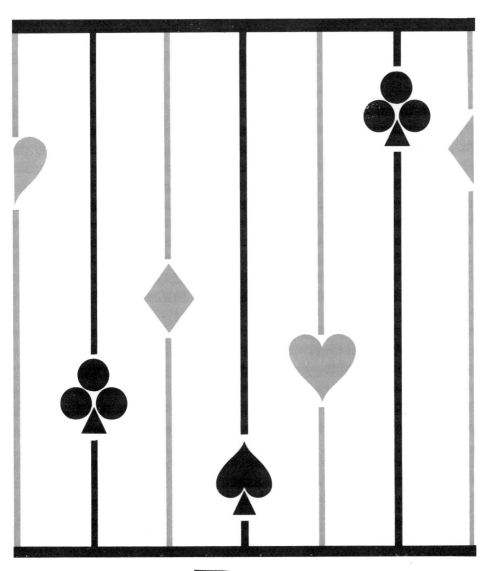

Desserts
and Sweets

POP CORN CAKE

This is my most treasured recipe. It brings back many happy memories of Christmas. It was a family tradition to make this cake for our holiday parties. I thank my sons, Kim and Carey, for their help in the making and the pounding!

2 cups unpopped popcorn
⅛ teaspoon salt
1 cup black walnuts, coarsely chopped (no substitutes)

2 cups medium Orleans molasses
Butter, the size of a walnut

Pop the corn. Put into a large roasting pan; carefully remove any unpopped kernels. Add salt and nuts; toss to mix.

Put molasses in a heavy saucepan; boil gently until molasses forms a soft ball in cold water (232-234 degrees on candy thermometer.) Add butter. Quickly stir molasses into popcorn mixture to cover all kernels.

Put mixture into two buttered 8½ × 4½ inch loaf pans. Press popcorn into pans with slightly wet hands. Pack down tightly and finish packing by pounding with a potato masher.

Wrap in wax paper. Let stand overnight. To serve, unmold by running a knife around sides. Place cake on a board and slice with serrated knife. The cake is easier to slice if chilled.

A wonderful Christmas present . . . if you can give it away.

My Mother, Cherry Kindel Orr
Nashville, Tennessee

BANANA CAKE

A big, beautiful birthday cake — a special request from my sons

1 cup butter	2 teaspoons baking powder
2½ cups sugar	2 teaspoons baking soda
4 eggs, beaten	2 cups buttermilk
4 to 5 bananas, sliced thin	2 teaspoons vanilla extract
4 cups cake flour	

Cream butter and sugar with an electric beater; add eggs and bananas. Beat mixture thoroughly on low speed. Sift flour once; resift with baking powder and baking soda. Add flour to butter mixture alternately with buttermilk, starting and ending with flour. Add vanilla. Pour batter into three greased layer cake pans. Place in cold oven; set at 350° and bake 25 to 30 minutes. When cake is cool, cover each layer, top and sides, with frosting.

Seven Minute Frosting:

2 egg whites, unbeaten	1½ teaspoons light corn
1½ cups sugar	syrup
5 tablespoons cold water	1 teaspoon vanilla extract
¼ teaspoon cream of tartar	Flaked coconut

In the top of a large double boiler place all ingredients but vanilla and coconut. Over rapidly boiling water, beat constantly with electric or rotary beater for 6 to 7 minutes. Remove from heat; add vanilla. Continue beating until icing is the right consistency to be spread. After cake is iced, sprinkle coconut on top and sides. Serves 14 to 16.

KAHLÚA CHOCOLATE CAKE

This is a treasure of a recipe

¾ cup butter
2 cups sugar
4 egg yolks
2 teaspoons vanilla extract
1 teaspoon baking soda
2 tablespoons water

1⅓ cups flour
¾ cup cocoa powder
½ cup Kahlúa
½ cup cold coffee
4 egg whites

Glaze:

½ cup confectioners' sugar,
sifted

¼ cup Kahlúa

Cream butter, sugar, egg yolks and vanilla until light and fluffy. Add baking soda which has been dissolved in water. Sift together flour and cocoa; add to creamed mixture alternately with combined Kahlúa and coffee, starting and ending with flour. Blend well. Fold in stiffly beaten egg whites. Pour batter into greased 12 cup Bundt pan. Bake at 325° for 50 to 60 minutes. Cool in pan on wire rack for 15 minutes; remove from pan. Combine glaze ingredients and spoon over warm cake. Serves 16.

Laurene Hefty
Orland, California

MANDARIN CAKE

A winner indeed!

1 (18.25 ounce) package
yellow cake mix
4 eggs, beaten
¼ cup Crisco oil
1 (11 ounce) can mandarin
oranges with juice

1 (12 ounce) carton Cool
Whip
1 (8¼ ounce) can crushed
pineapple, well drained

Beat first 4 ingredients together until well blended. Pour into three 8 inch greased and floured cake pans. Bake at 350° for 15 to 18 minutes. Cool. Combine Cool Whip and pineapple. Ice cake. Refrigerate several hours or overnight. Serves 12.

CHOCOLATE CAKE

There is no other!

1 cup butter
2 cups sugar
4 eggs
2 cups flour, sifted
¼ teaspoon salt
1½ teaspoons baking soda

⅔ cup buttermilk
1 teaspoon vanilla extract
3 (1 ounce) squares
   unsweetened chocolate,
   melted in ⅔ cup boiling
   water

Cream butter and sugar with electric beater until light and fluffy. Add eggs, one at a time; beat well after each addition. Sift flour with salt. Mix soda with buttermilk and add alternately with flour to creamed mixture, starting and ending with flour. Add vanilla and melted chocolate with water; stir until smooth.

Grease 9 × 13 inch pan. Pour batter into pan and bake at 325° for 50 to 55 minutes. Cool in pan. While slightly warm, frost with chocolate frosting. Yield: 20 (2 inch) squares. Cake freezes well.

Chocolate Frosting:

½ cup butter
1½ cups sugar
⅓ cup milk

¾ cup semi-sweet chocolate
   chips
¼ teaspoon vanilla extract

In heavy saucepan cook butter, sugar and milk to a full rolling boil. Boil for 2 minutes. Remove from heat; add chocolate chips and vanilla. Blend quickly. Beat until spreading consistency. (It won't take more than a minute or two.) Spread at once over chocolate cake.

Betty Cole
Ludington, Michigan

"14 KARAT" CAKE

A delicious moist cake for many occasions — picnics, covered-dish socials and everyday snacking

2 cups flour
2 teaspoons baking powder
1½ teaspoons baking soda
2 teaspoons cinnamon
1½ teaspoons salt
4 eggs, beaten
2 cups sugar
1½ cups vegetable oil

2 cups finely grated raw
  carrots
1 (8 ounce) can crushed
  pineapple, drained
1 (3½ ounce) can flaked
  coconut
½ cup chopped nuts

Sift together first five ingredients. Add eggs, sugar and oil; mix well. Fold in remaining ingredients and blend thoroughly.

Pour batter into three greased and floured 9 inch cake pans or two greased 6-cup Bundt pans. Bake at 350° for 35 to 40 minutes. Remove from oven; cool in pans a few minutes. Turn out on racks and cool. Fill layers and frost tops and sides of cake with Cream Cheese Frosting. Serves 14 to 16.

CREAM CHEESE FROSTING

½ cup butter, softened
1 (8 ounce) package cream
  cheese, softened

1 teaspoon vanilla extract
1 pound box confectioners'
  sugar

Combine butter, cream cheese and vanilla; blend. Gradually add sugar, beating well.

Pat Cherry
Vero Beach, Florida

BOURBON POUND CAKE
A very popular, very delicious cake

2 cups butter, softened
3 cups sugar
8 eggs, separated
3 cups flour, sifted
½ cup bourbon

4 teaspoons almond
  extract
½ cup slivered almonds
Confectioners' sugar

Cream butter and 2 cups sugar until light and fluffy. Add egg yolks, one at a time, beating after each addition. Add flour alternately with bourbon and flavoring, beating until smooth. Let egg whites warm to room temperature; beat until frothy. Slowly add 1 cup sugar and continue beating until stiff peaks form. Gently fold egg white mixture into batter. Sprinkle almonds on bottom of buttered and floured 10-inch tube pan; pour batter into pan. Bake at 350° about 1¼ hours, or until wooden pick inserted in center comes out clean. Cool; dust with confectioners' sugar. Serves 16.

SPICE CAKE
One of my favorites — you'll make this again and again

1 cup butter
2 cups sugar
2 eggs
3 cups flour
1 tablespoon baking soda
½ teaspoon salt
1 tablespoon cinnamon
1½ teaspoons nutmeg

1 teaspoon cloves
2½ cups applesauce
2 tablespoons light corn
  syrup
1 cup seedless raisins
1 cup chopped nuts
Confectioners' sugar

Cream butter and sugar; beat in eggs, one at a time. Sift flour, soda, salt and spices. Add to butter mixture alternately with combined applesauce and syrup. Fold in raisins and nuts. Pour batter into 2 greased 8 x 8 inch pans. Bake at 300° about 60 minutes. Cool. Sift on confectioners' sugar. Serves 12.

Sally Searles Grace
Ann Arbor, Michigan

HUMMINGBIRD CAKE

A very popular, very delicious cake ... moist and tender

2 cups sugar
3 eggs, beaten
1½ cups Crisco oil
3 cups flour, sifted
1 teaspoon baking soda
1 teaspoon salt
1 teaspoon cinnamon

5 bananas, mashed
1 (8¼ ounce) can crushed
  pineapple with juice
1½ teaspoon vanilla
  extract
1 cup pecans, chopped

Blend sugar, eggs and oil. Add flour, soda, salt and cinnamon. Mix thoroughly. Add remaining ingredients. Pour into three greased 8 inch cake pans. Bake at 350° for 25 to 30 minutes. Cool 15 minutes; remove from pans.

Cream Cheese Frosting:

12 ounces cream cheese,
  softened
¾ cup butter, softened
  (1½ sticks)

1 (16 ounce box) plus 1 cup
  confectioners' sugar
1½ teaspoons vanilla
1 cup pecans, chopped

Combine cream cheese and butter; gradually add sugar, vanilla and nuts. Beat until smooth and creamy. Spread frosting between layers and on top and sides of cake. Refrigerate. Serves 14.

SUNSHINE CAKE

When the occasion calls for a light, sweet dessert, this delicate cake is a perfect choice

8 egg whites
8 egg yolks
1 cup sugar
¼ cup orange juice, scant
2 tablespoons orange peel, grated

1 cup sifted cake flour
½ teaspoon baking powder
¾ teaspoon cream of tartar
Confectioners' sugar

In a large bowl of electric mixer, let egg whites warm to room temperature, about 1 hour. In a small bowl of electric mixer, beat egg yolks until very thick and lemon-colored, about 3 minutes. Add sugar and continue beating. Add orange juice and orange peel and beat again. Sift flour and baking powder and fold into yolk mixture. Beat egg whites until foamy, add cream of tartar and beat until stiff. Gradually and gently fold yolk mixture into beaten whites.

Pour batter into ungreased angel food cake pan. Bake at 350° for 30 minutes. To test, lightly touch center of cake with finger; cake should spring back and leave no imprint. Invert to cool. Sift confectioners' sugar over top of cake. Serves 12.

LEMON ROLL

In a word..."Sensational"

4 eggs, separated
¾ cup sugar, divided
1 teaspoon lemon extract
1 tablespoon vegetable oil

⅔ cup cake flour
1 teaspoon baking powder
¼ teaspoon salt
Confectioners' sugar

Lightly oil bottom and sides of a 15 x 10-inch jellyroll pan with vegetable oil; line with wax paper extending 2 inches beyond pan on each end. Lightly oil and flour wax paper. Set prepared pan aside.

Beat egg yolks at high speed with an electric mixer until thick and lemon colored. Gradually add ¼ cup sugar; blend at low speed. Stir in extract and oil.

Beat egg whites until foamy. Gradually add remaining ½ cup sugar, 1 tablespoon at a time, beating until stiff peaks form and sugar dissolves; fold into yolk mixture.

Combine flour, baking powder and salt; gradually fold into egg mixture. Spread batter evenly into pan. Bake at 350° 10 to 12 minutes.

Sift confectioners' sugar in 15 x 10-inch rectangle on tea towel. When cake is done, immediately loosen from sides of pan, and turn out onto towel. Carefully peel off wax paper. Roll up cake and towel together; cool completely on wire rack, seam side down.

Unroll cake; spread with filling, and carefully reroll. Place cake on platter, seam side down. Cover top and sides with Cool Whip, sprinkle with coconut. Refrigerate. Yield: 10 to 12 servings.

Filling:

⅓ cup fresh lemon juice
1 (14 ounce) can sweetened condensed milk

2 tablespoons grated lemon peel
1 (8 ounce) carton Cool Whip
Flaked coconut, optional

Dorothy Dickey
Asheville, North Carolina

LEMON REFRIGERATOR CAKE

A beautiful year-round company dessert

1 (10 inch) Angel Food
  cake (or chiffon)
1 envelope unflavored
  gelatin
¼ cup cold water
6 eggs, separated
1½ cups sugar

¾ cup lemon juice
2 teaspoons grated lemon
  peel
Pinch of salt
½ pint heavy cream,
  whipped
Maraschino cherries

Tear cake into small pieces. Soften gelatin in cold water. In top of double boiler, combine beaten egg yolks, ¾ cup sugar, lemon juice, lemon peel and salt. Cook over simmering water until mixture coats a spoon. Remove from heat and stir in gelatin. Cool. Beat egg whites until stiff, gradually adding remaining sugar. Fold into custard. Add cake to custard and mix gently covering all pieces. Pour mixture into an oiled tube pan. Chill overnight or at least 6 hours. Unmold and frost with whipped cream. Decorate with cherries. Serves 12.

MOM'S ALMOND POUND CAKE

Excellent flavor and texture

1 cup butter
2½ cups sugar
6 eggs
3 cups cake flour (sift
  before measuring)
1 cup dairy sour cream

⅛ teaspoon baking soda
1½ tablespoons almond
  extract
½ teaspoon salt
Confectioners' sugar

Cream butter and sugar. Add eggs, one at a time, beating well after each addition. Add flour, alternately, with ¾ cup sour cream. Dissolve baking soda in ¼ cup sour cream; add to batter and blend well. Stir in extract and salt. Pour into greased and floured tube pan. (or 2 loaf pans). Bake at 325° for 65 minutes. Cool 20 minutes and remove from pan. Sift on confectioners' sugar. Serves 12.

Amy Davenport
Dallas, Texas

CHIFFON CAKE

For 16 people and in the oven in 20 minutes! Have all ingredients ready before starting to mix.

2¼ cups cake flour, sift
  before measuring
1½ cups sugar
1 tablespoon baking
  powder
1 teaspoon salt
¾ cup water
¼ teaspoon almond extract

1 teaspoon vanilla extract
½ cup vegetable oil
5 egg yolks
7 egg whites, room
  temperature
½ teaspoon cream of tartar
Confectioners' sugar,
  sifted

In a large bowl of electric mixer, sift flour again with sugar, baking powder and salt. Add water, extracts, oil and unbeaten egg yolks. Beat until smooth; it will take about 1 minute. Beat egg whites and cream of tartar until stiff or until the batter can be cut with a knife.

Pour batter into beaten egg whites gradually, mixing as you go. Pour into ungreased 10 inch tube pan and bake at 325° for 60 to 65 minutes. When cake is done, invert cake to cool, about 1½ hours. Sift confectioners' sugar over top of cake.

OATMEAL CAKE

Moist and spicy with a chewy crisp topping of coconut and pecans

1 cup quick-cooking
  oatmeal
½ cup margarine
1¼ cups boiling water
1 cup sugar
1 cup brown sugar

2 eggs, beaten
1½ cups flour
½ teaspoon salt
1 teaspoon baking soda
1 teaspoon cinnamon

Place oatmeal, margarine and boiling water in bowl. Stir and set aside for 20 minutes. Combine all other ingredients. Add oatmeal mixture and blend thoroughly. Pour into 9 x 13 inch greased pan. Bake at 375° for 40 minutes. Serves 12 to 14.

Continued on next page

Topping:

6 tablespoons butter,
melted
½ cup brown sugar
¼ cup evaporated milk

¼ teaspoon vanilla extract
1 cup flaked coconut
½ cup chopped pecans

Combine topping ingredients and spread over warm cake. Place under broiler until topping bubbles; do not brown.

Effie Long White
Mason, Texas

KAHLÚA CHOCOLATE SWIRL CHEESE CAKE
...just as delicious as it sounds

Crust:

1½ cups chocolate wafer
cookie crumbs

6 tablespoons butter,
melted

Filling:

4 ounce Hershey milk
chocolate candy bar
¼ cup heavy cream
3 (8 ounce) packages cream
cheese, softened
1 cup sugar

¼ cup Kahlúa
¼ cup heavy cream
3 eggs, beaten
2 teaspoons vanilla extract
Hershey bar chocolate curls
Heavy cream, whipped

Mix crust ingredients and press into well-buttered 9 inch spring-form pan. Melt chocolate with ¼ cup cream, stirring until smooth; set aside. Combine cream cheese, sugar, Kahlúa, cream, eggs and vanilla. Mix well. Pour into crust. Drizzle chocolate mixture over cheese cake; run a knife through batter a few times to distribute.

Place spring-form pan into a large pan and pour boiling water around. Bake at 350° about 1½ hours. Cool; refrigerate several hours. Remove from pan. Press chocolate curls around sides and garnish with whipped cream. Serves 12.

June Starkey
Darby, Montana

NEW YORK-STYLE CHEESECAKE
The "Big Apple" is proud of this one!

1½ cups graham cracker
  crumbs
¼ cup sifted confectioners'
  sugar

6 tablespoons unsalted
  butter, melted

Combine crumbs, sugar and butter. Press into bottom and up sides of 9½ inch spring-form pan. Refrigerate 1 hour.

Filling:

5 (8 ounce) packages
  cream cheese, softened
1¾ cups sugar
3 tablespoons flour
2 teaspoons grated lemon
  peel

2 teaspoons grated orange
  peel
1 teaspoon vanilla extract
6 eggs
¼ cup heavy cream

Topping:
**Fresh or thawed frozen
  sliced strawberries**

Beat cream cheese with electric mixer until fluffy. Combine sugar, flour, lemon peel, orange peel and vanilla; slowly add to cheese, beating until smooth. Add eggs, one at a time, beating after each addition. Stir in cream.

Pour into crust and bake at 500° for 12 minutes. Reduce oven temperature to 250°; bake 60 to 70 minutes longer. Remove from oven and cool on rack for 2 hours. Remove side of pan; cover and refrigerate 8 hours or overnight.

Spoon strawberries over the top of cheesecake. Serves 16.

Leila MacAdam
Vero Beach, Florida

RUM CAKE

So easy you can't believe it can be so delicious! Serve it chilled

1 cup pecans, chopped
1 (18½ ounce) yellow cake
   mix with pudding
3 eggs

⅓ cup vegetable oil
½ cup cold water
½ cup dark rum

Grease 12 cup Bundt pan. Sprinkle nuts over bottom of pan. Mix all cake ingredients together at low speed. Increase to medium speed and beat for 3 to 4 minutes. Pour batter over nuts.

Bake at 325° for 55 to 60 minutes. Cool 15 minutes. Invert cake onto a pan lined with wax paper. Pierce entire top of cake and spoon and brush glaze over top and sides. Allow cake to absorb glaze; repeat until glaze is used up. Serves 16 to 18.

Glaze:

¼ pound butter
¼ cup water

¾ cup sugar
½ cup dark rum

Melt butter in saucepan. Stir in water and sugar. Boil 5 minutes, stirring constantly. Remove from heat; cool slightly; stir in rum.

June Starkey
Darby, Montana

KNOBBY APPLE CAKE

3 eggs, beaten	1 teaspoon baking soda
2 cups sugar	1 teaspoon salt
1¼ cups salad oil	1 teaspoon cinnamon
1 teaspoon vanilla	1 teaspoon nutmeg
3 cups peeled, chopped	3 cups flour
tart apples	1 cup pecans, chopped

Combine eggs, sugar, oil and vanilla. Mix well; add apples. Sift together dry ingredients. Add apple batter to flour mixture; add nuts, blending well. Pour into greased and floured 12-cup Bundt pan. Place in a cold oven set at 325°. Bake 60 to 75 minutes. Test with a wooden pick. Glaze cake. Serves 16.

Caramel Glaze:

½ cup butter	¼ cup evaporated milk
1 cup light brown sugar	

Combine ingredients; bring to a boil. Cool and spread on cake.

Marion Bruckner
Oyster Bay, New York

GINGERBREAD

1 cup brown sugar	2 teaspoons baking soda
½ cup butter	2 teaspoons ginger
2 eggs, beaten	1 teaspoon cinnamon
¾ cup molasses	½ teaspoon salt
2¾ cups flour	1 cup buttermilk

Cream sugar, butter and eggs. Add molasses; blend. Sift dry ingredients; add alternately with buttermilk. Beat well. Pour batter into greased 9 x 13-inch pan. Bake at 350° for 35 to 40 minutes. Serve warm.

MARZIPAN COOKIES
You will treasure this one

1 (8 ounce) can almond
 paste
½ cup butter, softened
½ cup sugar
¼ cup brown sugar

1 egg, slightly beaten
1¼ cups flour
½ teaspoon soda
½ teaspoon salt

Place almond paste in bowl of electric mixer. Beat to soften; add butter and sugars and mix until light and fluffy. Beat in egg. Stir in dry ingredients until well blended. Wrap dough in plastic wrap and refrigerate for 15 minutes. Drop by rounded teaspoonsful onto greased baking sheet. Bake at 375° for 7 to 9 minutes or until light brown. Remove to rack; cool. Store in tight container in refrigerator or freezer. Yield: 7 dozen.

JAM BITES
Serve warm or cold...They're sure to make a hit

¾ cup butter
5 ounces cream cheese
2 cups flour, sifted
½ teaspoon salt

Apricot jam
Confectioners' sugar,
 sifted

Cream butter and cheese. Blend in flour and salt; mix thoroughly. Roll out on floured board to ½ inch thickness. Cut into 2 x 1 inch strips. Make a deep groove down middle of each cookie with handle of knife, keeping ends closed. Place ¼ teaspoon jam in each groove. Bake at 350° about 20 minutes, or until delicately browned. Dust with confectioners' sugar while still hot. Yield: 2 dozen.

HOLIDAY ROSETTES

My Mother served these at our parties ... a lovely memory

2 eggs, beaten
1 cup milk
1 cup flour, sifted
1 tablespoon sugar
¼ teaspoon salt

2 tablespoons butter,
  melted
Confectioners' sugar,
  sifted

Combine first 6 ingredients; beat with an electric mixer until blended and smooth. Cover and refrigerate for 2 hours or more.

Heat about 2½ inches of oil to 375° in a deep-fat fryer or medium size saucepan. Prepare iron by immersing the head of it in hot oil.

Dip hot iron in batter, but do not let it run over top of iron for then it is difficult to get rosette off when cooked. Return batter-coated iron to oil, immersing it completely. As soon as rosette is formed (about 20 seconds), lift iron slowly up and down to release rosette from iron. Cook until golden, about 1 minute, turning once. Remove from oil and drain rosette on absorbent paper. Dust with confectioners' sugar. May freeze.

Reheat iron for a few seconds and repeat process. Stir batter occasionally.

Yield: 4 dozen

Note: Rosettes are shaped with a small iron made for the purpose.

LACE COOKIES

½ cup butter
1 cup light brown sugar
1 cup plus 2 tablespoons
    quick cooking oatmeal,
    uncooked

1½ tablespoons flour
½ teaspoon salt
1 egg, slightly beaten
½ teaspoon vanilla extract

Melt butter in saucepan. Add brown sugar and stir to combine. Remove from heat. Add remaining ingredients; mix well. Place heavy duty aluminum foil on a 14 x 16 inch aluminum baking sheet. Butter foil. Drop batter by level measuring teaspoon about 2 inches apart. Bake at 375° about 5 minutes, until golden brown. Remove from oven, cool for 5 minutes. Lift off with a spatula and transfer to racks to complete the cooling. Store in airtight containers in freezer. Yield: 5 dozen.

My Mother, Cherry Kindel Orr
Nashville, Tennessee

OATMEAL COOKIES
Grandmother's recipe and a favorite

1 cup butter or margarine,
    softened
1 cup sugar
1 cup dark brown sugar
2 eggs
1½ cups flour, (sift before
    measuring)

1 teaspoon salt
1 teaspoon baking soda
3 cups old-fashioned
    oatmeal, uncooked
1½ teaspoons vanilla
    extract

Cream butter and sugars in electric mixer. Add eggs, one at a time, beating well after each addition. Combine flour, salt and soda; add to butter mixture. Stir in oatmeal and vanilla. Drop batter on ungreased baking sheet by rounded teaspoonful. Bake at 350° about 8 minutes. Remove from oven and cool 1 minute. Use back of spatula to loosen cookies; transfer to racks and cool completely. Yield: 10 dozen.

Barbara Matthias
Winter Park, Florida

APRICOT BARS

Moist and chewy with a delectable taste of apricots

⅔ cup dried apricots
½ cup butter, softened
¼ cup sugar
1 cup flour, sifted
1 cup brown sugar
2 eggs, well beaten
⅓ cup flour

½ teaspoon baking powder
¼ teaspoon salt
½ teaspoon vanilla
½ cup pecans, chopped
Confectioners' sugar,
　optional

Rinse apricots and cover with water. Boil 10 minutes. Drain, cool and chop. Combine butter, sugar and flour and pack into a greased 8x8x2-inch pan. Bake at 350° until lightly browned, checking after 20 minutes. Combine brown sugar, eggs, ⅓ cup flour, baking powder, salt and vanilla; add pecans and apricots and spread over the baked layer. Bake in a 350° oven about 30 minutes. Cool in pan, cut into bars and sift confectioners' sugar over tops. Yield: 2 dozen.

Marguerite Williams
Thomasville, Georgia

ALMOND SQUARES

A wonderful pastry from Vienna

1 cup butter (no
  substitutes)
¾ cup sugar
1 egg, separated

4 ounces almond paste
1 teaspoon almond extract
2 cups flour
½ cup slivered almonds

Mix butter and sugar in electric mixer until fluffy. Add egg yolk, almond paste and almond extract. Beat well; add flour and beat until just blended. Do not overbeat. Smooth with a spatula into ungreased 11×7 inch pan. Beat egg whites until foamy and brush surface of the dough. Scatter almonds over top. Bake at 350° for 30 minutes. Cut into squares. Yield: 3 dozen.

ALMOND BUTTER COOKIES

½ cup butter, softened
¼ cup sugar
¾ teaspoon almond extract
1 cup flour, sifted
Pinch of salt

½ cup blanched almonds,
  finely chopped
Sugar
Blanched whole almonds

Mix butter and sugar in electric mixer until fluffy. Add almond extract; blend. Add flour and salt and mix until smooth. Stir in chopped almonds. Shape dough into 1 inch balls. Place on ungreased cookie sheet. Flatten dough, sprinkle sugar on top, and press whole almond into center of each cookie. Bake at 350° for 10 minutes, or until lightly browned. Cookies freeze well. Yield: 3 dozen.

GINGERSNAPS

6 tablespoons butter
1 cup sugar
¼ cup light molasses
1 egg, beaten
1 teaspoon vinegar
1⅔ cups flour

1½ teaspoons ginger
¾ teaspoon baking soda
½ teaspoon cinnamon
⅛ teaspoon cloves
Sugar for topping, optional

Cream butter and sugar; add molasses, egg and vinegar and mix well. Sift dry ingredients together and stir into butter mixture. Drop batter by rounded teaspoonsful, about 2 inches apart, onto a greased cookie sheet. Sprinkle with sugar. Bake at 325° for 9 to 12 minutes. Cool for 1 minute; remove to rack. Yield: 5 dozen.

LEMON BARS
Ever so good! I like these right out of the freezer

Crust:

1 cup butter, softened
2 cups flour, sifted

½ cup confectioners' sugar, sifted

Mix thoroughly and press into 10 x 14 inch ungreased pan. Bake at 350° for 15 to 20 minutes, or until lightly browned. Cool.

Filling:

4 eggs, beaten
2 cups sugar
6 tablespoons lemon juice
Grated peel of 2 lemons

¼ cup flour
½ teaspoon baking powder
Dash of salt
Confectioners' sugar

Combine all ingredients but confectioners' sugar; mix well. Pour on top of baked crust. Bake at 350° 20 to 25 minutes. When cool, sprinkle with sifted confectioners' sugar. Yield: 4 dozen.

MELTING MOMENT
The name says it all

½ cup butter, softened
2 tablespoons sugar
1 teaspoon vanilla extract

1 cup ground nut meats
1 cup cake flour, sifted
Confectioners' sugar

Cream butter and sugar until light and fluffy; add vanilla. Mix nuts with flour and add to butter mixture. Chill dough for ½ hour. Roll into balls or crescent shape. Bake on buttered cookie sheet at 300° for 25 to 30 minutes. When cool, sift confectioners' sugar over cookies. Store in airtight container. Yield: 4 dozen.

Bess Orr Cullen
Whitefish, Montana

#1 SUGAR COOKIES

1 cup butter
1 cup sugar
1 egg, beaten
1 teaspoon vanilla extract
2 cups plus 2 tablespoons
   flour

½ teaspoon baking soda
½ teaspoon cream of tartar
Pinch of salt
Sugar

Cream butter and sugar; add egg and vanilla and beat until fluffy. Sift flour, baking soda, cream of tartar and salt; add to butter mixture. Chill for 1 hour. Roll dough into small balls, dip in sugar and place on unbuttered cookie sheet. Press each ball thin with bottom of glass. Bake at 350° for 10 to 12 minutes. May freeze. Yield: 6 dozen.

Note: For the holidays, add green or red sprinkles.

BLACK WALNUT OATMEAL COOKIES

Oh, the flavor in these rich nuts...serve cookies right from the freezer

¾ cup unsalted butter,
  softened
1⅓ cups brown sugar
2 large eggs
1 teaspoon vanilla extract
1 cup flour
¾ teaspoon baking soda

½ teaspoon salt
¼ teaspoon nutmeg
2 cups old-fashioned
  oatmeal, uncooked
1 cup black walnuts,
  chopped

Cream butter and sugar in electric mixer. Beat until light and fluffy. Add eggs, one at a time, beating well after each addition; add vanilla. Sift together flour, soda, salt and nutmeg; add to butter mixture. Stir in oatmeal and black walnuts. Drop batter on greased baking sheet by teaspoonful, about 2 inches apart. Bake at 350° about 8 to 10 minutes. Remove from oven, let cool 1 minute, transfer to racks and cool. Yield: 8 dozen.

Mary Lourie
Winnetka, Illinois

POTATO CHIP COOKIES

Long a favorite

1 cup butter, softened (no
  substitutes)
½ cup sugar
1½ cups flour

1 teaspoon vanilla extract
¾ cup finely crushed fresh
  potato chips
Confectioners' sugar

Mix butter and sugar in electric mixer until fluffy. Add flour; mix until smooth. Fold in vanilla and potato chips. Drop on ungreased cookie sheet by small teaspoonfuls. Bake at 325° for 15 to 20 minutes, or until light brown. Cool and sprinkle with sifted confectioners' sugar. Yield: 6 dozen.

Alice Strom
Boynton Beach, Florida

PEANUT BUTTER COOKIES

1 cup butter
1 cup brown sugar
¾ cup sugar
2 eggs
1 cup creamy peanut
  butter

2 cups flour
2 teaspoons baking soda
½ teaspoon salt
1 cup oatmeal (quick or
  old-fashioned, uncooked)

Cream butter and sugars in electric mixer until light and fluffy. Add eggs and peanut butter; beat well. Sift flour, soda and salt. Add to creamed mixture, mixing well. Stir in oatmeal. Shape dough into 1 inch balls and place on ungreased baking sheet. Make crisscrosses on each with tines of fork. Bake at 350° for 8 to 10 minutes. Yield: 6 dozen.

BENNE WAFERS

"A touch of Charleston"
Crisp buttery cookies with distinctive flavor

1 cup sesame seeds
  (available at health food
  store)
½ cup margarine
1½ cups light brown sugar

1 egg, beaten
¾ cup flour
¼ teaspoon baking powder
1 teaspoon vanilla extract

Toast sesame seeds in skillet for 5 minutes, stirring frequently. Remove from skillet; reserve. Line ungreased cookie sheet with heavy foil. Mix margarine, sugar and egg with electric mixer. Add sesame seeds and remaining ingredients; blend well. Drop batter by half teaspoon onto cookie sheet, about 2 inches apart. Bake at 350° for 5 to 8 minutes or until light brown. Cool on cookie sheet; remove with back of spatula. Cookies should be thin and crisp. Yield: 15 dozen.

Nan Swansen
Black Mountain, North Carolina

CHOCOLATE PEPPERMINT SQUARES

You will love these

2 (1 ounce) squares
    unsweetened chocolate
½ cup butter
2 eggs
1 cup sugar

1 teaspoon vanilla extract
½ cup flour
¼ teaspoon baking powder
¼ teaspoon salt
½ cup chopped pecans

In top of double boiler, melt chocolate and butter. Cool. Beat eggs until frothy. Stir in sugar; add chocolate mixture and vanilla. Add remaining ingredients. Mix well. Pour into 9 × 13 inch buttered pan. Bake at 350° for 15 minutes. Cool.

Frosting:

2 tablespoons butter,
    melted
1 cup confectioners' sugar,
    sifted

1 tablespoon cream
¾ teaspoon peppermint
    flavoring

Combine all ingredients. Frost cooled cake. Refrigerate.

Glaze:

1 (1 ounce) square
    unsweetened chocolate

1 tablespoon butter

Melt chocolate and butter, stirring well. Drizzle over frosted cake. Chill. Cut into 1 inch squares. Store in refrigerator. Yield: 5 dozen.

Lillian Paxson
Vero Beach, Florida

SINFUL BROWNIES
They are

1 (14 ounce) bag caramels
⅔ cup evaporated milk
1 (6 ounce) package semi-
  sweet chocolate chips

1 (18.25 ounce) package
  deluxe Devil's Food cake
  mix
¾ cup butter, melted

In top of double boiler melt caramels, ⅓ cup evaporated milk and chocolate chips. To cake mix add melted butter and ⅓ cup evaporated milk; blend. Spread half of batter in greased 9 × 13 inch aluminum pan. Bake at 350° for 6 to 8 minutes. Remove from oven and spread melted caramel-chocolate mixture over cake. Crumble remaining cake mixture on top. Bake 5 minutes; spread top batter more evenly. Return to oven and bake an additional 25 minutes. When cool, cut into squares. Yield: 4 dozen.

Barbara Morrison
Vero Beach, Florida

CREAM CHEESE BROWNIES
Right out of the freezer they taste like caramels!

4 (1 ounce) squares
  unsweetened chocolate
1 cup butter or margarine,
  softened
1 (8 ounce) package cream
  cheese, softened

2½ cups sugar
4 eggs
1 cup flour, sifted
½ teaspoon salt
2 teaspoons vanilla extract
1 cup walnuts, chopped

Melt chocolate and butter in top of double boiler. Remove from heat and cool. Beat cheese, sugar and eggs with electric beater until blended. Add chocolate mixture. Blend well. Add flour, salt and vanilla; mix thoroughly. Stir in walnuts. Pour batter into well-greased 9 × 13 inch pan. Bake at 350° for 45 to 50 minutes. When cool, cut into squares. Serve chilled. Yield: 3½ dozen.

Mary Tatham
Tequesta, Florida

CARAMEL BROWNIES

Attention butterscotch lovers

½ cup butter
2 cups brown sugar
2 eggs
1 teaspoon vanilla extract

1 cup flour
2 teaspoons baking powder
½ teaspoon salt
1 cup pecans, chopped

Combine butter, sugar, eggs and vanilla in large bowl of electric mixer. Beat until smooth. Add sifted dry ingredients; blend. Fold in nuts. Pour into buttered 9 × 9 inch pan. Bake at 350° for 25 to 30 minutes. Cool slightly. Cut into squares. Yield: 2 dozen.

Mary Clark
San Diego, California

FUDGE BROWNIES

*For bridge players and brownies and boy scouts and baseball players
and big boys too! The best!*

1 cup butter
4 (1 ounce) squares
  unsweetened chocolate
4 eggs, well beaten
2 cups sugar

1 cup flour, sifted
¼ teaspoon salt
2 teaspoons vanilla extract
1 cup chopped nuts
Chocolate glaze, optional

Melt butter and chocolate in top of double boiler. Remove from heat and cool. Beat eggs and sugar with an electric mixer. Add chocolate mixture; blend well. Add flour, salt and vanilla. Mix thoroughly. Stir in nuts. Pour batter into buttered 9 × 13 inch pan. Bake at 350° for 25 to 30 minutes. Cool and cut into squares. Yield: 3½ dozen.

Chocolate glaze:

Melt 3 ounces chocolate chips or 1 (1 ounce) square semisweet chocolate with 1½ tablespoons butter. Stir until smooth. Spread glaze on top of brownies. Allow glaze to set.

TEREZ'S COOKIES

Thin-crisp-delicious

1 cup butter
1¾ cups sugar
¼ cup dark brown sugar
2 eggs
3½ cups cake flour

2½ teaspoons baking
 powder
½ teaspoon salt
2 teaspoons vanilla extract
1 cup pecan pieces

Cream butter and sugars with electric beater; add eggs and mix well. Sift dry ingredients; add to butter mixture. Mix thoroughly. Add vanilla and pecans. Chill dough. When firm, form into three long rolls. Slice very thin. Place on buttered baking sheets and bake at 350° about 10 minutes. Cookie dough may be frozen and baked as needed. Yield: 6 dozen.

Hilda Hoffman
Washington, D.C.

TOFFEE SQUARES

1 cup butter
1 cup brown sugar
1 egg yolk, beaten
2 cups flour, sifted

1 teaspoon vanilla extract
1 (8 ounce) sweet milk
 chocolate Hershey bar
½ cup pecan, chopped

In electric mixer, cream butter and sugar until light; add egg yolk. Add flour blending well; add vanilla. Spread thinly on 15½ × 10½ inch greased cookie sheet. Bake at 350° for 15 to 17 minutes. Remove from oven. Break chocolate into squares and place on surface of cookie while warm. Spread over entire top. Sprinkle pecans over all, pressing in with sheet of wax paper. Cut while warm. Yield: 54 (1½ inch squares).

Mi Mi Garnett
Evanston, Illinois

SPRITZ COOKIES

1 cup butter
¾ cup sugar
1 egg, beaten
2½ cups flour, sifted
½ teaspoon baking powder

⅛ teaspoon salt
1 teaspoon almond extract
1 egg white
Blanched almonds,
 slivered

Cream butter and sugar until fluffy. Add egg and beat. Mix dry ingredients and add to butter mixture. Add flavoring. Mix well. Put dough through cookie press onto a buttered baking sheet. Brush with unbeaten egg white; sprinkle with almonds. Bake at 375° for 8 to 10 minutes. Yield: 5 dozen.

BUTTERSCOTCH COOKIES

1 cup butter, softened
¾ cup sugar
¾ cup brown sugar
2 eggs
1 teaspoon vanilla extract
1¼ cups flour
1 teaspoon baking soda
½ teaspoon cinnamon

½ teaspoon salt
3 cups old-fashioned or
 quick cooking oatmeal,
 uncooked
1 (12 ounce) package
 Nestle Toll House
 butterscotch morsels

Cream butter and sugars in electric mixer. Add eggs and vanilla and beat until creamy. Sift together flour, cinnamon and salt; gradually add to butter mixture. Stir in oatmeal and butterscotch morsels. Drop batter by rounded tablespoonful onto greased baking sheet about 2 inches apart. Bake at 375° for 8 to 10 minutes. Cool 1 minute before removing from baking sheet. Yield: 4 dozen.

Ruth Keller
Asheville, North Carolina

FORGOTTEN COOKIES

The young people won't let you forget!

2 egg whites
½ cup sugar
1 teaspoon vanilla extract

¾ cup chocolate chips or
1 cup pecan pieces

Beat egg whites until stiff, gradually adding sugar. Fold in vanilla and chocolate chips or pecans. Drop meringue batter, about ½ teaspoon at a time, onto ungreased cookie sheet, an inch apart. Place in 350° oven. Turn off heat and forget! . . . several hours or overnight. Remove from oven and store in tightly closed container. Yield: 5 dozen.

Martha Wolfer
Cheyenne, Wyoming

SCOTCH SHORTBREAD

Delicious . . . an authentic Scottish recipe

1 cup butter, softened
½ cup fine granulated
   sugar

2½ cups flour, sifted

Cream butter and sugar; gradually add flour blending thoroughly. On buttered baking sheet, pat dough out to ½ inch thick*; cut into triangles. Pierce the dough all over with a fork in even rows and close together. Bake at 275° about 40 minutes, or until bottoms are slightly browned. Cool on racks. Yield: 5 dozen.

* The shortbread may be rolled into balls; flatten with stoneware cookie stamp on baking sheet. The stamp embosses designs on cookies.

Barbara Morrison
Vero Beach, Florida

FROSTED DELIGHTS

Cut into rather small squares for these are very rich

Crumb layer:

½ cup butter, softened
½ cup brown sugar

1 cup flour, sifted

Combine all ingredients and mix until texture of coarse meal. Pat into buttered 9 x 13 inch pan. Bake at 350° for 10 to 12 minutes, or until slightly brown.

Topping:

2 eggs, beaten
1 cup brown sugar
2 tablespoons flour
½ teaspoon salt

½ teaspoon baking powder
1 teaspoon vanilla extract
1 cup pecans, chopped

Combine topping ingredients; spread evenly over partially baked crumb layer. Continue baking for 25 minutes. When cool, ice with 1½ cups sifted confectioners' sugar thinned to a good spreading consistency with lemon juice. Yield: 3½ dozen.

BROWN EDGE WAFERS

A touch of lemon in these buttery tea cookies

½ cup butter, softened
½ cup sugar
1 egg
1 teaspoon vanilla extract

½ teaspoon grated lemon
   peel
1 cup flour
Granulated sugar, optional

Cream butter and sugar with electric beater until light and fluffy. Add egg, vanilla and lemon peel. Mix well. Add flour, mixing until just blended. Drop batter by teaspoonful onto greased cookie sheet. Bake at 375° about 8 minutes. Sprinkle with sugar. Cool on wire rack. Yield: 3 dozen.

Carey Jackson Sveen
Franklin, North Carolina

GIANT COOKIES

The best of the chocolate chips

1 cup butter
¾ cup brown sugar
¾ cup granulated sugar
2 eggs, beaten
1 teaspoon vanilla extract
1 teaspoon baking soda

1 teaspoon hot water
2¼ cups flour
1 teaspoon salt
2½ to 3 cups semi-sweet
   chocolate chips

In a large bowl, cream together butter, sugars, eggs and vanilla until light and fluffy. Add soda which has been dissolved in hot water. Sift together flour and salt; blend into creamed mixture. Add chocolate chips. Cover and refrigerate several hours or overnight.

Use an ice cream scoop to drop batter on greased baking sheet, averaging 9 cookies per sheet. Press balls with fingertips to form flat rounds. This way cookies do not spread as much in baking and they keep uniformly round. Bake at 350° for 8 to 10 minutes. Cool 1 minute before removing from baking sheet. Yield: 33 giant-size cookies.

CASHEW CRUNCH COOKIES

1 cup butter, softened
¾ cup light brown sugar
½ cup sugar
1 egg, beaten
1 teaspoon vanilla extract

2¼ cups flour
½ teaspoon baking soda
½ teaspoon cream of tartar
1½ cups cashew nuts,
   finely chopped

Mix butter and sugars in electric mixer until fluffy. Add egg and vanilla; blend. Sift dry ingredients; add to creamed mixture. Mix well. Stir in cashew nuts. Drop batter by rounded teaspoonfuls onto greased baking sheet. Bake at 350° for 8 to 10 minutes, or until lightly browned. Yield: 7 dozen.

BROWN BAG APPLE PIE

Here is an apple pie recipe that never fails to delight family and guests

6 cups tart apples	Topping:
Juice of ½ lemon	5 ounces flour
5 ounces sugar	½ cup sugar
3 tablespoons flour	¼ pound butter
1½ teaspoons cinnamon	
1 deep dish (9 inch) unbaked pie shell	

Peel and slice apples; sprinkle with lemon juice. Combine sugar, flour, cinnamon and apples; mix well and pour into pie shell. Mix flour and sugar in small bowl. Cut in butter until mixture resembles coarse crumbs. Spoon mixture over pie. Place pie in heavy brown bag and fold top of bag over twice; staple top or secure with paper clips. Bake at 400° for 60 minutes. Serves 6.

Lynn Morrison Beckley
Vero Beach, Florida

CRACKER PIE

3 egg whites	24 Ritz crackers, crushed
¾ cup sugar	1 cup chopped pecans
1 teaspoon almond flavoring	1 teaspoon butter, melted
1 teaspoon baking powder	1 cup heavy cream, whipped

Beat egg whites until stiff, slowly adding sugar; add almond flavoring and baking powder. Blend thoroughly. Fold in crackers and pecans. Melt butter in 9 inch pie pan; coat bottom and sides with butter. Add batter and bake at 325° for 30 minutes. Cool. Spread whipped cream over top of pie. Refrigerate several hours or freeze. Serves 6 to 8.

PEACH PRALINE PIE

Pecans and brown sugar give this summer Dixie pie a great flavor

½ cup sugar
2 tablespoons tapioca
4 cups sliced peeled
  peaches
1 teaspoon lemon juice
¼ teaspoon almond extract

¼ cup dark brown sugar
¼ cup flour (generous)
5 ounces chopped pecans
¼ cup butter, melted
1 (9 inch) unbaked pie
  shell

Combine sugar and tapioca in large bowl. Add peaches which have been mixed with lemon juice and almond extract. Set aside for 15 minutes. Combine brown sugar, flour, pecans and butter in small bowl; mix until crumbly. Sprinkle one third over bottom of pie shell; cover with peach mixture and sprinkle with remaining pecan mixture. Bake at 425° for 30 minutes, or until crust is lightly browned. Cool pie in pan on rack. Serves 8.

Bobbie Morrison
Vero Beach, Florida

CHERRY CRUNCH

A well-flavored easy cherry pastry

1 (21 ounce) can Comstock
  cherry pie filling
1 tablespoon sugar
1 tablespoon lemon juice
¾ teaspoon nutmeg

½ teaspoon almond extract
¼ pound butter or
  margarine, softened
1 (9 ounce) box Jiffy
  yellow cake mix

Spread cherry pie filling in a buttered 9×5 inch loaf pan. Sprinkle sugar, lemon juice, nutmeg and almond extract over pie filling. Combine butter and cake mix; spread over cherry mixture. Bake at 350° for 40 minutes. Serves 6.

Ruth Breese
Vero Beach, Florida

ANGEL PIE

A spectacular finish

Meringue:

4 egg whites	Pinch of salt
¼ teaspoon cream of tartar	1 teaspoon vanilla extract
1 cup sugar	

Beat egg whites until frothy. Add cream of tartar and beat until stiff, gradually adding sugar and salt. Fold in vanilla. Spread in 9 inch buttered pie pan covering bottom and sides; shape with back of spoon, making the bottom ¼ inch thick and the sides 1 inch thick. Bake at 275° for 1 hour, leave in oven to cool for 1 hour.

Filling:

4 egg yolks	¼ cup lemon juice
½ cup sugar	2 cups heavy cream
2 tablespoons grated lemon peel	Toasted almonds for garnish

Beat egg yolks until lemon-colored, gradually adding sugar, lemon peel and lemon juice. Cook in top of double boiler over hot water (not touching pan) until thick, stirring constantly. This will take between 5 and 8 minutes. Cool. Fold in 1 cup of cream, whipped. Spread over meringue and cover with 1 cup of cream, whipped. Sprinkle toasted almonds over top. Refrigerate a minimum of 8 hours. May be made the day before serving. Serves 8.

Hilda Hoffman
Washington, D.C.

LEMON CURD TARTS

Lemon curd may be kept for many weeks in the refrigerator. It is delicious as a cake filling, on meringues, gingerbread...almost anything

Lemon Curd:

4 teaspoons freshly grated lemon peel
½ cup fresh lemon juice

¾ cup sugar
6 tablespoons butter
4 eggs, beaten

Combine peel, lemon juice and sugar in top of double boiler. Add butter; heat over simmering water until butter has melted. Add eggs and cook, stirring constantly, until mixture is thick, about 15 minutes. Remove from heat; cool. Fill tarts and refrigerate. Yield: 2 cups.

Cream Cheese Pastry:

1 (3 ounce) package cream cheese, softened

½ cup butter, softened
1 cup flour, sifted

Beat together cream cheese and butter. Stir in flour. Cover and chill mixture for 40 minutes. Shape into 1 inch balls. Press onto bottom and up sides of ungreased mini-muffin pans. Pierce the dough with a fork. Bake at 400° for 10 to 12 minutes. Cool. May freeze. Yield: 24 tart shells.

APPLE CRISP

6 cups tart apples
¾ cup brown sugar
¾ cup flour
Pinch of salt

½ teaspoon cinnamon
½ cup butter
Whipped dessert topping, optional

Place sliced apples in buttered 8 x 8 inch baking dish. Combine sugar, flour, salt, cinnamon and butter; mix until crumbly. Sprinkle mixture over apples and bake at 350° for 40 to 45 minutes, or until top is nicely browned. If desired, serve with whipped dessert topping. Serves 6.

PUMPKIN CHIFFON PIE WITH GINGERSNAP CRUST

Something special

Crust:

1¼ cups gingersnap crumbs
4 tablespoons butter,
   melted

Mix together and pack into sides and bottom of 9 inch pie pan. Bake at 325° for 10 minutes. Cool.

Filling:

1½ cups canned pumpkin
1 cup brown sugar
3 egg yolks
½ teaspoon salt
½ teaspoon ginger
¼ teaspoon allspice
2 teaspoons cinnamon
1 tablespoon gelatin

¼ cup cold water
3 egg whites, beaten
2 teaspoons sugar
1 cup heavy cream,
   whipped
Additional gingersnap
   crumbs

Combine pumpkin, brown sugar, egg yolks, salt, ginger, allspice and cinnamon. Cook in top of double boiler until consistency of custard. Remove from heat. Add gelatin dissolved in cold water. Cool. Fold in stiffly beaten egg whites to which sugar has been added. Turn into a crumb lined pie pan and chill until firm. To serve, top with whipped cream and additional crumbs. Serves 8.

PUMPKIN PIE

It will be the best you've ever eaten, I'm sure!

1⅓ cups canned pumpkin
½ cup dark brown sugar
½ cup white sugar
2 eggs, slightly beaten
1¼ cups half and half
  cream

1 tablespoon melted butter
¼ teaspoon salt
1 teaspoon cinnamon
½ teaspoon ground cloves
1 deep dish (9 inch)
  unbaked pie shell

Combine all ingredients. Pour mixture into pie shell. Bake at 375° for 60 minutes. Serves 6.

Lorilee Weinhold
Sarasota, Florida

SOUTHERN PECAN PIE

Seven testers said it was delicious

1 cup sugar
½ cup white corn syrup
½ cup butter, melted
3 eggs, well beaten

1 cup pecan halves
1 (9 inch) unbaked pie
  shell

Combine sugar, syrup and butter. Add eggs. Place pecan halves in pie shell; add mixture. Bake at 400° for 10 minutes. Reduce heat to 350° and continue baking for 30 to 35 minutes. Serves 6 to 8.

NO CRUST COCONUT PIE

Makes two pies. Enjoy one, share one!

1¾ cups sugar
½ cup self-rising flour
4 eggs, well beaten
¼ cup butter, melted

1 teaspoon vanilla extract
2 cups milk
7 to 8 ounces coconut
  (fresh or flaked)

Mix sugar and flour. Add eggs, then remaining ingredients. Pour into two greased 9 inch foil pie tins. Bake at 350° for 35 to 40 minutes, or until brown on top. Serves 6.

HEAVENLY CHOCOLATE PIE

½ cup slivered almonds, toasted
1 (9 inch) baked pie shell
1 envelope unflavored gelatin
¼ cup cold water
½ cup unsweetened cocoa, sifted
1 cup confectioners' sugar, sifted
2 cups heavy cream
1 teaspoon vanilla extract
Additional heavy cream, whipped
Toasted almonds for garnish

Sprinkle almonds over bottom of pastry shell. Set aside. Soften gelatin in cold water; dissolve over hot water. Remove from heat. Combine cocoa, confectioners' sugar, heavy cream and vanilla. Beat until light and fluffy; gradually add dissolved gelatin and continue beating until mixture forms stiff peaks. Turn into baked pastry shell. Refrigerate several hours before serving. Garnish with whipped cream and toasted almonds. Serves 6.

SUPERB FUDGE PIE

It really is! and you'll like it served warm too

½ cup butter
3 (1 ounce) squares unsweetened chocolate
4 eggs, well beaten
3 tablespoons white corn syrup
1½ cups sugar
¼ teaspoon salt
1 teaspoon vanilla extract
1 (9 inch) unbaked pie shell
Ice cream or whipped cream for topping

In top of double boiler, melt butter and chocolate. Cool. Place eggs in mixing bowl; add syrup, sugar, salt and vanilla and mix well. Stir in chocolate mixture; blend. Pour into pie shell. Bake at 350° for 25 to 30 minutes, or until top is crusty and filling is set but somewhat soft inside. Do not over-bake. Top with ice cream or whipped cream. Serves 8.

LEMON MERINGUE PIE

1½ cups sugar
⅓ cup cornstarch
Pinch of salt
1½ cups water
5 egg yolks
½ cup fresh lemon juice
  with pulp

1 tablespoon grated lemon
  peel
2 tablespoons butter or
  margarine
1 (9 inch) deep-dish baked
  pie shell

Meringue:

5 egg whites (room
  temperature)
¼ teaspoon cream of tartar

6 tablespoons sugar
½ teaspoon vanilla extract

In a large heavy saucepan, combine sugar, cornstarch and salt. With a wire whisk, gradually stir in water. Heat to boiling over medium heat, stirring constantly, until thick and bubbly. Boil 1 minute. Remove from heat.

Beat egg yolks until thick and lemon-colored. Stir a small amount of hot mixture into egg yolks, then return yolks to hot mixture. Add lemon juice, lemon peel and butter to thickened filling, stirring constantly. Cool 1 more minute. Pour into cooled baked pie shell.

Beat egg whites and cream of tartar until frothy. Gradually add sugar and continue beating until stiff. Add vanilla; mix. Spread meringue over filling to edges of pastry. Bake at 350° for 12 to 15 minutes, until golden brown. Cool away from drafts. Serves 8.

CHESS PIE

Very rich — your reputation as a cook is made!

1½ cups sugar
1 tablespoon flour
½ cup butter, melted
1½ teaspoons white
  vinegar

1 teaspoon vanilla extract
3 eggs, beaten
1 (9 inch) unbaked pie
  shell

Mix sugar and flour together; add to melted butter. Stir in vinegar, vanilla and eggs; whisk thoroughly. Pour into pie crust. Bake at 350° for 35 minutes, or until a knife inserted into center comes out clean. Serves 6 to 8.

Lillian Paxson
Vero Beach, Florida

PERFECT PIE CRUST

Always tender, even with excess handling

2 cups flour
1½ teaspoons sugar
1 teaspoon salt
7 ounces Crisco, room
  temperature

¼ cup water
1½ teaspoons white
  vinegar
1 egg

Combine flour, sugar and salt in medium-size bowl. Mix well. Add shortening; mix with fork until crumbly. In small bowl beat water, vinegar and egg; add to flour mixture and stir to form a ball. Divide dough in half; shape each half into a ball and chill for 30 minutes or longer. Each ball makes one pie shell. Dough can be frozen. Roll out dough between pieces of wax paper. Remove top paper. Invert pastry into 9 inch pie pan; peel off paper. For baked pie shell, pierce bottom and sides with fork. Bake at 450° for 12 to 15 minutes. Yield: 2 pie crusts.

Karen Brown
Bobbie Shellen
Vero Beach, Florida

GRAND MARNIER CHOCOLATE MOUSSE

Ambrosial

1 (12 ounce) package semi-
   sweet chocolate chips
4 eggs

4 tablespoons Grand
   Marnier
1½ cups milk, scalded

In container of blender, combine half of all ingredients. Blend at high speed for 2 minutes. Repeat with remaining ingredients. Spoon into crystal bowl or 8 dessert cups. Cover with plastic wrap and chill several hours.

Topping:

1 cup heavy cream
2 teaspoons confectioners'
   sugar, sifted

1 teaspoon Grand Marnier
Grated chocolate for
   garnish, optional

Whip cream until stiff, gradually adding confectioners' sugar. Fold in Grand Marnier. Refrigerate. When ready to serve, garnish mousse with whipped cream and grated chocolate. Serves 8.

Cherry Jackson Sveen
Franklin, North Carolina

POTS DE CRÈME AU CHOCOLAT

Little effort . . . great reward

8 ounces semi-sweet
   chocolate chips
½ pint half and half cream,
   scalded

3 egg yolks
1 teaspoon vanilla extract
Pinch of salt
2 ounces Crème de Cacao

Place chocolate chips in blender. Pour near-boiling cream on top; cover and blend 5 seconds. Stop blender; add remaining ingredients. Blend just to combine. Fill pots de crème pots or demi-tasse cups two-thirds full. Chill several hours. Serves 8.

Paul Abbott
Vero Beach, Florida

CHOCOLATE DELIGHT

Absolutely wonderful! An exceptional dessert

Crust:

¼ **pound butter**
1 **cup flour**

½ **cup walnuts, chopped**

Mix together. Press into 9 x 13 inch buttered baking pan. Bake at 375° for 15 minutes. Cool

Filling:

1 **cup confectioners' sugar**
1 **(8 ounce) package cream cheese, softened**

1 **cup Cool Whip (from a 12 ounce carton)**

Using an electric mixer, blend together and spread over crust.

Topping:

2 **(3½ ounce) packages instant chocolate pudding***
3 **cups milk**

Remaining Cool Whip
Chopped walnuts for garnish, optional

Place pudding and milk in electric mixer. On low speed beat until thick, about 1 to 2 minutes. Spread mixture on top of filling. Cover with remaining Cool Whip. Cover and chill several hours or overnight. Serves 15.

* May substitute 2 packages instant lemon pudding. (Lemon Delight)

Elinor Simms
Hot Springs, Arkansas

HOT CHOCOLATE SOUFFLÉ

To prepare a dish for sweet soufflé, use a straight-sided ovenproof baker. Grease the bottom and sides well with butter. Dust the inside with confectioners' sugar

2 tablespoons butter	4 egg yolks
1 tablespoon cornstarch	7 egg whites
½ cup milk	¼ teaspoon cream of tartar
½ cup semi-sweet	3 tablespoons sugar
chocolate chips	½ pint heavy cream,
4 tablespoons sugar	whipped

In large saucepan melt butter, add cornstarch and stir until foamy. In top of double boiler, heat milk, chocolate and 4 tablespoons sugar until chocolate is melted; stir until smooth.

Add hot milk mixture to cornstarch mixture, stirring constantly until well blended. Beat egg yolks until light. Beat part of sauce into yolks, then add yolk mixture to rest of sauce and stir custard over low heat to permit yolks to thicken. Remove from heat and cool.

Whip egg whites with cream of tartar until soft peaks form; add sugar, 1 tablespoon at a time, and continue beating until stiff but not dry. Fold cooled chocolate mixture into egg whites. Pour mixture into 1½ quart soufflé dish*.

Bake at 350° about 45 minutes; test by inserting a silver knife part way into center of soufflé; if it comes out clean, soufflé is done. If any soufflé adheres to knife, bake 5 minutes more. Do not overbake; overbaking causes soufflé to fall. Serve immediately with whipped cream. Serves 5.

* Note: Cut a piece of foil large enough to encircle soufflé dish with 3-inch overlap; fold in half lengthwise. Wrap around outside of dish; secure with cord. Butter inside of foil collar.

Alice Cook
Asheville, North Carolina

LEMON FLUFF

The ideal light dessert that is easy to make

½ cup fresh lemon or lime juice
1 tablespoon lemon peel, grated

4 egg yolks, beaten
1 (14 ounce) can sweetened condensed milk
1 egg white, stiffly beaten

Mix together lemon juice, peel, egg yolks and milk. Fold into egg white. Pour custard into 6 sherbert glasses.

Meringue:

3 egg whites
2 tablespoons sugar

Lemon peel, finely grated for garnish

Whip egg whites until stiff, gradually adding sugar. Place meringue on top of each custard; garnish. Chill several hours. Serves 6.

Eleanor Pennington
Land O'Lakes, Wisconsin

LEMON SPONGE

*This delicious pudding has a cakelike texture on top
and a tart lemon sauce beneath*

½ cup sugar
2 tablespoons flour
¼ teaspoon salt
2 eggs, separated
1 cup half and half cream

3 tablespoons fresh lemon juice
2 teaspoons lemon peel, finely grated

Combine sugar, flour and salt. Beat egg yolks. Add cream, lemon juice and peel; mix well. Combine with dry ingredients; blend. Beat egg whites until stiff but not dry and fold into lemon mixture. Pour into buttered custard cups or 1 quart casserole; set in pan of hot water. Bake at 350° for 35 to 45 minutes or until knife inserted in center comes out clean. Serve hot. Serves 4.

CHARLOTTE RUSSE

One of the most delicate and delicious of the charlottes...you'll love it!

2 dozen lady fingers,
  unfilled
2 envelopes unflavored
  gelatin
½ cup cold water
2 cups milk, scalded

6 egg yolks, beaten
1 cup sugar
1 teaspoon vanilla extract
2 cups heavy cream,
  whipped
Fresh whole strawberries

Open lady fingers into halves; do not separate. Arrange halves upright around sides of buttered 9 inch spring-form pan (cut sides toward center). Separate and press remaining halves into bottom of pan to form a compact layer.

Soften gelatin in cold water; set aside. Scald milk in a sauce-pan. Bring to boiling point but do not boil. Beat egg yolks and sugar together until smooth; slowly stir in scalded milk. Cook in top of double boiler until custard begins to thicken. Remove from heat; add gelatin and stir until dissolved. Blend in vanilla and cool.

When thoroughly cool, fold in whipped cream. Pour into lined buttered spring-form pan. Chill several hours. To serve, remove rim and place on serving platter. Garnish with strawberries. Serves 8.

AMARETTO CHEESE BALL

1 (8 ounce) package cream
  cheese, softened
8 teaspoons Amaretto di
  Saronna

⅓ cup slivered almonds,
  toasted
Peeled apple wedges
  dipped in lemon juice

Combine cheese and Amaretto; mix well. Refrigerate to stiffen slightly. Make into a ball and stud with almonds. Chill. Serve with fruit. Serves 6.

191

APPLE DUMPLINGS

Long a favorite

1 (10 ounce) package
  Pepperidge Farm Puff
  Pastry Shells
2 to 3 tart apples, peeled
6 tablespoons sugar
½ teaspoon cinnamon

¼ teaspoon ground nutmeg
4 tablespoons butter,
  melted
Sharp Cheddar cheese,
  sliced

Roll each pastry shell into a 5 inch circle. Cut apples into small cubes. Combine sugar, cinnamon and nutmeg; add to apples and mix. Place about 2 tablespoons of apple mixture in center of each pastry; drizzle 1 teaspoon butter over each one. Gather up corners of pastry and pinch together in center and along edges; seal firmly. Place dumplings, seam side down, in 11 × 7 inch buttered baking dish. Brush with remaining butter. Bake at 400° about 25 minutes. Serve with cheese. Serves 6.

Cherry Jackson Sveen
Franklin, North Carolina

DESSERT CHEESE BALLS

Very pretty and tasty too!

1 (8 ounce) package cream
  cheese
2 tablespoons half and half
  cream
5 tablespoons nutmeats,
  finely chopped

2 teaspoons lime or lemon
  juice
Pinch of salt
Parsley, finely chopped
2 red Delicious apples,
  cored and cut in rings

Soften cream cheese; blend in cream, nutmeats, lime juice and salt. Chill. Form into balls and roll in parsley. Place in center of apple rings. Serves 4.

LEMON MOUSSE
Light as a cloud and just as heavenly

1 (6 ounce) package lemon
   gelatin
2 cups boiling water
1 (12 ounce) can lemon-
   lime carbonated drink
Peel of 2 lemons, grated

Juice of 2 lemons
2 cups heavy cream,
   whipped
Fresh raspberries or
   strawberries

Dissolve gelatin in boiling water. Add lemon-lime drink, lemon peel and juice. Chill until slightly thick, then beat until foamy. Fold into whipped cream. Turn into 2 quart serving dish. Chill until firm. Serve with fresh berries. Serves 8 to 10.

Tina Wehmeyer
Asheville, North Carolina

PINEAPPLE TORTE

1 (8 ounce) can crushed
   pineapple
1 egg, beaten
1 cup flour
1 cup sugar
1 teaspoon baking soda

Pinch of salt
¼ cup brown sugar
½ cup nuts, chopped
Whipped cream or ice
   cream for topping

Combine pineapple and egg. Add flour, sugar, soda and salt; mix well. Place in buttered 8 x 8 inch baking pan. Sprinkle brown sugar and nuts on top. Bake at 350° for 30 minutes. Serve warm with topping. Serves 6.

GREEN GRAPES WITH SOUR CREAM
Deliciously different

2 pounds seedless green
  grapes, stemmed
1½ cups dairy sour cream

⅔ cup dark brown sugar
1 strawberry for each
  serving

Wash grapes and dry well. Chill several hours. Fold in sour cream. Spoon mixture into parfait glasses. Sprinkle brown sugar over each. Garnish with strawberries. Serves 8.

Muff Craven
Concord, North Carolina

FROSTED GRAPES

2 egg whites
1½ pounds seedless green
  grapes

Superfine granulated sugar
Large whole strawberries,
  with stems on

Beat egg whites until just frothy; separate grapes into small bunches. With soft brush, coat grapes with egg white. Quickly roll in sugar to coat well. Place on rack to dry. If necessary, roll grapes in sugar to coat once again. Place in freezer a few minutes. Arrange in serving dish with strawberries. Serves 6 to 8.

HOT BRANDIED GRAPEFRUIT
A nice first course too

2 grapefruits
4 tablespoons dark brown
  sugar

2 teaspoons butter
2 tablespoons brandy

Halve grapefruits. Remove seeds with tip of sharp knife. Cut around each section to loosen pulp from the peel. Combine remaining ingredients. Spread on top of grapefruit halves. Broil about 10 minutes, or until golden, or bake at 450° for 20 minutes. Serve hot. Serves 4.

SWEDISH CREAM

The ideal light dessert that is very easy to make and glamorous in appearance

2⅓ cups heavy cream
1 cup sugar
1 package unflavored
  gelatin

1 pint dairy sour cream
1 teaspoon vanilla extract
Fresh fruit
Mint leaves for garnish

In a large saucepan, mix heavy cream, sugar and gelatin together. Heat gently, stirring constantly with a whisk until gelatin is completely dissolved. Cool until slightly thickened. Fold in sour cream and vanilla.

Pour into 1 quart oiled ring mold and chill until firm. Turn out and heap fresh fruit (peaches, strawberries, or raspberries) in the center and around edge. Garnish with mint leaves. Serves 6.

Lazelle Rafferty
Little Compton, Rhode Island

MACAROON BOMBE

A favorite for entertaining

¾ cup sugar
1½ tablespoons flour
1 egg, slightly beaten
2 cup milk
1 (10 ounce) jar
  maraschino cherries,
  chopped

1 (8 ounce) can crushed
  pineapple, drained
2 cups crumbled almond
  macaroons,* no
  substitutes
½ cup pecans, chopped
2 cups heavy cream,
  whipped

In heavy saucepan mix sugar and flour. Add egg and milk; blend. Oven medium heat, cook until thick, stirring constantly (15 to 20 minutes). Cool. Stir in fruit, cookie crumbs and nuts. Fold in whipped cream. spoon into refrigerator trays. Freeze until firm. Serves 12.

* Almond macaroons which have been frozen crush more easily in a blender or food processor.

BISCUIT TORTONI

Easy to make and worth every calorie

1 pint vanilla ice cream
¾ cup crumbled almond
  macaroons
1 cup heavy cream,
  whipped

Additional macaroon
  crumbs for topping
Maraschino cherries

Combine softened ice cream and macaroon crumbs. Fold whipped cream into macaroon mixture. Pack in individual cups. Sprinkle tops with macaroon crumbs. Place in freezer. Before serving, garnish the top with a maraschino cherry. Serves 6.

COFFEE TORTONI

Light and luscious

1 egg white
1 tablespoon instant coffee
  (not freeze dried)
⅛ teaspoon salt
⅓ cup sugar
1 cup heavy cream

1 teaspoon vanilla extract
⅛ teaspoon almond extract
¼ cup toasted almonds,
  chopped
Chocolate curls for
  garnish, optional

Combine egg white, coffee and salt in electric mixer; beat until stiff. Add 2 tablespoons sugar, continue beating until satiny in texture. In separate bowl, whip cream until it holds peaks, gradually add remaining sugar, vanilla and almond extract. Fold egg white mixture into whipped cream mixture and add toasted almonds. Line 6 cup muffin tin with paper muffin cups. Pour in mixture and freeze for at least 2 hours. Garnish. Serves 6.

Betty Robinson
Kenilworth, Illinois

SCHAUM TORTE

Your best bridge-playing friends will put up with you!
and go home happy

2 cups sugar
6 egg whites
1 teaspoon baking powder
¼ teaspoon salt
2 teaspoons vinegar
2 teaspoons water
2 teaspoons vanilla extract
1 quart fresh strawberries, sliced

2 cups heavy cream, whipped
3 tablespoons confectioners' sugar, sifted
1½ teaspoon vanilla extract
Whole strawberries, for garnish

Sift sugar. Set aside. With electric beater, at medium speed, beat egg whites, baking powder, salt, vinegar, water and 2 teaspoons vanilla until very stiff. Continue beating and add sugar 1 tablespoon at a time. When all sugar has been added, continue beating for several minutes.

Put batter in two buttered 10 inch cake pans, with removable rims. Bake at 275° about 1½ hours. Leave in oven to cool. When meringues are cool, place one on a serving platter. Place strawberries on top; cover with other meringue.

Whip the cream until stiff; fold in confectioners' sugar and 1½ teaspoons vanilla. Cover top and sides of meringues with whipped cream. Refrigerate several hours. Decorate with whole strawberries around bottom of platter. Serves 12.

A FANCY FINALE

Brandy Alexander:

4 ounces brandy
2½ ounces dark crème de
    cacao
6 scoops vanilla ice cream
Dash of nutmeg on top,
    optional

Velvet Hammer:

4 ounces dark crème de
    cacao
2 ounces Triple Sec
6 scoops vanilla ice cream

Golden Cadillac:

3 ounces white crème de
    cacao
3 ounces Galliano
6 scoops vanilla ice cream

Grasshopper:

2 ounces white crème de
    cacao
2 ounces white crème de
    menthe
4 scoops vanilla ice cream

Hummer:

1 ounce brandy
1 ounce light rum
½ ounce Triple Sec
1½ ounces Kahlúa
4 scoops vanilla ice cream

Mocha:

3 ounces Kahlúa
3 ounces dark crème de
    cacao
6 scoops vanilla ice cream

Whispers:

3 ounces brandy
3 ounces Kahlúa
6 scoops coffee ice cream
Whipped cream, optional

White Russian:

2 ounces Kahlúa
4 ounces vodka
6 scoops vanilla ice cream

For each dessert drink selected, soften ice cream slightly.
Place ingredients in blender, about half at a time; blend a few
seconds. Pour into chilled champagne or wine glasses. Serves ?

HOT FUDGE SAUCE

4 (1 ounce) squares
  unsweetened chocolate
10 tablespoons butter
1½ cups sugar

½ cup cocoa
1 teaspoon vanilla extract
1 cup half and half cream

In top of double boiler melt chocolate in butter; add sugar and cocoa. Simmer for 45 minutes, stirring occasionally. Add vanilla and cream and simmer the mixture for 10 minutes. Serve hot over ice cream. Store in glass jar in refrigerator. Reheat in pan of hot water or microwave. Yield: 3 cups.

CARAMEL SAUCE

Serve warm on ice cream, cake or apple dumplings!

5½ tablespoons butter
1 cup sugar
1 cup half and half cream

⅓ cup light corn syrup
Pinch of baking soda

In a large saucepan melt butter. Add remaining ingredients and bring to a boil. Boil slowly until mixture is caramel colored and begins to thicken, about 20 to 25 minutes. Store in glass jar in refrigerator. Reheat in pan of hot water or microwave. Yield: 2 cups.

RED RASPBERRY SAUCE

2 (10 ounce) packages
  frozen raspberries,
  thawed

4 teaspoons sugar
4 teaspoons cornstarch

Place raspberries in food processor. Process for 45 seconds. Pour through a wire-mesh strainer to remove seeds. Combine raspberry purée, sugar and cornstarch in small saucepan. Cook mixture, stirring with a whisk, until slightly thickened. Cover and refrigerate. Yield: 1½ cups.

OLD-FASHIONED CHOCOLATE FUDGE
Our favorite

2 cups sugar	Dash of salt
¾ cup milk	2 tablespoons butter
2 (1 ounce) squares unsweetened chocolate	1 teaspoon vanilla extract ½ cup coarsely chopped
1 teaspoon corn syrup	nuts

Line 9 x 5 inch loaf pan with foil; extend foil over edges of pan. Butter foil; butter sides of heavy 2 quart saucepan.

Heat sugar, milk, chocolate, corn syrup and salt in saucepan over medium heat, stirring constantly, until chocolate is melted and mixture begins to boil. Using a candy thermometer, cook to 234°.

Remove from heat; add butter and vanilla and cool, without stirring, to 110°. Beat until candy is thick and no longer glossy. Quickly stir in nuts. Turn into prepared pan. Score into 1 inch pieces. Cool until firm. Yield: 1¼ pounds.

Kimberly Orr Cook
Asheville, North Carolina

Carey Orr Cook
Menlo Park, California

Made for their grandfather, Carey Orr
Chicago, Illinois

THE BEST PRALINES

¾ cup butter
2 cups sugar
1 teaspoon baking soda

1 cup buttermilk
2 cups pecan halves
1 teaspoon vanilla extract

Combine butter, sugar, soda and buttermilk in large, heavy pan. Cook to 240°. Stir frequently. Remove from stove and with electric beater, beat for 5 minutes. Add pecans and vanilla. Continue beating by hand until mixture drops out easily onto wax paper. Cool. Wrap individually in clear plastic. Yield: 4 dozen

Helen Corbitt
Dallas, Texas

TOASTED ALMOND BARK

2 cups sugar
⅔ cup milk
1 tablespoon light corn
   syrup
¼ teaspoon salt

2 tablespoons butter
1 teaspoon vanilla extract
1 cup unblanched almonds,
   toasted

Combine sugar, milk, corn syrup and salt in 2 quart heavy saucepan. Stir until sugar is dissolved and mixture comes to a boil. Continue cooking, without stirring, to the softball stage, 236°. Remove from heat, add butter but do not mix in. Cool to 110°.

Add vanilla and beat until mixture is smooth and creamy. Add toasted almonds. Pour candy onto a buttered heavy foil-lined baking sheet. Spread mixture to a thickness of ½ inch. Break into pieces when cool. Store in covered tin lined with wax paper. Yield: 1½ pounds.

Note: to toast almonds, spread over bottom of pan. Bake at 350°, stirring occasionally, until toasted; about 5 to 7 minutes.

CARAMEL SNAPPERS

1¼ cups pecan halves
1 (14 ounce) package
  caramels

1 (8 ounce) Hershey bar
3 tablespoons butter

Place cluster of 3 pecans on buttered cookie sheet. Flatten caramels to 1½ inch squares. Place one caramel in center of each pecan group. Bake clusters at 325° for 8 minutes.

Melt Hershey bar and butter in top of double boiler, stirring occasionally until smooth. Remove nut-caramel mixture from oven, coat each cluster with melted chocolate. Let stand in cool place until firm, about an hour; or place in freezer for 15 minutes. Store in refrigerator. Yield: 28 "Turtles".

ROCKY ROAD CANDY

A so-easy, always popular, candy

1 (12 ounce) package semi-
  sweet chocolate chips
2 tablespoons butter
1 (14 ounce) can sweetened
  condensed milk (Eagle
  Brand)

2 cups dry roasted peanuts
1 (10½ ounce) package
  miniature marshmallows
Dash of salt

Line a 13 x 9 inch baking pan with waxed paper. In heavy saucepan, place chocolate, butter and milk. Cook over low heat, stirring with wooden spoon, until ingredients are melted. Remove from heat. Put remaining ingredients into large bowl. Pour chocolate over mixture; stir until all ingredients are coated. Spoon into prepared pan and pat firmly to make a smooth layer.

Refrigerate 1½ hours, or until chocolate is firm. Lift out of pan; peel off paper. Cut into 1½ inch squares. Store in covered container. Yield: 4 dozen.

CANDY CRISPS

My grandsons were willing testers! They gave the recipe a "10"

40 saltine crackers
1 cup butter
1 cup light brown sugar

1 (12 ounce) package semi-
sweet or milk chocolate
chips

Spray 15½ × 10½ inch jelly roll pan with Pam. Line bottom with crackers. Melt butter, add brown sugar and bring to a boil. Boil 4 minutes (no longer). Pour butter mixture evenly over crackers. Bake at 400° for 9 to 10 minutes. Remove from oven and sprinkle chocolate chips over crackers; spread evenly. Refrigerate a few minutes, then score. When cool, break into pieces. Store in tins and refrigerate.

Margaret Hanes
Atlanta, Georgia

CALIFORNIA BRITTLE

A great toffee . . . A happy project for the family

1 pound butter
2 cups sugar
6 tablespoons water
12 small Hershey bars
   (plain)

2 cups finely chopped
   pecans

Place butter, sugar and water in large, heavy saucepan. Stir constantly to 300° on candy thermometer. Remove from heat. Pour into buttered 15½ × 10½ inch pan and spread thin. Spread Hershey bars over mixture; add chopped pecans. Press pecans into chocolate slightly with a sheet of wax paper. When cool, break into pieces. Store in airtight container. Yield: 2 pounds

Phyl Miller
Johnston City, Tennessee

DIVINITY FUDGE

Choose a dry day

2 cups sugar
½ cup light corn syrup
½ cup hot water
2 egg whites

⅛ teaspoon salt
1 teaspoon vanilla extract
1 cup pecans, chopped

In a heavy saucepan, place sugar, corn syrup and water; stir to dissolve sugar. Bring to a boil, without stirring, to 265° on candy thermometer. Wipe sugar crystals away from sides of pan several times during cooking.

While syrup is in last stages of boiling, beat egg whites and salt to stiff peaks. Remove hot syrup from stove and pour over egg whites in a fine stream, beating constantly with an electric beater. Continue beating until mixture begins to lose gloss and thickens. Fold in vanilla and pecans. Drop by teaspoonful onto wax paper. Yield: 1 pound.

CHERRY CORDIALS

24 to 30 maraschino
  cherries with stems,
  reserve liquid
3 ounces cherry liquid
3 ounces bourbon

6 ounces semi-sweet
  chocolate chips
2 teaspoons vegetable
  shortening

Place cherries, cherry liquid and bourbon in a jar; cover. Let age, at room temperature, for 2 weeks or longer. Drain and freeze cherries.

To make cordials, melt chocolate and shortening in top of double boiler over low heat. Dry frozen cherries on paper towel and quickly dip, one at a time, into chocolate, swirling around by stem until completely coated. Place cherries on a rack which is covered with wax paper; refrigerate. Cordials may be frozen.

SPICED SUGARED NUTS

1 cup sugar
5 tablespoons water
1 tablespoon cinnamon

1 teaspoon vanilla extract
2 cups pecan halves

Bring to a boil sugar, water, cinnamon and vanilla. When mixture is boiling merrily, add pecans and let the whole come to a lively boil again. Remove from stove and stir constantly until syrup starts to turn to sugar. Pour out on lightly buttered cookie sheet; separate pecans. Cool

Kim and Carey Cook

GLAZED ALMONDS

1 cup natural whole
  almonds
½ cup sugar

2 tablespoon butter
½ teaspoon vanilla extract

Line a baking sheet with foil; butter foil. In a heavy 9 inch skillet, combine almonds, sugar and butter. Cook and stir over medium heat until sugar melts and turns a golden brown color (about 20 minutes). Remove from heat and add vanilla. Pour almonds onto foil; cool about 20 minutes. Break into clusters. Yield: ½ pound.

GLAZED PECANS

4 cups pecan halves,
  unsalted
½ cup margarine, melted

4 tablespoons light corn
  syrup
Salt to taste

Combine pecans, margarine and corn syrup. Bake in heavy skillet at 250° for 50 to 60 minutes. Stir occasionally to evenly glaze. Pour out on brown paper; separate pecans. Sprinkle lightly with salt. Refrigerate or freeze.

Betty Cole
Ludington, Michigan

SUGARED PEANUTS

2 cups dry roasted peanuts   ½ cup water
1 cup sugar

Boil peanuts, sugar and water until water evaporates and nuts begin to look sugary, about 12 minutes. Pour out into a buttered foil-lined baking sheet with sides. Bake at 300° for 25 to 30 minutes, stirring twice. Pour out on wax paper.

TOASTED PECANS

¼ cup butter   **½ teaspoon Tabasco**
1 teaspoon Worcestershire   **2 teaspoons garlic salt**
**   sauce**   **2 cups large pecan halves**

Melt butter in 13 x 9 inch baking pan; add spices. Coat pecans in mixture and bake at 350° about 15 minutes, or until brown. Stir and shake nuts occasionally as they toast. Pour out on brown paper; separate pecans. Store in an airtight container.

SWEDISH NUT MEATS

1½ cups whole blanched   **1 cup sugar**
**   almonds**   **Dash of salt**
2 cups walnut pieces   **¼ pound margarine**
2 egg whites

Place nuts in 15½ x 10½ inch baking pan; toast at 325° for 10 minutes. Stir often. Beat egg whites until stiff. Fold in sugar, salt and nut meats. Melt margarine in roasting pan. Spread nut mixture in pan by patting with wooden spoon. Bake at 325° about 30 minutes, stirring 4 or 5 times, until margarine has disappeared. Remove from oven. Cool and separate into clusters. Yield: 1¾ pounds.

Lorilee Weinhold
Sarasota, Florida

ONE HALF GALLON OF BLOODY MARY MIX

Into a half gallon jug put the following ingredients:

60 ounces V-8 juice
¼ cup lemon juice
2½ ounces Worcestershire
sauce

6 drops Tabasco
1½ teaspoons celery salt
1½ teaspoons salt

Shake well and refrigerate.

Leila Stringer
Anderson, South Carolina

PEAR RELISH

This is so good you can eat it right out of the jar

4 cups firm pears, peel,
core, cut in small cubes
3 bell peppers (2 green, 1
red), cut in small pieces
2 cups onion, grated
2 cups cider vinegar

1 cup sugar
½ cup flour
½ teaspoon turmeric
½ teaspoon celery seed
1½ teaspoons dry mustard
1½ teaspoons salt

Combine all ingredients. In a heavy saucepan, bring mixture to a boil and cook for 5 minutes. Stir occasionally. Seal in jars or refrigerate. Yield: 4 pints.

Sally Marshall
Columbia, South Carolina

FROZEN AMARETTO CRÈME

1 cup heavy cream
¼ cup Amaretto de Saronno
1 pint vanilla ice cream

⅓ cup toasted almonds,
finely chopped

Beat cream until stiff peaks form. Add Amaretto and softened ice cream. Blend well. Spoon into parfait glasses or dessert compotes. Sprinkle with almonds and freeze until firm. Serves 6 to 8.

BRIDGE HANDS

THE EARLY PLAY AT SUIT AND NOTRUMP

Many times victory or defeat rests on decisions made by the declarer very early in the play of a hand.

The average player wins the first trick and then begins to think about the problem at hand. Frequently, it is too late! There is a simple way to avoid this kind of mistake. Before playing to the first trick, take time out to plan your whole campaign. A little planning can produce big dividends.

An experienced player studies the dummy after the opening lead has been made, gathers the clues available, the lead, the bidding, etc. He can forgive any dummy (partners frequently overbid); he is interested in only one thing—winning the number of tricks needed for his contract.

At notrump contracts, the declarer counts his sure tricks, decides which suit to attack to develop additional winners, and studies the entry situation.

At suit contracts, the declarer counts his losers. Frequently he can trump a loser in the dummy before drawing trump. There may be a long suit in the dummy which can be established to discard losers in the declarer's hand. Again, look for the entries; they may be the high trumps in the dummy.

The importance of extracting the opponents' trumps is not to be overlooked. If the declarer can see the number of tricks needed for his contract, he should lead trumps immediately. Leading trumps should be postponed when the trumps in the dummy are needed for ruffing purposes or needed as entries for a long side-suit to be developed to discard losers.

I hope you will be rewarded by studying the following lesson hands.

East dealer
Neither side vulnerable

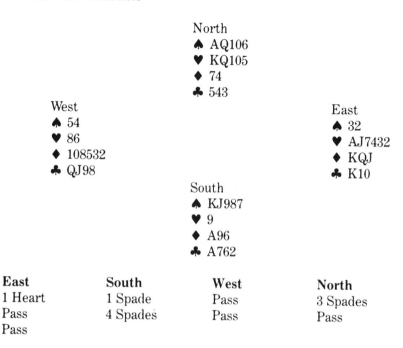

North
♠ AQ106
♥ KQ105
♦ 74
♣ 543

West
♠ 54
♥ 86
♦ 108532
♣ QJ98

East
♠ 32
♥ AJ7432
♦ KQJ
♣ K10

South
♠ KJ987
♥ 9
♦ A96
♣ A762

East	South	West	North
1 Heart	1 Spade	Pass	3 Spades
Pass	4 Spades	Pass	Pass
Pass			

Opening lead: 8 of hearts

Declarer counts four losers: one heart, one diamond and two clubs. The club losers can be discarded on two high hearts if declarer makes the winning play of the five of hearts on the opening lead. East wins the jack and returns the diamond king, won by declarer's ace. The king and ace of spades are led. The king of hearts is played; if East covers with the ace, declarer trumps, gives up a diamond, and wins the club return with the ace. A diamond is trumped in the dummy and two clubs are discarded on the queen and ten of hearts. If East does not cover the king of hearts, declarer discards clubs. Makes four, losing one heart, one diamond and one club.

Mini-lesson: The overcall by South promises a five card suit, or longer, and a range of 9-15 points.

The jump raise of an overcall is not forcing. The bid shows about 12-13 points.

North dealer   Deal #2
North-South vulnerable

<pre>
                              North
                              ♠ AQ1094
                              ♥ 8
                              ♦ A3
                              ♣ KQ1084
        West   East
        ♠ 76   ♠ 8532
        ♥ A5   ♥ 7643
        ♦ KQJ85   ♦ 976
        ♣ 7653   ♣ A2
                              South
                              ♠ KJ
                              ♥ KQJ1092
                              ♦ 1042
                              ♣ J9
</pre>

North	East	South	West
1 Spade	Pass	2 Hearts	Pass
3 Clubs	Pass	3 Hearts	Pass
4 Clubs	Pass	4 Hearts	Pass
Pass	Pass		

Opening lead: King of diamonds

Declarer allows the king of diamonds to win the first trick. If declarer wins
the opening lead with the ace, there are four losers: one heart, two diamonds and one club. By allowing West to win the king of diamonds, South
can trump a diamond in the dummy. If West shifts to a trump at trick two,
a high one or a low one, declarer drives out the ace of hearts and still has
control of the diamond suit. After pulling the remaining trumps, the declarer discards the losing diamond on a high spade in the dummy.

Mini-lesson: The bidding by North shows at least five spades and five
clubs. With five clubs and four spades, North would open the bidding with
one club.

The response by South, at the two level in a new suit, is forcing for one
round and promises ten or more high card points.

212

South dealer   Deal #3
East-West vulnerable

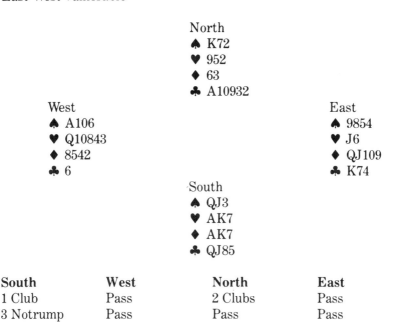

North
♠ K72
♥ 952
♦ 63
♣ A10932

West
♠ A106
♥ Q10843
♦ 8542
♣ 6

East
♠ 9854
♥ J6
♦ QJ109
♣ K74

South
♠ QJ3
♥ AK7
♦ AK7
♣ QJ85

South	**West**	**North**	**East**
1 Club	Pass	2 Clubs	Pass
3 Notrump	Pass	Pass	Pass

Opening lead: 4 of hearts

Declarer counts his winners: two hearts, two diamonds and four or five clubs, depending upon the position of the club king.

South wins the first trick with the king of hearts. A hold-up play, allowing East to win the jack, is dangerous; East may shift to a diamond, and declarer could be set, losing one spade, one heart, two diamonds and one club.

At trick two declarer leads the jack of spades. The only entry that West can have to establish his heart suit is the ace of spades. If West does not win his ace, declarer shifts to the clubs, taking the finesse, and although it loses, declarer has nine tricks and his contract. If West wins the ace of spades and continues hearts, South wins, takes the club finesse which loses, but East has no heart to return. If declarer improperly takes the club finesse at trick two and it loses, East returns a heart; if declarer ducks, West will force out the ace. When South leads a spade, West wins his ace, plus the good hearts, and the contract is defeated.

Mini-lesson: To raise one club to two, the responder needs four card support. The single raise shows 7-10 points and is a non-forcing bid.

South dealer   Deal #4
Both sides vulnerable

                              North
                              ♠ Q1052
                              ♥ AJ7
                              ♦ 643
                              ♣ Q74

        West   East
        ♠ 874   ♠ 6
        ♥ 10832   ♥ K64
        ♦ K82   ♦ J1097
        ♣ 853   ♣ A10962

                              South
                              ♠ AKJ93
                              ♥ Q95
                              ♦ AQ5
                              ♣ KJ

South	West	North	East
1 Spade	Pass	2 Spades	Pass
4 Spades	Pass	Pass	Pass

Opening lead: 2 of hearts

The opening lead is won in the dummy with the ace. Declarer can lose one
heart, one diamond and one club, but cannot afford to lose two diamonds.
If South finesses the opening heart lead and the king is in the East hand,
East may shift to a diamond.

Declarer leads three rounds of trump with the ace, king and ten. Clubs
are led, forcing out the ace. East may cash the king of hearts and shift to
a diamond; declarer takes the finesse of the queen which loses, but the
other losing diamond can be discarded on the queen of clubs. Makes four,
losing one heart, one diamond and one club.

Mini-lesson: Trump support for any suit, other than clubs, promises at
least three trumps with an honor or four small. The single raise shows 7-
10 points and is a non-forcing bid.

214

South dealer   Deal #5
Neither side vulnerable

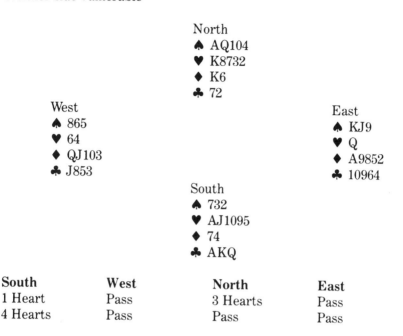

North
♠ AQ104
♥ K8732
♦ K6
♣ 72

West
♠ 865
♥ 64
♦ QJ103
♣ J853

East
♠ KJ9
♥ Q
♦ A9852
♣ 10964

South
♠ 732
♥ AJ1095
♦ 74
♣ AKQ

South	West	North	East
1 Heart	Pass	3 Hearts	Pass
4 Hearts	Pass	Pass	Pass

Opening lead: Queen of diamonds

Declarer counts four possible losers: two spades and two diamonds. If the opening lead is covered with the king, East wins the ace, returns a diamond, West winning, and West returns a spade. South will go set, losing two spades and two diamonds.

The winning play is the six of diamonds at trick one. If West shifts to a spade, declarer wins with the ace, pulls the trumps and discards the losing diamond on the third high club. If West continues diamonds, East will be end played. Declarer wins the club shift by East at trick three, leads two rounds of trumps, cashes the remaining high clubs and leads a spade, finessing the ten. East wins the jack and must either lead a spade into dummy's ace-queen or lead a diamond or club which enables declarer to discard a spade loser as he trumps in the dummy. Makes four.

Mini-lesson: A jump raise by the responder shows 13-16 points, four trumps or more and is forcing to game.

If the responder has passed, a jump raise of partner's suit shows 11-12 points and is not forcing.

North dealer   Deal #6
East-West vulnerable

                         North
                         ♠ AK42
                         ♥ 94
                         ♦ AQ732
                         ♣ J2

     West   East
     ♠ 53   ♠ 7
     ♥ KQ10732   ♥ J65
     ♦ K4   ♦ J108
     ♣ AQ10   ♣ 976543

                         South
                         ♠ QJ10986
                         ♥ A8
                         ♦ 965
                         ♣ K8

North	East	South	West
1 Diamond	Pass	1 Spade	2 Hearts
2 Spades	Pass	4 Spades	Pass
Pass	Pass		

Opening lead: King of hearts

Declarer counts five possible losers: one heart, two diamonds and two clubs.

West is allowed to win the first trick. This hold-up play by the declarer is made to avoid the possibility of East winning a heart trick and shifting to a club. Another danger exists in the diamond suit. If East has the king of diamonds, West surely has the ace-queen of clubs for his vulnerable over-call. Therefore, the diamond finesse must be successful in order to make the contract. Declarer wins the second heart lead and pulls trumps with the ace and queen. A low diamond is played, finessing the queen. A trump is led to declarer's jack and another diamond led; when West follows with the king, declarer plays low from the dummy. By this ducking play, East is kept out of the lead, and the dangerous club shift is avoided. Makes four, losing one heart, one diamond and one club.

Mini-lesson: A response at the one level in a new suit may have as few as six points, including high card points and distributional points, or as many as seventeen or eighteen points. The change of suit is forcing for one round.

216

East dealer   Deal #7
North-South vulnerable

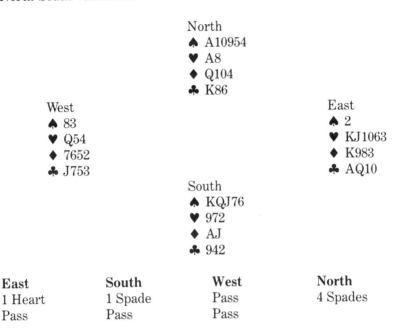

North
♠ A10954
♥ A8
♦ Q104
♣ K86

West
♠ 83
♥ Q54
♦ 7652
♣ J753

East
♠ 2
♥ KJ1063
♦ K983
♣ AQ10

South
♠ KQJ76
♥ 972
♦ AJ
♣ 942

East	South	West	North
1 Heart	1 Spade	Pass	4 Spades
Pass	Pass	Pass	

Opening lead: 4 of hearts

Declarer counts five possible losers: one heart, one diamond and three clubs. By allowing East to win the first heart, West may be unable to regain the lead for the dangerous club shift.

At trick two, East returns a heart won by dummy's ace. Declarer leads the king and ace of spades. A low diamond is led, and the jack is finessed, which wins. Declarer cashes the ace of diamonds, trumps a heart in the dummy, and leads the queen of diamonds, covered by the king, and declarer discards a losing club from his hand. East must either lead a club, which makes the king in the dummy a winner or lead a heart or a diamond, which allows declarer to discard a losing club as the dummy trumps. Makes four, losing one heart, one diamond and one club.

Mini-lesson: Holding three or more of your partner's suit headed by the king, queen, jack or ten, lead the lowest card. The underlined card is the proper lead: K7_2 Q95_3 J8_4 105_2. Holding the ace of your partner's suit, always lead the ace against a suit contract.

Against a notrump contract, if you have three or more of your partner's suit headed by the ace, lead the lowest card.

217

North dealer   Deal #8
Both sides vulnerable   North
                               ♠ KQ8
                               ♥ AQJ107
                               ♦ J2
                               ♣ A85

        West   East
        ♠ 7652   ♠ 1094
        ♥ 842   ♥ K6
        ♦ K1073   ♦ Q965
        ♣ 104   ♣ KQJ9

                               South
                               ♠ AJ3
                               ♥ 953
                               ♦ A84
                               ♣ 7632

North	**East**	**South**	**West**
1 Heart	Pass	1 Notrump	Pass
2 Notrump	Pass	3 Notrump	Pass
Pass	Pass		

Opening lead: 3 of diamonds

Declarer counts six winning tricks. The heart suit will develop the additional tricks needed for game. By analyzing the opening lead, and using the rule of eleven, declarer knows that the diamonds are divided evenly; West has four and East has four. Declarer wins the opening lead with the ace and takes the heart finesse, which loses to East. The defense can win three diamond tricks, and the declarer claims the balance of tricks. Makes three. The danger of a hold-up play at trick one, allowing East to win the queen of diamonds, is that a club shift may be made; this will defeat the contract. The defense will win one heart, one diamond and three clubs.

Mini-lesson: A one notrump response to an opening bid of one in a suit shows 6-10 high card points and is a non-forcing bid. It is not the cheapest response; a new suit bid at the one level is not only cheaper but more descriptive.

The Rule of Eleven is an exact mathematical calculation applicable whenever the card led is the leader's fourth highest of a suit. Here is the way it works: Subtract the denomination (number) of the card led from eleven; the result gives the number of *higher* cards than the one led in the other three hands. Counting the cards in his own hand and in the dummy which are higher than the one led, both declarer and the leader's partner can determine the number of such cards in the concealed hand of the other.

REBIDS BY OPENER

The rebid by the opener is probably the most important of all bids. The opening bid of one in a suit does not pretend to clarify the strength of the hand held by the opener. Such a bid may be made on as few as 13 points or as many as 20 to 23 points. It is the opener's second bid, after his partner's response, that will help clarify the precise strength and type of distribution. This will enable the partnership to determine how high to play and where to play.

The opener's hand will fall within the following four classifications:

A minimum hand (13 to 16 points)

With hands in this minimum range, you may or may not elect to bid again, unless partner's response to your opening bid is forcing.

A good hand (16 to 19 points)

You should make a constructive rebid. Avoid making any rebid which your partner might construe as discouraging.

A very good hand (19 to 21 points)

You should make a jump rebid in notrump, jump in your own suit or jump in partner's suit.

The powerhouse hand (21 points and up)

You should make a jump shift rebid which describes the strength of the hand and is forcing to game.

You will note that the upper limit of each classification coincides with the lower limit of the next higher classification. Point count cannot do everything. The true count of any hand is not really established until the bidding is over. A king, worth 3 points, can be rendered worthless one bid later. The decision on these "judgment points" should be made as the bidding progresses.

South dealer   Deal #9
East-West vulnerable

<pre>
                              North
                              ♠ KQJ6
                              ♥ Q43
                              ♦ A108
                              ♣ 973
        West   East
        ♠ 10987432   ♠ 5
        ♥ 6   ♥ 9872
        ♦ J   ♦ K75432
        ♣ K1084   ♣ J5
                              South
                              ♠ A
                              ♥ AKJ105
                              ♦ Q96
                              ♣ AQ62
</pre>

South	West	North	East
1 Heart	Pass	1 Spade	Pass
3 Clubs	Pass	4 Hearts	Pass
4 Spades	Pass	5 Diamonds	Pass
6 Hearts	Pass	Pass	Pass

Opening lead: Jack of diamonds

Declarer counts three possible losers, one diamond and two clubs; however, the three high spades in the dummy will provide discards for the club losers.

The ace of diamonds wins the first trick as declarer follows suit with the queen. Four rounds of trumps are led, the ace of spades cashed and the six of diamonds led to the eight. If East takes the king, the ten of diamonds is an entry for the high spades; if East ducks the eight of diamonds, spades are led, discarding three club losers. Makes six.

Mini-lesson: The jump shift by the opener after a one level response shows about 21 points or more. The bid is forcing to game. With equal length in partner's suits, the responder is obligated to return to the first suit bid by partner. North, who has promised only 6 points with his response at the one level, jumps in the heart suit to show good values.

After the trump suit is agreed upon and the required number of points are held by the partnership to be in the slam zone, cue bidding may be used to show aces. The four spade bid by South shows the ace; the five diamond bid by North shows the ace.

North dealer
Both sides vulnerable

North
- ♠ QJ1092
- ♥ 43
- ♦ 643
- ♣ KJ6

West
- ♠ 863
- ♥ Q872
- ♦ J7
- ♣ Q1084

East
- ♠ AK7
- ♥ 1096
- ♦ Q1098
- ♣ 732

South
- ♠ 54
- ♥ AKJ5
- ♦ AK52
- ♣ A95

North	East	South	West
Pass	Pass	1 Heart	Pass
1 Spade	Pass	2 Notrump	Pass
3 Notrump	Pass	Pass	Pass

Opening lead: 4 of clubs

Declarer counts six winners: two hearts, two diamonds and two clubs. By giving the defense the ace and king of spades, South can develop three additional tricks. Using the rule of eleven, declarer counts three clubs in the dummy higher than the four and three in his own hand higher. Therefore, East has only one club higher than the one led.

The six of clubs is played from the dummy, covered by the seven and won by declarer's ace. This play gives declarer two entries to the dummy, the king and jack of clubs. South leads a spade at trick two, and East ducks. A second spade is led and the king wins. East returns the ten of diamonds which South wins. A club is led to the jack and another spade played driving out the ace. Declarer wins any return by East and the king of clubs is the entry to cash the high spades in the dummy. Makes four.

If South does not win the first trick with the ace of clubs, East can defeat the contract by refusing to win the first spade lead.

Mini-lesson: The 2 notrump jump rebid by the opener, after a response in a new suit at the one level, shows a balanced hand, the unbid suits protected and 19-20 high card points. The bid is highly invitational but not forcing.

221

South dealer   Deal #11
Neither side vulnerable

North
♠ K109
♥ A853
♦ 863
♣ Q92

West   East
♠ 654   ♠ 32
♥ KQ109   ♥ J762
♦ AQ105   ♦ KJ
♣ 108   ♣ 76543

South
♠ AQJ87
♥ 4
♦ 9742
♣ AKJ

South	West	North	East
1 Spade	Pass	2 Spades	Pass
3 Spades	Pass	4 Spades	Pass
Pass	Pass		

Opening lead: King of hearts

Declarer counts four losing diamonds in his hand; however, the dummy has only three diamond losers. There are no other losing tricks in the North hand; the three low hearts can be trumped by South.

The opening lead is won with the ace. Dummy's three hearts are trumped in declarer's hand with the ace, queen and jack of spades, retaining the seven and eight as entries to the dummy to continue the ruffing. The jack of clubs is overtaken with the queen; the king of spades takes the remaining trump from West as declarer discards one of his losing diamonds. Makes four, winning in all six spade tricks, one heart and three clubs.

Mini-lesson: The play on this hand is called a dummy reversal. There are two requirements: the dummy's trumps must be good enough to draw the adverse trumps; the declarer's hand must have a short suit.

East dealer　　　　　　　　　　　　　　　　　Deal #12
North-South vulnerable

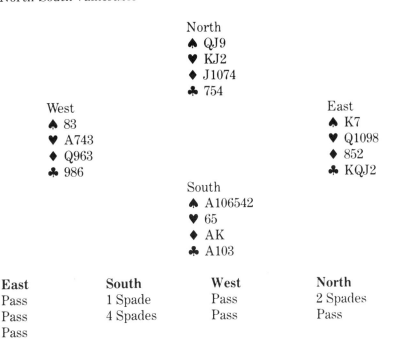

North
- ♠ QJ9
- ♥ KJ2
- ♦ J1074
- ♣ 754

West
- ♠ 83
- ♥ A743
- ♦ Q963
- ♣ 986

East
- ♠ K7
- ♥ Q1098
- ♦ 852
- ♣ KQJ2

South
- ♠ A106542
- ♥ 65
- ♦ AK
- ♣ A103

East	South	West	North
Pass	1 Spade	Pass	2 Spades
Pass	4 Spades	Pass	Pass
Pass			

Opening lead: 9 of clubs

West elected to lead the "top of nothing." Declarer counts his losers: one possible spade, one or two hearts and two clubs. The spade finesse must win, for there are three sure losers, one heart and two clubs.

The jack of clubs is won with the ace. At trick two, declarer leads a heart, West plays low, and the king is played from the dummy. The reason for this play is that East is known to hold the king, queen and jack of clubs from the opening lead; the king of spades has to be in the East hand for the contract to be made. East, having passed as the dealer, is unlikely to have the ace of hearts; that would give him thirteen high card points and an opening bid. Makes four.

Mini-lesson: After a raise from partner, the opener revalues his hand if it contains a long trump suit. The following adjustment is in order:

　　Add 1 point for the fifth trump
　　Add 2 additional points for the sixth and each subsequent trump

North dealer   Deal #13
Both sides vulnerable

                          North
                          ♠ K52
                          ♥ K8
                          ♦ J73
                          ♣ AQ1086
        West   East
        ♠ J106   ♠ AQ87
        ♥ Q73   ♥ 105
        ♦ KQ1092   ♦ 8654
        ♣ 74   ♣ 953
                          South
                          ♠ 943
                          ♥ AJ9642
                          ♦ A
                          ♣ KJ2

North	East	South	West
1 Club	Pass	1 Heart	Pass
1 Notrump	Pass	3 Hearts	Pass
4 Hearts	Pass	Pass	Pass

Opening lead: King of diamonds

Declarer counts four possible losers: three spades and one heart. By giving
a heart trick to East, the declarer avoids the dangerous spade shift by
West.

The ace of diamonds wins the opening lead. Declarer leads a low heart,
West follows with the three, the eight is played from the dummy and East
wins the ten. The diamond return is trumped by South. A heart is led to
the king, a diamond trumped, and the ace of hearts draws the remaining
trump. Two spades are discarded on the long club suit in the dummy. Makes
five.

Mini-lesson: The one notrump rebid by the opener indicates a minimum
and balanced hand.

Any jump by the responder, if not a passed hand, is forcing to game.

224

North dealer   Deal #14
Neither side vulnerable

<pre>
                        North
                        ♠ AQ
                        ♥ 7653
                        ♦ AQ
                        ♣ AK1098
      West   East
      ♠ KJ762   ♠ 1053
      ♥ 108   ♥ 2
      ♦ 10753   ♦ KJ984
      ♣ 62   ♣ Q543
                        South
                        ♠ 984
                        ♥ AKQJ94
                        ♦ 62
                        ♣ J7
</pre>

North	East	South	West
1 Club	Pass	1 Heart	Pass
4 Hearts	Pass	4 Notrump	Pass
5 Spades	Pass	6 Hearts	Pass
Pass	Pass		

Opening lead: 3 of diamonds

There are two possible losers, one spade and one diamond; however, neither the spade finesse nor the diamond finesse is needed. Declarer can
discard two spades and one diamond on the club suit.

The ace of diamonds wins the opening lead. Trumps are drawn in two
rounds. Declarer cashes the ace and king of clubs and plays the ten of clubs.
If East plays low, declarer discards his losing diamond. This play is called
a Banker's Finesse . . . it costs nothing! If West wins the queen of clubs,
South later discards two spades on the two remaining clubs. If East covers
with the queen, declarer trumps high; he now leads the four of hearts to
the seven and discards one diamond and one spade on the two high clubs
in the dummy. The queen of diamonds is trumped, and the spade finesse
taken. Makes seven.

Mini-lesson: The jump to game by North promises four or more trumps
and about 20 points. South, with a rebid valuation of 15 points, (one for
the fifth trump and two for the sixth trump), knows that the partnership
is in the slam zone and uses the Blackwood Convention to ask for aces.

225

North dealer

North-South vulnerable

Deal #15

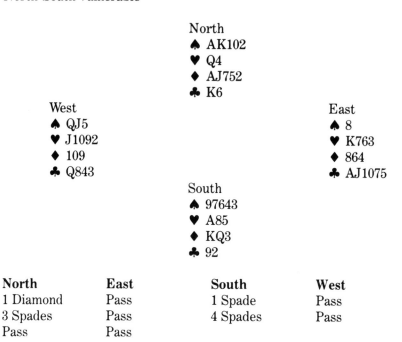

North
- ♠ AK102
- ♥ Q4
- ♦ AJ752
- ♣ K6

West
- ♠ QJ5
- ♥ J1092
- ♦ 109
- ♣ Q843

East
- ♠ 8
- ♥ K763
- ♦ 864
- ♣ AJ1075

South
- ♠ 97643
- ♥ A85
- ♦ KQ3
- ♣ 92

North	East	South	West
1 Diamond	Pass	1 Spade	Pass
3 Spades	Pass	4 Spades	Pass
Pass	Pass		

Opening lead: Jack of hearts

Declarer counts four possible losers: one spade, one heart and two clubs. If West is not allowed to regain the lead, the declarer can discard one or two clubs on the diamond suit.

The jack of hearts is covered with the queen; East follows with the king, and South plays low. East returns a heart, and declarer wins the ace. A low spade is led; West plays low, and the ten is played from the dummy. If the ten loses to an honor in the East hand, the ace and king will pick up the outstanding trumps. Declarer pulls the remaining trumps and discards both clubs on the long diamonds in the dummy. Makes six.

If South makes the error of winning the ace of hearts at trick one and loses a trump trick to East (he could have held the jack or queen of spades), East will return a heart which West wins. A club lead by West then sets the contract.

Mini-lesson: The jump by North promises four or more trumps, a good hand with 16-19 points (an average of 17 or 18 points), and is not forcing after a response at the one level.

South Dealer   Deal #16
East-West vulnerable

                          North
                          ♠ A109
                          ♥ 654
                          ♦ Q10
                          ♣ KQJ104
         West   East
         ♠ 876   ♠ K432
         ♥ K1083   ♥ QJ97
         ♦ A84   ♦ 763
         ♣ 852   ♣ 93
                          South
                          ♠ QJ5
                          ♥ A2
                          ♦ KJ952
                          ♣ A76

South	West	North	East
1 Diamond	Pass	2 Clubs	Pass
2 Notrump	Pass	3 Notrump	Pass
Pass	Pass		

Opening lead: 3 of hearts

Declarer counts seven winners: one spade, one heart and five clubs. The additional tricks needed for game can come from the diamond suit after giving the opponents the ace, or from a successful finesse in the spade suit.

The clue to declarer's choice is the opening lead. Using the rule of eleven, South knows that the hearts are divided four-four in the opponents' hands.

The winning play is to give up the diamond ace immediately. East and West can win their ace and three heart tricks; declarer claims the balance, making three notrump.

If the spade finesse is taken, the defense will win one spade, three hearts and the ace of diamonds, setting the contract.

Mini-lesson: The 2 notrump rebid by the opener, after a response in a new suit at the two level, shows a minimum of 15 high card points, a balanced hand and the unbid suits protected. The bid is forcing to game except where responder makes a simple rebid of his own suit over 2 notrump.

                        North
                        ♠ 832
                        ♥ K107
                        ♦ Q3
                        ♣ AK843

West   East
♠ Q1074   ♠ KJ95
♥ Q43   ♥ A65
♦ 974   ♦ 8652
♣ J106   ♣ Q7

                        South
                        ♠ A6
                        ♥ J982
                        ♦ AKJ10
                        ♣ 952

South	West	North	East
1 Diamond	Pass	2 Clubs	Pass
2 Diamonds*	Pass	3 Diamonds	Pass
3 Notrump	Pass	Pass	Pass

Opening lead: 4 of spades

Declarer counts seven winners: one spade, four diamonds and two clubs. There is no reason to hold-up the ace of spades. Using the rule of eleven, the declarer knows that the outstanding spades are divided four-four in the opponents' hands.

At trick two, declarer leads the nine of hearts, West plays low, dummy follows with the seven, and East may or may not win his ace. If he does not, the finesse is repeated. East and West can win three spade tricks, and declarer claims the balance. Makes three.

Leading the ace and king of clubs and giving up a club will set declarer, for the defense can score three spades, the ace of hearts and one club.

Mini-lesson: *Goren says, "It is better to mislead partner about your suit than to mislead him about the strength of your hand." A 2 notrump rebid by declarer would indicate a holding of 15-17 high card points. Put a heart in your diamond suit and rebid it. Don't admit that you did it.

North dealer   Deal #18
North-South vulnerable

                              North
                              ♠ K643
                              ♥ K7
                              ♦ AQ853
                              ♣ 83

West   East
♠ Q9   ♠ A1075
♥ 1083   ♥ J964
♦ J107   ♦ K9
♣ Q9762   ♣ J104

                              South
                              ♠ J82
                              ♥ AQ52
                              ♦ 642
                              ♣ AK5

North	East	South	West
1 Diamond	Pass	1 Heart	Pass
1 Spade	Pass	2 Notrump	Pass
3 Notrump	Pass	Pass	Pass

Opening lead: 6 of clubs

Declarer counts six winners: three hearts, one diamond and two clubs. The
diamond suit may develop the additional tricks needed for game.

South wins the ten of clubs with the king. The normal play in diamonds is
to duck one round and take the finesse of the queen on the second round.
However, declarer can improve his chances immeasurably by learning the
art of leading towards the closed hand.

At trick two, declarer leads a heart to the king and plays the three of
diamonds. Depending upon the experience and caliber of the players in
the game, South will win four diamond tricks if East plays the king. He
will probably go set if East doesn't hesitate and then plays low. There is
nothing to lose by the play. Against a large percentage of the players, declarer will make his contract.

Mini-lesson: The opener always shows a biddable four card major suit on
his rebid, if he can do so at the one level.

North dealer   Deal #19
East-West vulnerable

North
♠ QJ82
♥ AJ62
♦ K2
♣ 862

West
♠ 73
♥ KQ1097
♦ Q87
♣ K95

East
♠ 4
♥ 854
♦ J10965
♣ J1074

South
♠ AK10965
♥ 3
♦ A43
♣ AQ3

North	East	South	West
Pass	Pass	1 Spade	Pass
3 Spades	Pass	6 Spades	Pass
Pass	Pass		

Opening lead: King of hearts

Delcarer counts two possible losers; however, the jack of hearts will end play West, who will be forced to lead a club into the ace-queen or give declarer a sluff and a ruff.

The ace of hearts wins the opening lead. A low heart is trumped with the nine. A low spade is led to the eight, and another heart is trumped with the ten. The ace of spades takes the outstanding trump away from West. Declarer leads a diamond to the king, a diamond back to the ace, and the losing diamond is trumped in the dummy. The jack of hearts is led, South discards the three of clubs, and West is end played. If West leads a heart, it will be trumped in the dummy as declarer discards the queen of clubs; if West elects to lead a club, the loser in that suit is eliminated. Makes six.

Mini-lesson: The jump raise by North, after he has passed, promises four or more trumps, about 11-12 points, and is not forcing.

South has 22 points, adding 1 point for the fifth trump and 2 points for the sixth trump. The combined count puts the partnership in the slam zone.

North dealer   Deal #20
Both sides vulnerable

North
♠ Q109
♥ KJ932
♦ AK
♣ 853

West   East
♠ 652   ♠ 3
♥ 74   ♥ Q106
♦ J9752   ♦ 108643
♣ KQJ   ♣ 10942

South
♠ AKJ874
♥ A85
♦ Q
♣ A76

North	East	South	West
1 Heart	Pass	2 Spades	Pass
3 Spades	Pass	4 Notrump	Pass
5 Diamonds	Pass	5 Notrump	Pass
6 Hearts	Pass	6 Spades	Pass
Pass	Pass		

Opening lead: King of clubs

Declarer counts three possible losers: one heart and two clubs. The high diamond in the dummy will take care of one loser.

The ace of clubs wins the first trick. Two rounds of trumps are led with the ace and king. The queen of diamonds is won in the dummy with the king; the ace of diamonds discards a heart. Declarer leads a heart to the ace, a heart to the king and trumps a heart high. South plays a trump to the queen and discards two clubs on the long heart suit. Makes seven.

Mini-lesson: When the opener has a choice of rebidding his own suit or of supporting his partner's suit, he usually should raise partner's suit.

The jump shift by the responder is forcing to game and strongly suggests a slam. The bid shows about 19 points or more. If the responder has a solid suit of his own or very good trump support for his partner, he may jump shift with 17 points.

THE FINESSE

The finesse is the first play learned by a beginning bridge player as a method of increasing the number of tricks he may be able to win. It is an elementary play and a very important play; the greatest of experts use finesses. Mathematically speaking, a finesse is a 50-50 proposition; it will be successful 50% of the time. Unless there is a better play available, the finesse stands to gain everything and lose nothing.

The beginner loves to take finesses; he is happy with a 50% chance of success. The expert's first choice is not the finesse. He is on the alert for a line of play that offers a better chance of success. Frequently the bidding will yield a clue as to the possible success or failure of an intended finesse. The skillful player will be able to locate cards from this bidding information or from discards of the opponents during the play.

A line of play which is frequently available to the declarer is the end play. This is a play taking place toward the end of the hand, usually at the tenth or eleventh trick. The preparation for an end play may begin as early as the first or second trick. It is an advanced technique with which declarer frequently can produce one additional trick. This is done by forcing the defenders to lead a key suit which presents declarer with a trick he might not make on his own.

Another line of play is the safety play. A safety play is exactly what its name implies: it is a play made to reduce to a minimum the risk of losing the contract. It is a method of protecting against a bad break. The expert will make any play that will give a modicum of safety to his contract. He will sacrifice one trick in order to run the least possible risk of losing two tricks; thus a finesse may be refused and a trick given up to avoid the loss of an additional trick if the finesse should fail.

There are necessary finesses and unnecessary finesses; the winning player will learn to distinguish between them.

North dealer   Deal #21
Neither side vulnerable

North
♠ Q6
♥ AJ82
♦ AK64
♣ K104

West   East
♠ KJ95   ♠ 108432
♥ 5   ♥ 43
♦ QJ108   ♦ 972
♣ Q832   ♣ 765

South
♠ A7
♥ KQ10976
♦ 53
♣ AJ9

North	East	South	West
1 Notrump	Pass	3 Hearts	Pass
4 Diamonds*	Pass	4 Notrump	Pass
5 Hearts	Pass	6 Hearts	Pass
Pass	Pass		

Opening lead: Queen of diamonds

Declarer counts two possible losers: one spade and one club There is no
need to guess which way to finesse for the queen of clubs. There is an end
play available which will force the opponents to lead a club, or lead another
suit, which will give the declarer a sluff and a ruff. The king of diamonds
wins the opening lead. Declarer cashes the king and queen of trumps and
leads a diamond to the ace. A diamond is trumped, the dummy re-entered
with a heart and the last diamond is trumped. Declarer leads the ace of
spades and exits with a spade. West must either lead a spade, on which a
club is discarded from either hand and trumped in the other, or make a
club lead, which eliminates the guess in that suit. Makes six.

Mini-lesson: The one notrump opening is made with a balanced hand, 16-
17-18 high card points, and at least three suits are protected. Any jump
by the responder is forcing to game.

*The four diamond bid by North is called a feature bid. The bid shows a
good fit for partner's suit, a near-maximum notrump opening and controls
in the suit bid. It is the same as raising partner's suit and pinpoints outside
strength.

South dealer   Deal #22
North-South vulnerable

                              North
                              ♠ AJ1085
                              ♥ A3
                              ♦ A64
                              ♣ K42

        West   East
        ♠ 743   ♠ void
        ♥ KQJ84   ♥ 109652
        ♦ Q5   ♦ 10983
        ♣ J85   ♣ Q1076

                              South
                              ♠ KQ962
                              ♥ 7
                              ♦ KJ72
                              ♣ A93

South	West	North	East
1 Spade	Pass	3 Clubs	Pass
3 Diamonds	Pass	3 Spades	Pass
4 Notrump	Pass	5 Spades	Pass
6 Spades	Pass	Pass	Pass

Opening lead: King of hearts

Declarer counts two possible losers: one diamond and one club. The diamond suit may set up for a club discard.

The ace of hearts takes the first trick. Declarer leads three rounds of trump and trumps a heart. A safety play is made in the diamond suit. The king of diamonds is led and a low diamond led to the ace; when the queen falls, declarer loses one club. If the queen of diamonds does not fall, declarer will win the ace and a low diamond will be played towards the jack. If East has the queen, the losing club in the dummy will be discarded on the jack. If West has the queen, the club loser will be discarded on the fourth diamond in declarer's hand. If West has four diamonds to the queen, the contract cannot be made. Makes six.

Mini-lesson: The North hand is too strong for a jump raise in partner's suit. This bid is limited to 13-16 points. The responder makes a temporizing bid and supports spades on his next bid. The jump shift may be made with 17 points and very good trump support for partner's suit.

North dealer   Deal #23
East-West vulnerable

North
♠ 7
♥ KJ2
♦ AQ765
♣ Q853

West   East
♠ Q1084   ♠ KJ6
♥ 83   ♥ 765
♦ KJ103   South   ♦ 942
♣ K97   ♠ A9532   ♣ AJ104
                               ♥ AQ1094
                               ♦ 8
                               ♣ 62

North	East	South	West
1 Diamond	Pass	1 Spade	Pass
2 Clubs	Pass	2 Hearts	Pass
2 Notrump*	Pass	3 Hearts	Pass
4 Hearts	Pass	Pass	Pass

Opening lead: 3 of hearts

When planning a crossruff, the declarer will find it easier to count his winners. South counts nine winning tricks: one spade, five hearts in the South
hand, two hearts in the North hand by trumping spades and one diamond.
The diamond finesse must be successful to win ten tricks.

Declarer wins the trump lead with the nine and at trick two he leads a
diamond, finessing the queen. The ace of diamonds is played and declarer
trumps a diamond. The ace of spades is cashed and the crossruff proceeds,
trumping spades in the dummy and diamonds in declarer's hand. Makes
four. With any lead but a trump, the diamond finesse is not needed. There
are ten winners: five hearts in the South hand, three hearts in the North
hand, by ruffing spades, and two aces.

Mini-lesson: With two five card suits, South bids the higher ranking suit
first and rebids the lower ranking.

*To raise partner's second bid suit at your first opportunity, four card
trump support is needed.

The trump lead is proper when the bidding has indicated that the dummy
has a short suit. The bidding by North indicates a shortness in his partner's
first bid suit, spades. Another time when the trump lead is recommended
is on a hand in which any other lead may be beneficial to the declarer.

235

South dealer   Deal #24
Both sides vulnerable

North
♠ 653
♥ A653
♦ AJ73
♣ 83

West   East
♠ AJ8   ♠ Q1092
♥ 9   ♥ Q107
♦ 10862   ♦ 94
♣ J10965   ♣ K742

South
♠ K74
♥ KJ842
♦ KQ5
♣ AQ

South	West	North	East
1 Heart	Pass	2 Hearts	Pass
4 Hearts	Pass	Pass	Pass

Opening lead: Jack of clubs

Declarer counts four possible losers: three spades and one heart. If South can keep the East player from gaining the lead, the dangerous spade shift will be avoided.

After winning the opening lead with the ace, South plays a low heart to the ace and returns a heart. When East follows with the ten, declarer plays the jack; if this loses, declarer makes four, losing two spades and one heart. When the finesse wins, declarer makes his game with an overtrick.

Mini-lesson: A one notrump opening is never made with a five card major suit and 18 high card points.

North dealer   Deal #25
North-South vulnerable

                              North
                              ♠ Q1085
                              ♥ J632
                              ♦ A2
                              ♣ AQ2

West   East
♠ 64   ♠ J2
♥ A97   ♥ K108
♦ J1097   ♦ 6543
♣ J764   ♣ K983

                              South
                              ♠ AK973
                              ♥ Q54
                              ♦ KQ8
                              ♣ 105

North	East	South	West
1 Club	Pass	1 Spade	Pass
2 Spades	Pass	4 Spades	Pass
Pass	Pass		

Opening lead: Jack of diamonds

Declarer counts four possible losers: three hearts and one club. After winning the opening diamond lead with the ace, South pulls trumps with the ace and king, cashes the king and queen of diamonds, discarding the two of clubs from dummy. A club is led to the ace and the queen of clubs is given to the defenders. After winning the king of clubs, East is end-played. If East elects to lead a heart, only two tricks will be lost in that suit; if he leads a diamond or a club, declarer will discard a heart from his hand as he trumps in the dummy. Makes four.

Mini-lesson: A bid of one club may be used to open the bidding holding only three clubs headed by an honor. The reason for this opening is that occasionally a hand is dealt where you have the required count to open the bidding, but there is no biddable suit; or you hold only one four card biddable suit and will have no convenient rebid should partner change suits. The one club bid is not forcing; pass if you hold fewer than six points.

South dealer   Deal #26
East-West vulnerable

                              North
                              ♠ Q42
                              ♥ AQJ86
                              ♦ 64
                              ♣ Q76
        West   East
        ♠ 75   ♠ 963
        ♥ K1092   ♥ 73
        ♦ A107   ♦ KJ852
        ♣ J1098   ♣ K52
                              South
                              ♠ AKJ108
                              ♥ 54
                              ♦ Q93
                              ♣ A43

South	West	North	East
1 Spade	Pass	2 Hearts	Pass
2 Spades	Pass	3 Spades	Pass
4 Spades	Pass	Pass	Pass

Opening lead: Jack of clubs

Declarer counts five possible losers: one heart, two diamonds and two
clubs. In order to make the contract, the heart finesse must win. On the
opening lead the queen of clubs is played, covered by the king, and South
wins the ace. At trick two, a heart is led, West plays low and the finesse
of the jack wins. A spade is led to the king and another heart played
finessing the queen. A low heart is trumped by declarer.* South cashes
the ace of spades and leads a spade to the queen. Declarer discards two
losing diamonds or two losing clubs on the ace of hearts and the fifth heart.
Makes four.

Mini-lesson: The response of two hearts over a one spade opening promises
a five card or longer suit. With only four hearts, the responder with nine
other cards in his hand will have other bids available.

*This is an important play—only four heart tricks are needed.

6 cards outstanding will be divided: 3-3   36% of the time
                                      4-2   48% of the time
                                      5-1   15% of the time
                                      6-0   1% of the time

North dealer   Deal #27
Both sides vulnerable

                              North
                              ♠ K1053
                              ♥ A2
                              ♦ A43
                              ♣ Q865

        West   East
        ♠ 74   ♠ 2
        ♥ 9843   ♥ J765
        ♦ KQ107   ♦ 9652
        ♣ K72   ♣ 10943

                              South
                              ♠ AQJ986
                              ♥ KQ10
                              ♦ J8
                              ♣ AJ

North	East	South	West
1 Club	Pass	2 Spades	Pass
3 Spades	Pass	4 Notrump	Pass
5 Hearts	Pass	6 Spades	Pass
Pass	Pass		

Opening lead: King of diamonds

Declarer counts two possible losers: one diamond and one club. The opening diamond lead is won with the ace. Two rounds of trumps are led and
then three rounds of hearts, discarding a diamond from the dummy. South
gives the jack of diamonds to West who is end-played. West has three
choices—all losers—a heart or a diamond lead will be trumped in the
dummy as declarer discards his losing club (this is called a ruff and sluff);
if West leads a club, the loser in that suit is eliminated. Makes six, losing
one diamond.

Mini-lesson: The finesse in the club suit is a 50% play; half the time the
jack will win and half the time it will lose; the endplay is a 100% play.

North dealer   Deal #28
East-West vulnerable

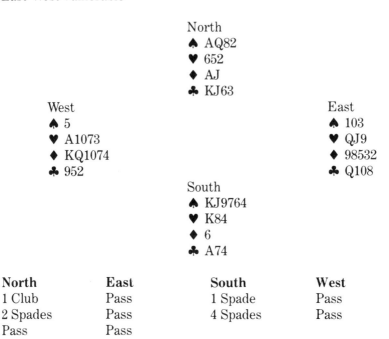

North
- ♠ AQ82
- ♥ 652
- ♦ AJ
- ♣ KJ63

West
- ♠ 5
- ♥ A1073
- ♦ KQ1074
- ♣ 952

East
- ♠ 103
- ♥ QJ9
- ♦ 98532
- ♣ Q108

South
- ♠ KJ9764
- ♥ K84
- ♦ 6
- ♣ A74

North	East	South	West
1 Club	Pass	1 Spade	Pass
2 Spades	Pass	4 Spades	Pass
Pass	Pass		

Opening lead: King of diamonds

Declarer counts four possible losers: three hearts and one club. The king of diamonds is won with the ace. Declarer leads two rounds of trumps with the ace and king. The ace and king of clubs are played and the jack of diamonds led, on which South discards his losing club. This play will guarantee the game contract with any combination of cards which may be held by East and West.

1. On the actual hand: If West leads a club, dummy covers whatever is led; East follows with the queen and declarer trumps. South will discard one losing heart on the thirteenth club in the dummy.

2. If West has four clubs, and leads that suit, the jack in the dummy will be a winner and provide a discard for a losing heart.

3. If West has no clubs, he must lead a heart, which makes the king in declarer's hand a winner, or lead a diamond which will be trumped in the dummy as declarer discards a losing heart.

Mini-lesson: The opener holding four spades and four clubs, bids the club suit first.

LEADS, SIGNALS AND DEFENSE

Most experts agree that defensive play is the most difficult phase of bridge. The object of the defending side is the same as the object of the declarer; to win as many tricks as possible. The intitial lead is of paramount importance in the defenders' opening campaign to defeat the declarer. If chosen properly, the opening lead gives the defense crucial timing and frequently will spell the difference between victory and defeat. There is a great scope for judgment in the choice of this lead. To judge well, the defenders with an ear to the bidding have the advantage of knowing something about the declarer's hand. Also, there are fundamental principles available; these consist of a system of conventional leads and a system of signals. With the application of these principles, the defenders convey to each other the proper defense.

Whether the final contract is in a suit or in notrump, if the partner of the opening leader has bid a suit, it is generally best to lead that suit. When partner has not bid a suit, the lead of an unbid suit is best.

Hands should be classified; a chosen lead may be a proper one against a notrump contract but an improper one against a suit contract. Against a notrump contract it is essential to develop winning tricks out of low cards, to establish your suit before the declarer establishes his suit. Therefore, your longest suit usually should be selected as the opening lead.

When defending against a contract, the defenders must rely on a system of signals in order to be successful. Information that is needed for the defense of the hand can be given by the size of the cards that are played on various tricks. The play of an unnecessarily high card indicates strength in the suit or a desire to have that suit led or continued; a low card indicates weakness in the suit. This is called the Attitude Signal and generally is used when following to your partner's lead or when making a discard.

Another necessary signal is the Count Signal and usually is applied when following to a lead by the declarer. It is a method by which a defender can indicate to his partner the length held in a particular suit. With an even number of cards play high-low; with an odd number of cards play the lowest.

Basic defense starts with an ear to the bidding, signals by partner, inferences drawn from the play, and the number of tricks that can be counted for the declarer.

North
♠ 985
♥ AQ4
♦ Q2
♣ Q10963

West
♠ 74
♥ 876532
♦ 1064
♣ 72

East
♠ AQ32
♥ 9
♦ KJ93
♣ A854

South
♠ KJ106
♥ KJ10
♦ A875
♣ KJ

East	South	West	North
1 Diamond	1 Notrump	Pass	3 Notrump
Pass	Pass	Pass	

Opening lead: 4 of diamonds

The overcall of 1 notrump by South shows the same values as an original 1 notrump opening bid. The notrump bidder must have the opponent's suit stopped.

West makes the proper lead of a low card of partner's suit holding three to the ten. The deuce is played from the dummy, East follows with the jack and declarer wins the ace. At trick two declarer leads the king of clubs, East winning with the ace. The king of diamonds smothers the queen; a low diamond is led to partner's ten. West returns a spade which East wins with the ace and the nine of diamonds is the setting trick. Down one.

Many beginning players will make the improper lead of the ten of diamonds, the top of partner's suit; declarer will cover with the queen, East follows with the king and the ace wins. Declarer now has an additional stopper with the eight and will lose only two diamond tricks and two aces, making his contract.

Mini-lesson: The opener, holding three four-card biddable suits, bids the suit below the singleton.

Leading partner's suit . . . review Deal #7.

North dealer   Deal #30
Neither side vulnerable

                            North
                            ♠ 95
                            ♥ KQ74
                            ♦ 104
                            ♣ AK1074
        West   East
        ♠ A8   ♠ 743
        ♥ 9832   ♥ 65
        ♦ AK9832   ♦ QJ7
        ♣ 8   ♣ J9652
                            South
                            ♠ KQJ1062
                            ♥ AJ10
                            ♦ 65
                            ♣ Q3

North	East	South	West
1 Club	Pass	1 Spade	2 Diamonds
Pass	Pass	3 Spades	Pass
4 Spades	Pass	Pass	Pass

Opening lead: King of diamonds

Good defense by East and West will set South in an otherwise ironclad
contract. Declarer counts three losers: one spade and two diamonds. The
king of diamonds wins the first trick as East follows with the queen. At
trick two, West leads the eight of clubs, South winning with the queen.
The queen of trumps is led, West wins with the ace and returns the two
of diamonds for East to win with the jack. East returns a club which West
trumps, setting the contract one trick.

Mini-lesson: The queen is never used as a high-low signal. Therefore, if
the defender follows suit with the queen on his partner's lead of the king,
the defender either has a singleton or the jack of the suit led. It is an
accepted convention that when the suit is continued, the leader must un-
derlead his ace; partner will win the trick either with the jack or by
trumping.

North
- ♠ QJ2
- ♥ 874
- ♦ 92
- ♣ AK952

West
- ♠ 1086
- ♥ A105
- ♦ Q1053
- ♣ 1064

East
- ♠ 97
- ♥ J962
- ♦ AK76
- ♣ QJ8

South
- ♠ AK543
- ♥ KQ3
- ♦ J84
- ♣ 73

South	West	North	East
1 Spade	Pass	2 Clubs	Pass
2 Spades	Pass	3 Spades	Pass
4 Spades	Pass	Pass	Pass

Opening lead: 3 of diamonds

Declarer counts four possible losers: two hearts and two diamonds. If the heart ace is in the East hand, the contract is assured. If not, South will play for the outstanding clubs to be divided three-three. Only two rounds of trumps will be led, the clubs tested and the queen of spades retained in the dummy as an entry to the good clubs.

However, East has other plans. Using the rule of eleven, East knows that South has three diamonds higher than the opening lead. By forcing the dummy to ruff a diamond at trick three, the entry for the club suit is eliminated. This good defense sets the hand. Down one.

Mini-lesson: The South hand revalues to 15 points.

Adding for length when partner raises your suit . . . Review Deal #12.

The rule of eleven . . . Review Deal #8.

North dealer   Deal #32
East-West vulnerable

```
                              North
                              ♠ A92
                              ♥ AK
                              ♦ AK5
                              ♣ J6532
        West                                           East
        ♠ K65                                          ♠ J1087
        ♥ 964                                          ♥ 72
        ♦ J83                                          ♦ Q1094
        ♣ AQ108                                        ♣ K94
                              South
                              ♠ Q43
                              ♥ QJ10853
                              ♦ 762
                              ♣ 7
```

North	East	South	West
1 Club	Pass	1 Heart	Pass
2 Notrump	Pass	3 Hearts	Pass
4 Hearts	Pass	Pass	Pass

Opening lead: 4 of hearts

Declarer counts four possible losers: two spades, one diamond and one club. If the king of spades is in the East hand, the contract is assured. An additional chance is to develop a winner in the club suit. If the clubs do not break favorably, the spade play for the king in East's hand is still available.

The opening trump lead is won with the king. At trick two, a low club is led, won by West with the eight. Another trump is led, won by the ace and a second round of clubs played, declarer trumping with the ten. The queen of hearts takes the remaining trump from West. South plays a diamond to the king and a third round of clubs is trumped. A diamond back to the ace and the fourth round of clubs is trumped. The dummy is entered with the ace of spades and the diamond loser in declarer's hand is discarded on the thirteenth club. Makes four, losing two spades and one club.

Mini-lesson: East will have the king of spades 50% of the time. The outstanding seven clubs held by East and West will be divided as follows:

    4-3   62%
    5-2   31%
    6-1   6½%
    7-0   ½%

245

South dealer   Deal #33
Neither side vulnerable

                              North
                              ♠ AKQ73
                              ♥ 52
                              ♦ 863
                              ♣ 852
        West   East
        ♠ J2   ♠ 10986
        ♥ 943   ♥ 106
        ♦ K1042   ♦ J975
        ♣ KJ76   ♣ 1094
                              South
                              ♠ 54
                              ♥ AKQJ87
                              ♦ AQ
                              ♣ AQ3

South	West	North	East
2 Hearts	Pass	2 Spades	Pass
3 Hearts	Pass	4 Hearts	Pass
4 Notrump	Pass	5 Diamonds	Pass
5 Notrump	Pass	6 Diamonds	Pass
6 Hearts	Pass	Pass	Pass

Opening lead: 3 of hearts

Declarer has three potential losers: one diamond and two clubs; but on the
other hand he has eleven sure winners.

When the dummy has a long suit that cannot be established by ruffing due
to lack of entries, and there is no ruffing to be done in the dummy, declarer
should count winners as if the hand were being played at notrump. With
six heart winners and two minor suit aces, declarer needs four spade
tricks, not five!

Declarer draws the trumps and ducks a spade, East winning. South wins
the club return with the ace, runs the trumps and cashes four spade winners, discarding a diamond and two clubs. Makes six. If the spades don't
break 4-2 (percentage is that they will), declarer can fall back on the diamond finesse.

Mini-lesson: Playing strong two bids, the opening two demand bid is forcing to game. The opener must have four quick tricks and be within one
trick of game in his own hand.

246

North dealer   Deal #34
North-South vulnerable

                            North
                            ♠ A32
                            ♥ 5
                            ♦ 8754
                            ♣ AKJ92
        West   East
        ♠ 106   ♠ J8754
        ♥ A74   ♥ 983
        ♦ AKQJ3   ♦ 102
        ♣ Q53   ♣ 864
                            South
                            ♠ KQ9
                            ♥ KQJ1062
                            ♦ 96
                            ♣ 107

North	**East**	**South**	**West**
1 Club	Pass	1 Heart	2 Diamonds
Pass	Pass	4 Hearts	Pass
Pass	Pass		

Opening lead: King of diamonds

Excellent defense will set the game contract, although at first glance it
looks as though declarer will only lose one heart and two diamonds. On the
king and queen of diamonds East follows with the ten and then the two;
this is called an echo. West in analyzing the defense, and with an ear to the
bidding, cannot figure to win anything in the spade suit or the club suit.
Certainly declarer has strength in spades, having jumped to game. He does
not have any points in the diamond or club suits. He does not have either
major suit ace. If there is a future for the defense, it has to be in a trump
promotion. At trick three, West leads the three of diamonds, East trumps
with the eight of hearts, overtrumped by the ten. When declarer plays the
king of hearts (it would be smart of South to lead the queen of hearts
hoping West might duck), West wins the ace and returns a fourth diamond,
trumped by East with the nine, overtrumped with the jack—and the setting trick is the seven of hearts! Down one.

Mini-lesson: This trump promotion play is called an uppercut. The play
consists of using otherwise useless trumps on partner's lead, in order to
force out declarer's high trumps; in so doing you promote a trump trick for
partner.

East dealer   Deal #35
East-West vulnerable

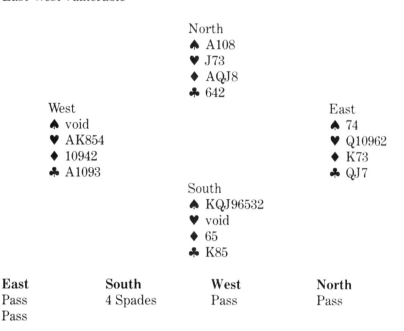

```
                              North
                              ♠ A108
                              ♥ J73
                              ♦ AQJ8
                              ♣ 642
          West                                      East
          ♠ void                                    ♠ 74
          ♥ AK854                                   ♥ Q10962
          ♦ 10942                                   ♦ K73
          ♣ A1093                                   ♣ QJ7
                              South
                              ♠ KQJ96532
                              ♥ void
                              ♦ 65
                              ♣ K85
```

East	South	West	North
Pass	4 Spades	Pass	Pass
Pass			

Opening lead: King of hearts

Declarer counts four possible losers: one diamond and three clubs. On the
opening lead of the king of hearts, South makes the winning play of discarding the five of diamonds. With this play, South can keep East from
gaining the lead and the dangerous club shift will be avoided. West continues with a heart which is trumped by South. Two rounds of spades are
led and the ace and queen of diamonds played. If East doesn't play the
king of diamonds, South discards a losing club. This play is the Banker's
Finesse . . . it costs nothing. If East plays the king, South trumps and
leads a spade to the dummy and discards a club on the good jack of diamonds. If West has the king of diamonds, he will win the queen with the
king as declarer discards a losing club; however, the king of clubs is safe
from attack. Declarer can discard another club loser on the jack of diamonds or score his king of clubs if West leads that suit. Makes four.

Mini-lesson: Pre-emptive bids are not made with good hands. They are
relatively weak in high cards and contain a very long trump suit. The bid
is an attempt to keep the opponents out of the bidding for the pre-emptive
bidder has little, if any, defensive strength. The pre-emptive bidder should
be prepared, if doubled, to lose no more than 500 points. If not vulnerable,
he may overbid by three tricks; if vulnerable, he may overbid by two
tricks. Because of the favorable location of key cards, East and West can
make 6 hearts!

North
- ♠ AQ10
- ♥ J1087
- ♦ 76
- ♣ AJ108

West
- ♠ 842
- ♥ 54
- ♦ AKJ1052
- ♣ K4

East
- ♠ 7653
- ♥ A9
- ♦ Q843
- ♣ Q96

South
- ♠ KJ9
- ♥ KQ632
- ♦ 9
- ♣ 7532

West	**North**	**East**	**South**
1 Diamond	Double	3 Diamonds	4 Hearts
Pass	Pass	Pass	

Opening lead: King of diamonds

Declarer counts one heart loser, one diamond loser and should lose only one club by a finesse of the ten and later finessing the jack. On this hand, when the king of club falls on the second lead of the suit, the finesse is not necessary. However, West had a plan for the defense; after winning the king of diamonds, he led the king of clubs. Declarer won the ace and played the jack of trumps, hoping that East might duck—thinking there was a finesse position. East stepped up with the ace, cashed the queen of clubs and returned a club which West trumped. This good defense set the contract one trick.

Mini-lesson: The double by North is a take-out double. A double in order to be a take-out, must be at the doubler's first opportunity to bid. It is a conventional bid asking partner to name his best suit. The doubler has an opening bid (13 points and up), and either support for the other three suits, two suits, one of which is a good five card suit, or a strong six card suit with a very good hand. The jump raise by East over the double is called a "barricade bid." The bid shows at least four trumps and about 8 to 10 points in support of partner's suit. It is not a forcing bid. Holding 10 high card points or more, with or without support for partner's suit, East would redouble.

North dealer   Deal #37
North-South vulnerable

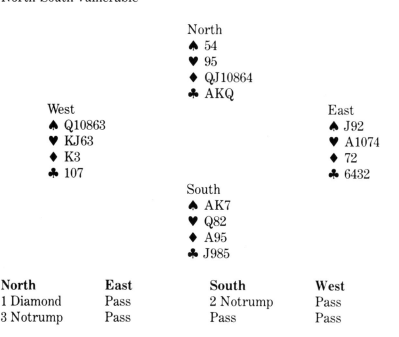

North
♠ 54
♥ 95
♦ QJ10864
♣ AKQ

West
♠ Q10863
♥ KJ63
♦ K3
♣ 107

East
♠ J92
♥ A1074
♦ 72
♣ 6432

South
♠ AK7
♥ Q82
♦ A95
♣ J985

North	East	South	West
1 Diamond	Pass	2 Notrump	Pass
3 Notrump	Pass	Pass	Pass

Opening lead: 6 of spades

Declarer counts seven winners. If the diamond finesse is successful, South
will win twelve tricks. When the diamond finesse loses to West, good defense will set the contract.

The king of spades wins the first trick. Declarer leads a club to the queen
and returns the queen of diamonds, won by West with the king. West can
count ten tricks for the declarer: two spades, five diamonds and three
clubs. The only hope for the defense is in the heart suit. West leads the
three of hearts* which East wins with the ace. East returns the four and
the defense wins four heart tricks and one diamond to set the contract.

Mini-lesson: *When a defender switches suits (West led a spade on his
opening lead and now has switched to the heart suit) . . . he wants his
second suit led back if he leads a low card in his second suit; but he wants
his first suit returned if he leads a high card in his second suit.

The jump to two notrump by the responder shows a balanced hand, 13-15
high card points and the unbid suits protected. The bid is forcing to game.
If the responder has passed, the jump to two notrump shows 11-12 high
card points and is not forcing.

South dealer   Deal #38
East-West vulnerable

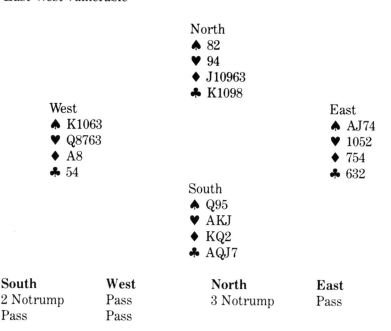

North
♠ 82
♥ 94
♦ J10963
♣ K1098

West
♠ K1063
♥ Q8763
♦ A8
♣ 54

East
♠ AJ74
♥ 1052
♦ 754
♣ 632

South
♠ Q95
♥ AKJ
♦ KQ2
♣ AQJ7

South	West	North	East
2 Notrump	Pass	3 Notrump	Pass
Pass	Pass		

Opening lead: 6 of hearts

Declarer counts seven winners: three hearts and four clubs. The diamond suit will produce the extra tricks needed for game if South can keep the opponents from switching to the spade suit.

To give West the impression that East has the jack of hearts, South wins the ten of hearts with the king. The king of diamonds is played, then the queen, which West wins. Hoping that the king of spades is the entry for cashing his good hearts after South wins the ace, West returns the three of hearts expecting East to play the jack! Instead, South wins the jack of hearts and makes his game contract plus two overtricks. The Bridge World calls this "a touch of larceny." If South wins the opening lead with the jack of hearts, West will realize that there is no future in the heart suit and he will shift to the three of spades. The defense will win four spade tricks and one diamond to set the game contract.

Mini-lesson: A two notrump opening bid shows 22-23-24 high card points. The hand must be balanced in distribution and all four suits must be protected. The bid is not forcing.

When following suit to a lead, play the lowest of touching equals. For example: Holding AKQ follow with the queen; holding KQJ or QJ follow with the jack; holding QJ10 or J10 follow with the ten.

251

South dealer   Deal #39
Both sides vulnerable

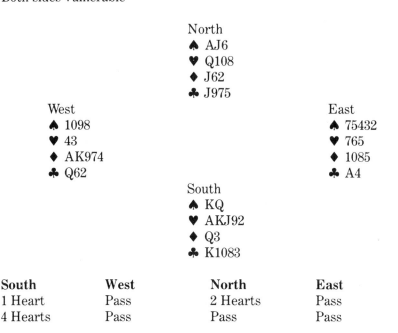

North
♠ AJ6
♥ Q108
♦ J62
♣ J975

West
♠ 1098
♥ 43
♦ AK974
♣ Q62

East
♠ 75432
♥ 765
♦ 1085
♣ A4

South
♠ KQ
♥ AKJ92
♦ Q3
♣ K1083

South	West	North	East
1 Heart	Pass	2 Hearts	Pass
4 Hearts	Pass	Pass	Pass

Opening lead: King of diamonds

Declarer counts four possible losers: two diamonds and two clubs. A touch of larceny may work! On the opening lead of the king of diamonds, declarer follows with the queen. Afraid to lead the ace and have South trump, making the jack in the dummy good for a possible discard, West shifts to the ten of spades. South wins with the queen, pulls the trumps and discards his losing diamond on the high spade in the dummy. South takes the club finesse which loses to the queen, another club is lost to the ace and South claims his contract, losing one diamond and two clubs.

Mini-lesson: With a 4-3-3-3 distribution, adequate trump support but only three trumps, the responder bids one notrump with six or seven points, gives a single raise of partner's suit holding nine or ten points, and with eight points uses his judgment. Two aces are better than four queens and tens and nines are good fillers and important cards.

North
♠ Q943
♥ 7
♦ KQ53
♣ AJ64

West
♠ 52
♥ AKQ1052
♦ 1042
♣ K2

East
♠ A86
♥ J986
♦ 8
♣ Q10985

South
♠ KJ107
♥ 43
♦ AJ976
♣ 73

North	East	South	West
1 Diamond	Pass	1 Spade	2 Hearts
2 Spades	3 Diamonds*	3 Spades	4 Hearts
4 Spades	Pass	Pass	Pass

Opening lead: 2 of diamonds

Declarer counts three losers: one spade, one heart and one club. With the normal lead of the king of hearts, there is no defense that will set the contract. Declarer will win any shift, drive out the ace of trumps, pull the remaining trumps and concede a club, making four.

With control in spades, the cue bid by East of the opponent's suit* suggests a lead to his partner in case they defend the hand. The bid guarantees a fit in partner's suit; it is the same as raising partner's suit but shows a feature for the defense. With an opening diamond lead, South will be set one trick. When East wins the ace of trumps, he returns a low heart which West wins. West returns a diamond which is trumped by East, and a club trick is collected later in the play.

Mini-lesson: When raising partner's suit, holding four trumps or more, promote the honors in that suit by 1 point. However, there is a limit to the promotion, and if 4 points have already been counted in the trump suit, no promotion takes place.

When raising partner's suit, the distributional points also change. The void suit counts 5 points (instead of 3); the singleton counts 3 points (instead of 2); the doubleton does not change and remains at 1 point.

South dealer   Deal #41
East-West vulnerable

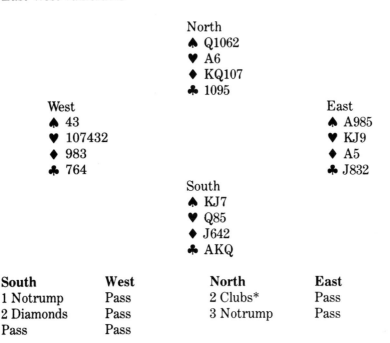

North
♠ Q1062
♥ A6
♦ KQ107
♣ 1095

West
♠ 43
♥ 107432
♦ 983
♣ 764

East
♠ A985
♥ KJ9
♦ A5
♣ J832

South
♠ KJ7
♥ Q85
♦ J642
♣ AKQ

South	West	North	East
1 Notrump	Pass	2 Clubs*	Pass
2 Diamonds	Pass	3 Notrump	Pass
Pass	Pass		

Opening lead: 3 of hearts

Declarer has five winners: two hearts and three clubs. Four tricks must be developed in the spade and diamond suits.

On the opening lead declarer plays the six of hearts and East makes the winning play of the jack. East knows that West does not have a high card point in his hand; South has sixteen points for his notrump opening and between the dummy and his own hand East can count the remaining twenty four high card points in the deck. South wins the jack of hearts with the queen and leads a diamond to the king. East wins the ace and returns the king of hearts which dummy wins. The two of spades is led, East steps up with the ace, returns the nine of hearts which West over-takes with the ten, and he cashes two additional heart tricks to set the contract one trick.

Mini-lesson: *The Stayman Convention is an artificial two club response to an opening 1 notrump bid. Its purpose is to find a four-four major suit fit. The two club response requests partner to bid any biddable major suit. With no biddable four card major suit, the opener bids two diamonds.

South dealer
Neither side vulnerable

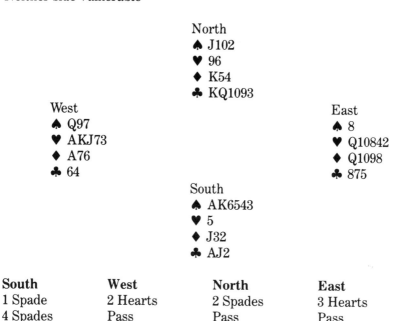

North
- ♠ J102
- ♥ 96
- ♦ K54
- ♣ KQ1093

West
- ♠ Q97
- ♥ AKJ73
- ♦ A76
- ♣ 64

East
- ♠ 8
- ♥ Q10842
- ♦ Q1098
- ♣ 875

South
- ♠ AK6543
- ♥ 5
- ♦ J32
- ♣ AJ2

South	West	North	East
1 Spade	2 Hearts	2 Spades	3 Hearts
4 Spades	Pass	Pass	Pass

Opening lead: King of hearts

Declarer has four possible losers: one spade, one heart and two diamonds. The overcall at the two level by West would suggest that the ace of diamonds is in that hand. On the king of hearts East plays the two, a signal discouraging a heart continuation. East knows that the declarer has a singleton heart or is void in hearts, for the overcall by West promises a five card or longer suit.

At trick two, West plays the ace of diamonds, East signals with the ten; another diamond lead by West sets up the queen for East and along with the queen of trumps, the defense win four tricks, one spade, one heart and two diamonds.

If West leads anything but a diamond at trick two, declarer will make his game contract.

Mini-lesson: The bid by North is called a free raise. The count for this bid is about 8-11 points.

255

North dealer   Deal #43
Both sides vulnerable

North
♠ K54
♥ QJ9
♦ 108
♣ Q10764

West   East
♠ J83   ♠ Q1092
♥ 52   ♥ 63
♦ J92   ♦ KQ7543
♣ AKJ95   ♣ 2

South
♠ A76
♥ AK10874
♦ A6
♣ 83

North	East	South	West
Pass	Pass	1 Heart	Pass
2 Hearts	Pass	4 Hearts	Pass
Pass	Pass		

Opening lead: King of clubs

Declarer counts four losers: one spade, one diamond and two clubs. Depending upon the defense by East and West, the queen of clubs may set up for a discard of a spade or a diamond loser.

On the lead of the king of clubs, East plays the two.* At trick two, West makes the only play that will defeat the contract . . . a low club which East trumps. South has two additional losers, a spade and a diamond, and is set one trick on good defense.

Mini-lesson: *When the king is led and the queen of that suit is in the dummy, the partner of the leader must play high-low (called an echo) to show a doubleton. Therefore, the two of clubs played by East, shows one or three.

The South hand revalues to 20 points. Review Deal #12.

South dealer   Deal #44
North-South vulnerable

                                North
                                ♠ Q106
                                ♥ 93
                                ♦ KJ1063
                                ♣ KJ6
West   East
♠ A73   ♠ 82
♥ QJ105   ♥ A8742
♦ 85   ♦ A72
♣ 9542   ♣ 1073
                                South
                                ♠ KJ954
                                ♥ K6
                                ♦ Q94
                                ♣ AQ8

South	West	North	East
1 Spade	Pass	2 Diamonds	Pass
2 Notrump	Pass	3 Spades	Pass
4 Spades	Pass	Pass	Pass

Opening lead: Queen of hearts

Declarer counts three losers: one spade, one heart and one diamond. The
opening lead is won by East with the ace. East realizes that the only hope
for the defense to win three more tricks to defeat the contract, is for West
to have a trump winner and a shortness in the diamond suit. It is unlikely
that West has a singleton diamond and a trump winner, for with that holding he probably would have chosen a diamond for his opening lead.

At trick two, East leads the two of diamonds, won by dummy's ten. A low
spade is led, the jack losing to the ace in the West hand. West returns a
diamond to partner's ace, and a diamond ruff sets the game contract.

Mini-lesson: The two notrump rebid by the opener . . . Review Deal #16.

South dealer   Deal #45
Both sides vulnerable

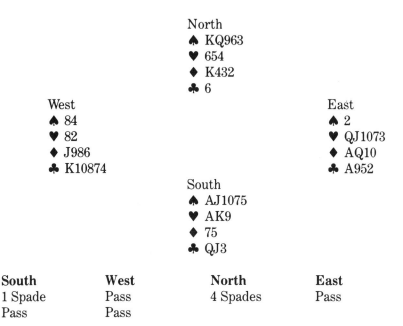

North
♠ KQ963
♥ 654
♦ K432
♣ 6

West
♠ 84
♥ 82
♦ J986
♣ K10874

East
♠ 2
♥ QJ1073
♦ AQ10
♣ A952

South
♠ AJ1075
♥ AK9
♦ 75
♣ QJ3

South	West	North	East
1 Spade	Pass	4 Spades	Pass
Pass	Pass		

Opening lead: 8 of hearts

Declarer counts four possible losers: one heart, two diamonds and one club. West elected to lead the "top of nothing" in the other major; East follows with the ten and declarer wins with his ace. Two rounds of trumps are led with the ace and king, and the six of clubs is played from the dummy. If East timorously grabs his ace declarer will make his contract. After winning his ace, East returns the queen of hearts, won by South who now plays a "ruffing finesse" with the queen of clubs. If West covers, it will be trumped in the dummy and the losing heart will be discarded on the jack of clubs; if West does not cover, South will discard the losing heart.

If East makes the proper play of a low club when the singleton is led, West will win the king and declarer will not be able to discard his heart loser. This defense will set the contract one trick. If South has the king of clubs, East might lose his ace; however, he will get a heart trick in exchange.

Mini-lesson: The jump by North is called a triple raise. The bid shows five trumps or more, a singleton or a void and no more than 9 high card points. The bid is used for major suits only.

East dealer   Deal #46
Neither side vulnerable

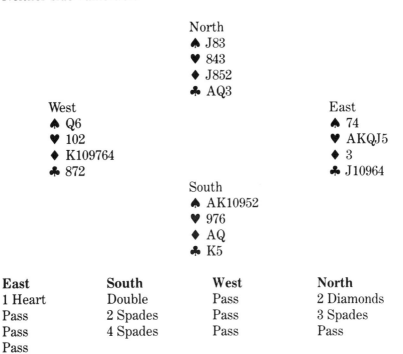

North
♠ J83
♥ 843
♦ J852
♣ AQ3

West
♠ Q6
♥ 102
♦ K109764
♣ 872

East
♠ 74
♥ AKQJ5
♦ 3
♣ J10964

South
♠ AK10952
♥ 976
♦ AQ
♣ K5

East	South	West	North
1 Heart	Double	Pass	2 Diamonds
Pass	2 Spades	Pass	3 Spades
Pass	4 Spades	Pass	Pass
Pass			

Opening lead: 10 of hearts

Declarer counts four possible losers: one spade and three hearts. East wins
the opening heart lead with the jack and continues with the king and
queen. On the third lead of hearts, West discards his lowest diamond, the
four. This discard is a signal to East that West does not want a diamond
shift; East can see the two of diamonds in the dummy and the three of
diamonds in his own hand. Looking at the clubs in the dummy, there cannot
be any future in that suit. At trick four, East leads the ace of hearts; this
insures a spade trick for West. If declarer trumps with the nine, West over-
trumps; if declarer trumps with the king, the queen will be a winner. This
defense sets the contract one trick.

Mini-lesson: The South hand is too strong for a simple overcall of one
spade. It is also too strong for an intermediate jump overcall. Strong jump
overcalls are no longer used; with a strong hand, a player can make a take-
out double and then show his own suit. The bidding by South, doubling
and then bidding his own suit at the two level, shows 16-18 points and a
good five card or longer suit.

259

West dealer   Deal #47
East-West vulnerable

                              North
                              ♠ AQJ107
                              ♥ KQ92
                              ♦ 105
                              ♣ 65
            West   East
            ♠ 98   ♠ 632
            ♥ 543   ♥ 7
            ♦ A84   ♦ QJ732
            ♣ AKJ43   ♣ Q1082
                              South
                              ♠ K54
                              ♥ AJ1086
                              ♦ K96
                              ♣ 97

West	North	East	South
1 Club	Double	3 Clubs	4 Hearts
Pass	Pass	Pass	

Opening lead: King of clubs

Declarer counts four possible losers: two diamonds and two clubs. Unless East and West are knowledgeable players and understand signals, South will make his game contract. Two diamonds can be discarded on the long spades after the trumps have been taken away from the opponents.

On the opening lead of the king of clubs, East plays the ten. At trick two West leads a low club to his partner's queen. East shifts to the queen of diamonds and the defenders win two more tricks, setting the game contract one trick.

Mini-lesson: The play of the ten of clubs by East is called an "equal honor" signal. As the name suggests, the signal is used when partner leads an honor card and you have an honor of equal value.

When you have supported partner's suit, the message is clear; if you want the suit continued, play your next to highest card on partner's honor lead; therefore, the ten denies the jack but promises the queen. If you have not supported partner's suit, your high-low play may show a doubleton.

The jump raise by East over the take-out double . . . Review Deal #36

East dealer   Deal #48
East-West vulnerable

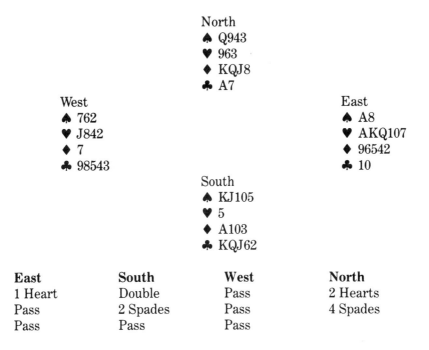

North
♠ Q943
♥ 963
♦ KQJ8
♣ A7

West
♠ 762
♥ J842
♦ 7
♣ 98543

East
♠ A8
♥ AKQ107
♦ 96542
♣ 10

South
♠ KJ105
♥ 5
♦ A103
♣ KQJ62

East	South	West	North
1 Heart	Double	Pass	2 Hearts
Pass	2 Spades	Pass	4 Spades
Pass	Pass	Pass	

Opening lead: 7 of diamonds

The cue bid of the opponent's suit, in response to a take-out double by partner, is the only forcing bid that can be made by the responder. The bid shows about 13 points or more. Holding both major suits, the cue bid may be shaded to 11-12 points. It is a forcing bid and may not be passed until the cue bidder raises partner's suit or bids notrump. A jump in a suit in response to partner's take-out double is not forcing; therefore, the cue bid of the opponent's suit is used to force partner to bid again.

South counts two losers: one spade and one heart. The opening lead is won with the jack. A low spade is led, East steps up with the ace as West follows with the six. East returns a diamond which West trumps with the two (trump echo). West leads the two of hearts won by East with the queen; another diamond is led, West trumps with the seven and the game contract is set one.

Mini-lesson: When a defender plays high-low in the trump suit, either in ruffing or in following to trump leads by declarer, he indicates a holding of three trumps. The signal is used to indicate to partner the ability to ruff a trick.

261

South dealer   Deal #49
North-South vulnerable

                          North
                          ♠ J4
                          ♥ 10732
                          ♦ KQJ3
                          ♣ Q64

        West   East
        ♠ K7   ♠ 85
        ♥ Q64   ♥ KJ98
        ♦ 10874   ♦ A92
        ♣ J1093   ♣ K872

                          South
                          ♠ AQ109632
                          ♥ A5
                          ♦ 65
                          ♣ A5

South	West	North	East
1 Spade	Pass	1 Notrump	Pass
3 Spades	Pass	4 Spades	Pass
Pass	Pass		

Opening lead: Jack of clubs

Declarer counts four possible losers: one spade, one heart, one diamond and one club. The jack of clubs is covered with the queen, East plays the king and declarer wins his ace. At trick two, South plays a diamond, West follows with the eight (the count signal), the jack is played from the dummy and East does not play the ace. The jack of spades is led for a finesse and West wins the king. West cashes the ten of clubs and South trumps the lead of the nine of clubs. The ace of spades pulls the remaining trumps. A second round of diamonds is led, West follows with the seven, and the queen loses to the ace. East returns a heart, South wins his ace but still must lose one heart and is set one on good defense.

If West plays his lowest card, the four, on the first diamond lead by South, East will play West for an odd number of cards in that suit (three or five) . . . possibly five . . . and win the first lead of diamonds and South will make his game.

Mini-lesson: The count signal is a method by which a defender can indicate to his partner the length held in a particular suit. The procedure is as follows: play high-low with a doubleton; play the lowest from three or five cards; play the second highest card followed by the third highest with four cards.

South dealer   Deal #50
Both sides vulnerable

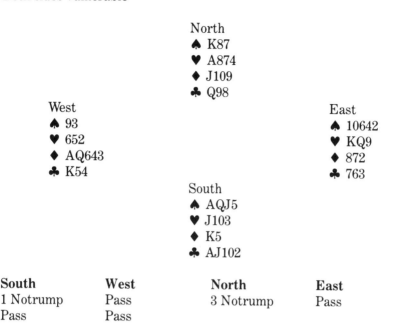

North
♠ K87
♥ A874
♦ J109
♣ Q98

West
♠ 93
♥ 652
♦ AQ643
♣ K54

East
♠ 10642
♥ KQ9
♦ 872
♣ 763

South
♠ AQJ5
♥ J103
♦ K5
♣ AJ102

South	West	North	East
1 Notrump	Pass	3 Notrump	Pass
Pass	Pass		

Opening lead: 4 of diamonds

Declarer counts his winners: four spades, one heart, one diamond and at least three clubs. The nine of diamonds is played from the dummy, East plays the two (the count signal) and declarer follows with the five. The nine of clubs is led for a finesse and West wins the king. If West doesn't lead the ace of diamonds, South will claim his contract. However, West knows that East has either one diamond or three diamonds from his play of the two at trick one. West cashes his four diamond tricks and sets the contract. If East has a singleton diamond, South has four to the king, and the diamonds in the West hand will not defeat the game.

Mini-lesson: When the dummy wins the first trick, third hand can give his partner the count signal: high-low with two or four; lowest with three or five.

The Stayman Convention is not used when the distribution of the hand is 4-3-3-3.

South dealer   Deal #51
East-West vulnerable

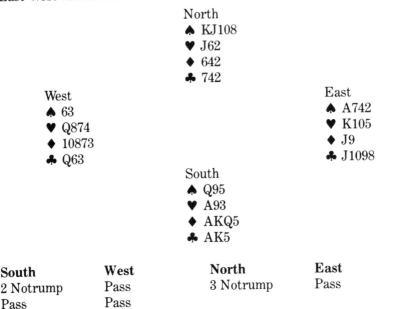

North
♠ KJ108
♥ J62
♦ 642
♣ 742

West
♠ 63
♥ Q874
♦ 10873
♣ Q63

East
♠ A742
♥ K105
♦ J9
♣ J1098

South
♠ Q95
♥ A93
♦ AKQ5
♣ AK5

South	West	North	East
2 Notrump	Pass	3 Notrump	Pass
Pass	Pass		

Opening lead: 4 of hearts

Declarer counts six winners: one heart, three diamonds and two clubs. The additional three tricks may come from the spade suit if the defenders win the first or second lead of that suit. One additional heart trick may be developed, depending upon the caliber of the player in the East seat. There may be four diamond winners if the suit breaks evenly.

On the opening lead, the two of hearts is played from the dummy, East properly follows with the ten and declarer plays low. The king of hearts is returned and declarer plays low again. The third heart lead is won with the ace. The queen of spades is led, West follows with the six (the count signal) and East allows the queen to win. South leads another spade, West follows with the three and East plays low again. The spade suit is now useless for lack of entries into the dummy. Declarer cashes two high clubs and three high diamonds and when the diamond suit does not break, the contract is set one trick.

Mini-lesson: The old whist rule of "third hand high" is generally right when a low card is led and the dummy has low cards. However, if dummy has an honor which the third hand player can beat, and that honor is not played, third hand should play his second-highest card if that is a nine or better.

264

South dealer   Deal #52
North-South vulnerable

                          North
                          ♠ 10953
                          ♥ K953
                          ♦ AK7
                          ♣ KJ

        West   East
        ♠ K6   ♠ 42
        ♥ 874   ♥ Q106
        ♦ J64   ♦ Q1085
        ♣ 107432   ♣ AQ95

                          South
                          ♠ AQJ87
                          ♥ AJ2
                          ♦ 932
                          ♣ 86

South	West	North	East
1 Spade	Pass	3 Spades	Pass
4 Spades	Pass	Pass	Pass

Opening lead: 3 of clubs

Declarer counts five possible losers: one spade, one heart, one diamond and two clubs. The queen and ace of clubs win the first two tricks and East shifts to the two of trumps; South loses the jack of spades to the king and wins the trump return with the nine in the dummy. The only hope for making the contract is for East to have the queen of hearts and for the suit to break three-three. The losing diamond can be discarded on the thirteenth heart.

The three of hearts is led, East plays the six, declarer follows with the jack which wins. The ace of hearts is led, West and North play low cards and East plays the queen! South leads the two of hearts, West follows with the eight, the nine is played from the dummy and East wins the ten! setting the contract one trick. Larceny on defense!

Mini-lesson: Always play the card that your opponent knows you hold.

265

Bridge: Teachers Visit Here
for Convention and Lectures

BY ALBERT H. MOREHEAD

This has been a week for the nation's bridge teachers to visit New York. The American Bridge Teachers' Association held its annual convention at the Statler-Hilton Hotel on Tuesday and Wednesday, and yesterday, Charles H. Goren's annual course of lectures to bridge teachers began at the Plaza Hotel.

The teachers' convention elected George Gooden of Carmel, California president of the association for the coming year.

The deal shown today was played at the Summer National North American Championships by the newly elected first vice president of the bridge teachers' association, Mrs. D. J. Cook of Winnetka, Illinois.

The contract was a reasonable one, makable if the heart finesse won with some chance to make it even if the finesse lost—a 3—3 heart break, for example, or a doubleton king of spades in East's hand, or other fortuitous circumstances. But it turned out to depend on the classic type of double squeeze, which Mrs. Cook executed handily.

The diamond opening was won by South's king, and South led her low club to dummy's jack so as to lead the heart three and finesse the heart jack.

West won this trick with the heart king and led a second round of clubs, which South took with the king.

South cashed the ace and queen of hearts, for if the suit had been evenly divided there would have been twelve tricks available without further trouble. But the suit did not break.

Then South led her last club to dummy, successfully finessed for the spade king, led her diamond to dummy's queen, and cashed the diamond ace and then the club ace.

This last club lead produced the squeeze on both defenders. East had the high heart and in order to keep it East had to come down to one spade. South then discarded the heart seven. West had the high diamond, which could not be discarded because dummy's diamond eight would then become good, so West too had to come down to one spade. South won the last two tricks with the ace and six of spades.

The only trick the defenders got was the king of hearts and the slam was made.

```
                 NORTH
                 ♠ Q54
                 ♥ 93
                 ♦ AQ83
                 ♣ AQJ2
WEST                           EAST
♠ 1083                         ♠ K972
♥ K5                           ♥ 10842
♦ J1096                        ♦ 742
♣ 9743                         ♣ 86
                 SOUTH
                 ♠ AJ6
                 ♥ AQJ76
                 ♦ K5
                 ♣ K105
```

Neither side was vulnerable. The bidding:

East	South	West	North
Pass	1 ♥	Pass	2 ♣
Pass	3 N.T.	Pass	6 N.T.
Pass	Pass	Pass	

West led the diamond jack.

'D.J.' Gets 12 Tricks by Astute Play

BY CHARLES GOREN

Neither side vulnerable. South deals.

NORTH
- ♠ J53
- ♥ AKQ2
- ♦ 74
- ♣ A954

WEST
- ♠ 106
- ♥ J853
- ♦ J82
- ♣ QJ103

EAST
- ♠ KQ2
- ♥ 10974
- ♦ Q65
- ♣ K87

SOUTH
- ♠ A9874
- ♥ 6
- ♦ AK1093
- ♣ 62

The bidding:

South	West	North	East
1 ♠	Pass	2 ♥	Pass
2 ♠	Pass	4 ♠	Pass
Pass	Pass		

Opening lead: Queen of ♣

Coming from the Chicago area and ranking high both as a bridge teacher and tournament player is my good friend D. J. Cook, a lady of great charm. Her father, Carey Orr, is one of the country's leading political cartoonists. "D. J." has carved out a very successful record of her own. In today's hand, she was the only player to score 12 tricks.

Mrs. Cook, seated South, opened the bidding with one spade. When her partner responded with two hearts, she was obliged to rebid the rather mangy spade suit. The alternative call of three diamonds would promise a much better hand. North decided not to dally further and proceeded at once to game in spades.

West opened the queen of clubs. The ace was put up from dummy in order to cash two high hearts, permitting declarer, to discard her club loser. Mrs. Cook crossed over to her hand with the ace of diamonds and led the nine of spades next. West followed with the six, dummy played the three, and East's queen of spades won the trick.

The king of clubs came back and declarer trumped. She now cashed the king of diamonds and then ruffed away the opponent's queen and jack on the next round to establish the diamond suit. The jack of spades was led from dummy, and East was helpless. He actually chose to duck and Mrs. Cook permitted the jack to ride. When the ten dropped from West's hand the contest was virtually over.

Declarer ruffed herself in with a heart, drew East's remaining trump with the ace of spades and played the good diamonds. Her only loser was one trump trick.

Sheinwold on Bridge

Singleton as Deuce

By ALFRED SHEINWOLD

Today we start a small study of the deuce, with hands that come from celebrated bridge teacher D.J. Cook, of Vero Beach, Florida. We begin with the lead of a deuce as a singleton.

East doesn't know that the deuce of clubs is a singleton since West would lead the deuce from four clubs or from K-x-x. East does best to take the ace and return the queen or jack.

In fact the deuce is a singleton and South has the king of clubs. If South plays the king at the second trick, West ruffs. Now reasonable defense limits South to six trumps, two top hearts and the ace of diamonds. Down one.

BETTER PLAY

South should, of course, find a better play at the second trick. He should play a low club, letting East win. East perseveres with another club honor, and South plays low again.

West must ruff to shut out dummy's trumps. Now South wins

any return and draws trumps. Sooner or later he gets his tenth trick with the carefully preserved king of clubs.

South dealer
Both sides vulnerable

NORTH
♠ 5 4
♥ A 5 4 2
♦ Q J 8 5 3
♣ 10 3

WEST
♠ 10 8 7 3
♥ J 9 7 6 3
♦ 9 7 4
♣ 2

EAST
♠ 9
♥ Q 8
♦ K 10 6 2
♣ A Q J 9 6 5

SOUTH
♠ A K Q J 6 2
♥ K 10
♦ A
♣ K 8 7 4

South	West	North	East
1 ♠	Pass	1 NT	2 ♣
4 ♠	All Pass		

Opening lead — ♣ 2

Sheinwold on Bridge

Deuce Denies Interest

By ALFRED SHEINWOLD

We continue our study of the deuce with a hand (contributed by bridge teacher D.J. Cook, of Vero Beach, Florida) in which a deuce is played to deny interest.

East takes the jack of diamonds and continues with another top diamond. West follows with the deuce, making it clear that he started with only two diamonds.

East continues with a third high diamond, giving West his chance to steer the defense.

STEERING METHOD

If West discards a high club, such as the eight or ten, he indicates an interest in the suit; but if West discards a low club, he denies interest in clubs. Since West has no interest at all in clubs, he makes the lowest possible discard — the deuce.

When West denies club strength East sees dummy's hearts and knows that the only chance for the setting trick is in trumps. East therefore continues with a fourth diamond to put West in overruffing position.

If South ruffs low, West overruffs. If South ruffs high, West's

ten of trumps becomes a natural trump trick.

West dealer
North-South vulnerable

NORTH
♠ 2
♥ A K Q 10 8
♦ 10 7 3
♣ 9 7 5 3

WEST
♠ 10 6 4 3
♥ J 7 6 3
♦ 4 2
♣ 10 8 2

EAST
♠ 7 5
♥ 9 5 2
♦ A K Q J 5
♣ Q J 4

SOUTH
♠ A K Q J 9 8
♥ 4
♦ 9 8 6
♣ A K 6

West	North	East	South
Pass	Pass	1 ♦	Dbl
Pass	2 ♥	Pass	4 ♠
All Pass			

Opening lead — ♦ 4

Sheinwold on Bridge

The Deuce Shows Three

By ALFRED SHEINWOLD

We continue our study of the deuce with hands from D.J. Cook, author of "Cook and Deal." The deuce, Mrs. Cook points out, may be used to give partner "the count."

South plays low from dummy at the first trick, and East wins with the king. East returns his low spade, and West drives out dummy's ace.

Whenever diamonds are led, East must win the third diamond if South has three diamonds; but East must win the second diamond if South has only two diamonds.

GIVES COUNT

How does East know how many diamonds South has?

West provides the count. If West has an odd number of diamonds he plays his cards normally, lowest card first; but if West has an even number of diamonds he plays higher than necessary on the first round of the suit.

When West plays the deuce on the first round of diamonds today,

he shows an odd number. East plays West for three diamonds, which means that South must have only two. East therefore wins the second round of diamonds, defeating the contract.

South dealer
Both sides vulnerable

```
                NORTH
                ♠ A 6 4
                ♥ 8 5 3
                ♦ Q J 10 9 7
                ♣ 9 4
WEST                        EAST
♠ Q 10 8 7 2                ♠ K 3
♥ K 7                       ♥ Q 10 6 4 2
♦ 8 5 2                     ♦ A 4 3
♣ 10 7 3                    ♣ 8 5 2
                SOUTH
                ♠ J 9 5
                ♥ A J 9
                ♦ K 6
                ♣ A K Q J 6
```

South	West	North	East
1 ♣	Pass	1 ♦	Pass
2 NT	Pass	3 NT	All Pass

Opening lead — ♠ 7

Sheinwold on Bridge

The Deuce Shows Four

By ALFRED SHEINWOLD

As we noted yesterday, the deuce shows three cards in a suit that somebody else has led. Today, in another hand from D.J. Cook, of Vero Beach, Florida, we see that the deuce usually shows that the leader has four cards in the suit.

Most players lead fourth-highest from a long, broken suit, showing three higher cards in that suit. When your lead is the deuce, you cannot have any card lower than your lead and therefore have a suit of exactly four cards.

SOUND DEDUCTION

Today's South can tell from the deuce that West has exactly four hearts, and this information guides him to the best line of play. South takes four diamonds and two hearts and then gets out with a heart.

The defenders can take two heart, two spades and two clubs, for a total of six tricks, but then must give declarer a spade or a club if he has discarded intelligently.

If South tries to develop a spade or a club by his own efforts, he gives the defenders a seventh trick.

South dealer
Both sides vulnerable

NORTH
♠ J 7 4 3
♥ K 7
♦ A 10 3 2
♣ J 8 3

WEST
♠ K 8 5
♥ Q 9 6 2
♦ 9 8 5
♣ K 9 4

EAST
♠ A 10 9
♥ J 10 8 4
♦ 7 6 4
♣ A 10 5

SOUTH
♠ Q 6 2
♥ A 5 3
♦ K Q J
♣ Q 7 6 2

South	West	North	East
1 ♣	Pass	1 ♦	Pass
1 NT	All Pass		

Opening lead — ♥ 2

Sheinwold on Bridge

The Deuce Shows Five

By ALFRED SHEINWOLD

As we saw yesterday, the lead of a deuce usually shows a four-card suit. Today, in another hand contributed by Mrs. D.J. Cook, we see a different meaning for the deuce.

East takes the king and ace of diamonds. West plays the deuce at the second trick, showing that he had three diamonds higher than the five for his fourth-highest opening lead and one card (the deuce) lower than the opening lead. To put it another way, his deuce shows a five-card suit.

HAS THE COUNT

Now East knows that South is out of diamonds. If East leads another diamond, South ruffs and goes to dummy with a club to try the heart finesse. Declarer takes the spade return with the ace, draws trumps and runs the clubs to discard his spade loser.

East's only chance is to switch to spades at the third trick in the hope that West has the queen and can drive out the ace. West gets in with a trump in time to lead another spade, defeating the contract.

North dealer
Both sides vulnerable

NORTH
♠ A 7 4 3
♥ 9 4
♦ J 6 4
♣ A K Q 10

WEST
♠ Q 8 6
♥ Q 7 3
♦ Q 10 8 5 2
♣ 9 8

EAST
♠ K 9 5 2
♥ 6 5
♦ A K 7
♣ 7 6 5 2

SOUTH
♠ J 10
♥ A K J 10 8 2
♦ 9 3
♣ J 4 3

North	East	South	West
1 ♣	Pass	1 ♥	Pass
1 ♠	Pass	4 ♥	All Pass

Opening lead — ♦ 5

Sheinwold on Bridge

Deuce for Preference

By ALFRED SHEINWOLD

Today we end a brief study of the deuce with a final hand contributed by D.J. Cook, of Vero Beach, Florida, author of "Cook and Deal," a fine collection of bridge hands and recipes.

East takes the first trick with the king of clubs. If East continues with the ace and a low club, South ruffs, draws trumps and discards a heart on the jack of clubs. The rest is easy.

After taking the king of clubs, East must lead a low club for West to ruff. East selects his lowest club, the deuce, to show that he has a preference for a return in the lower side suit (diamonds rather than hearts).

RUFFS DEUCE

West ruffs the deuce of clubs and obediently returns a diamond. East wins and leads another low club to kill dummy's club trick.

South ruffs and draws trumps, but dummy's jack of clubs is not set up, and South must eventually lose a heart trick. If West led a heart after ruffing the second club, South could make the contract by careful play.

East dealer
Both sides vulnerable

NORTH
- ♠ A 10 7 4
- ♥ A Q 7 6
- ♦ J
- ♣ J 10 6 3

WEST
- ♠ 5 3
- ♥ J 10 4 2
- ♦ Q 10 9 7 5 2
- ♣ 4

EAST
- ♠ 6 2
- ♥ K 9 8
- ♦ A 3
- ♣ A K 9 8 5 2

SOUTH
- ♠ K Q J 9 8
- ♥ 5 3
- ♦ K 8 6 4
- ♣ Q 7

East	South	West	North
1 ♣	1 ♠	Pass	4 ♠
All Pass			

Opening lead — ♣ 4

273

Index

A

276

277

283

284

V

VEAL

VEGETABLE

W

Z

COOK & DEAL
12 Busbee Road
Asheville, NC 28803

Please send ___ copies of COOK & DEAL $17.95 each $ _____

Add shipping and handling $2.00 each $ _____

North Carolina residents add sales tax $1.08 each $ _____

                                               TOTAL $ _____

NAME _____

ADDRESS _____

CITY _____ STATE _____ ZIP _____

COOK & DEAL
12 Busbee Road
Asheville, NC 28803

Please send ___ copies of COOK & DEAL $17.95 each $ _____

Add shipping and handling $2.00 each $ _____

North Carolina residents add sales tax $1.08 each $ _____

                                               TOTAL $ _____

NAME _____

ADDRESS _____

CITY _____ STATE _____ ZIP _____

COOK & DEAL
12 Busbee Road
Asheville, NC 28803

Please send ___ copies of COOK & DEAL $17.95 each $ _____

Add shipping and handling $2.00 each $ _____

North Carolina residents add sales tax $1.08 each $ _____

                                               TOTAL $ _____

NAME _____

ADDRESS _____

CITY _____ STATE _____ ZIP _____